Routledge Author Guides

Tennyson

Routledge Author Guides

GENERAL EDITOR: B. C. SOUTHAM, M.A., B. LITT. (OXON)
Formerly Department of English, Westfield College, University of London

Titles in the series

Routledge Author Guides

Tennyson

by
Paul Turner
University Lecturer in English Literature
Fellow of Linacre College, Oxford

Routledge & Kegan Paul
London, Henley and Boston

First published in 1976
by Routledge & Kegan Paul Ltd
39 Store Street,
London WC1E 7DD,
Broadway House,
Newtown Road,
Henley-on-Thames,
Oxon RG9 1EN and
9 Park Street,
Boston, Mass. 02108, USA
Photoset in Latinesque
and printed in Great Britain by
Weatherby Woolnough

ISBN 0 7100 8371 8

To Jane

General Editor's Preface

Nowadays there is a growing awareness that the specialist areas have much to offer and much to learn from one another. The student of history, for example, is becoming increasingly aware of the value that literature can have in the understanding of the past; equally, the student of literature is turning more and more to the historians for illumination of his area of special interest, and of course philosophy, political science, sociology, and other disciplines have much to give him.

What we are trying to do in the Routledge *Author Guides* is to offer this illumination and communication by providing for non-specialist readers, whether students or the interested general public, a clear and systematic account of the life and times and works of the major writers and thinkers across a wide range of disciplines. Where the *Author Guides* may be seen to differ from other, apparently similar, series, is in its historical emphasis, which will be particularly evident in the treatment of the great literary writers, where we are trying to establish, in so far as this can be done, the social and historical context of the writer's life and times, and the cultural and intellectual tradition in which he stands, always remembering that critical and intepretative principles are implicit to any sound historical approach.

BCS

Contents

Preface

Abbreviated references for all quotations from Tennyson are incorporated in the text, and the abbreviations are explained in the Notes on the Text (page xiii). The Bibliographical Notes at the end of the book list secondary sources, which are suggested as further reading on the subjects covered by individual chapters.

I am grateful to Lord Tennyson's Trustees, to Trinity College, Cambridge, to the Cambridge University Library, and to the Houghton Library at Harvard, for permission to quote from the poet's manuscripts; to Mr Richard Andrews for showing me a copy of an unpublished Tennyson letter about *Maud*; to Mr Gerald Gurney, for giving me further information about this letter, and permitting me to quote from it (page 144); to Professor Cecil Lang for allowing me to anticipate his publication of the complete letter in a forthcoming edition of Tennyson's correspondence; and to Professor John Jump for letting me copy the general layout of his *Byron* in this series.

For various forms of assistance in the preparation of my book, I owe thanks to so many people that I can mention only a small proportion of them: Sir Charles Tennyson, Professor Christopher Ricks, Mr Laurence Elvin, Mr James Maxwell, Miss Kathleen Geer, Mr E. G. Earl, Dr Elisabeth Leedham-Green, Mr T. Kaye, Dr Lilian Haddakin, Mr Christopher Lloyd, Dr Louis Ziff, Miss Marjorie Boulton, Professor Bernard Fleischmann, Professor Harry Levin, Professors Edward and Lillian Bloom, and Dr Park Honan. Mr Brian Southam first suggested and patiently encouraged the project; my colleagues at Oxford allowed me time and money for research; my students kept the subject alive, and broadened my view of it; and my wife gave every kind of support, and cheerfully accepted, over many years, the constant presence of Tennyson about the house.

Notes on the Text

When giving references for Tennyson's own words, written or spoken, I have used the following abbreviations:

Diary   William Allingham, *A Diary*, ed. H. Allingham and D. Radford, 1907.
Eversley   *The Works of Tennyson*, annotated by Alfred, Lord Tennyson, ed. Hallam, Lord Tennyson (The Eversley Edition), 9 vols, 1907–8.
Materials   [Hallam Tennyson], *Materials for a Life of A. T.*, 4 vols, privately printed, 1896.
Memoir   [Hallam Tennyson], *Alfred Lord Tennyson: A Memoir By His Son*, 2 vols, 1897.
Oxford   Tennyson, *Poems and Plays* (Oxford Standard Authors), 1965.
Poems   *The Poems of Tennyson*, ed. Christopher Ricks, 1969.
Reminiscence James Knowles, 'A Personal Reminiscence', *The Nineteenth Century*, vol. 33 (Jan. 1893), pp. 164–88.

Arabic numerals in brackets after a quotation from, or reference to, one of Tennyson's works indicate line-numbers. A preceding small Roman numeral indicates the section; and a sequence of large Roman numeral, small Roman numeral, Arabic numeral indicates act-, scene- and line-number in a play (e.g. *The Devil and the Lady*), or part-, section- and line-number in *Maud*, as printed in the Ricks edition (the Oxford edition has the same part- and section-numbers, but unfortunately prints no line-numbers).

References to long poems by other authors follow the usual conventions for classical literature; thus '*Aeneid*, iv, 285' means book four, line 285, and '*Inferno*, xxvi, 90' means canto 26, line 90. Plays (e.g. Shakespeare's) divided into acts and scenes are referred to in the same way as Tennyson's. In references to Malory, a large Roman numeral followed by a small Roman numeral indicates book- and chapter-number in Caxton's version (as printed in the Everyman edition). Translations from classical or other foreign languages are normally my own.

1

The Age

'Can anybody in his senses', asked a Victorian critic, 'imagine posterity speaking of our age as the age of Tennyson?' We may reasonably call it just that; for all its main features are reflected in his poetry.

I

Alfred Tennyson was born (6 August 1809) twenty years after the start of the French Revolution, towards the end of the Napoleonic Wars. In the tiny Lincolnshire village of Somersby, where he spent his childhood and adolescence, he heard nothing at the time of the battle of Waterloo (1815), though he later remembered seeing a coach drive past, with flowers and ribbons on the horses.

He grew up in a period of momentous change. The population of England and Wales was increasing rapidly (from less than nine million in 1801 to nearly eighteen million in 1851) and the whole structure of society was being transformed by the Industrial Revolution. As industry became mechanized, and attracted labour to factories, there was a massive migration from the country to the towns. In thirty years Birmingham and Sheffield doubled in size; Liverpool, Leeds, Manchester and Glasgow more than doubled, and by 1820 London had one and a quarter million inhabitants. By 1851, for the first time in history, more than half the population of the country was living in urban areas.

The horrors of town life, to be described by Tennyson in *Maud* and elsewhere, were primarily the result of overcrowding, when vast numbers of people, including Irish immigrants, suddenly converged on relatively small districts, without adequate housing, sanitation, water supplies or local government. And to the health risks created by untreated sewage and industrial waste was added that of chronic air pollution, from the sulphurous smoke belched out by coal furnaces and domestic fires.

Working conditions were equally bad. In factories and mines men, women, and even small children were made to work fantastically long hours for minimal wages, as employers, intoxicated by visions of profit from machinery, began to treat employees as mere 'appendages of the machine'. Then there was always the threat of being thrown out of work without warning, for improvements in techniques often led to over-production for existing markets, and so to periodic slumps.

In the absence of a police force (no serious steps were taken to provide one even for London until 1829), these dense concentrations of desperately poor, largely illiterate and justly resentful people were obviously dangerous, and made the middle classes increasingly afraid of mob violence. This fear had been awakened by the French Revolution, and by Tom Paine's best-selling defence of it, *The Rights of Man* (1791-2). In this he had also worked out in some detail an attractive scheme for a welfare state, which could be the reward of a radical change in society.

The Tory government tried to meet the situation with a repressive régime, in which Habeas Corpus was suspended (1817) and public meetings calling for Parliamentary Reform were treated as revolutionary outrages. In 1819 a peaceful and orderly gathering of about 60,000 men, women and children were charged by cavalry in St Peter's Fields, Manchester: eleven were killed, and hundreds were wounded by sabres or horses' hooves.

Some members of the ruling class, however, reacted more humanely to the problem. In 1820 the 'Gentlemen of Lanarkshire' invited Robert Owen, who had been managing a highly successful factory on philanthropic lines, to submit a plan 'for relieving Public Distress and Removing Discontent' among the 'Poor and Working Classes'. He produced a somewhat Utopian scheme for the establishment of self-supporting 'Villages of Co-operation'; and although he had little success with his various attempts to put his theories into action, he exerted a long-term influence on the development of the Co-operative Movement, of Socialism, and of Trades Unions.

In *A New View of Society* (1813) Owen had already called for 'a national system of training and education for the poor and uninstructed'. No coherent system of primary education was established until 1870; but the 1820s saw some progress in adult education, with the founding by Lord Brougham of the Society for the Diffusion of Useful Knowledge (1827), which published all kinds of cheap educational literature, including *The Penny Magazine* (1832–45) and *The Penny Cyclopaedia* (1833–44). Brougham also encouraged the formation of Mechanics' Institutes, where small libraries could be collected, and working men could meet for lectures and discussions. The London Institute was opened in 1824, and by 1860 there were over 600 of them. Tennyson used the annual festival of the Maidstone Mechanics' Institute as the scene of *The Princess* (1847). But advances in education were very slow: even in the 1840s only about two-thirds of the male population, and half of the female, were able to sign their names.

England in Tennyson's youth was thus a highly explosive mixture of ignorance, poverty, commercial exploitation, popular discontent, repressive government, progressive theorizing and reforming zeal. That disaster was averted and conditions gradually improved was largely due to two main types of thinking, Evangelical and Utilitarian.

The Evangelical movement, best represented by William Wilberforce's *A Practical View of the Prevailing Religious System of Professed Christians* (1797) aimed to replace nominal Christianity by a genuine personal religion which expressed itself by a high standard of moral behaviour. It tried to allay discontent among the under-privileged by persuading them that the miseries of their lot were divinely ordained; but it also urged the privileged classes to take practical steps for the relief of their fellow-men, and encouraged various kinds of humanitarian reform. Three years before Tennyson's birth Wilberforce's efforts had brought about the abolition of the slave trade; and although he showed no interest in the plight of industrial slaves at home (he advocated the Combination Acts of 1799 and 1800, which made trades unions illegal), another Evangelical, Lord Shaftesbury, was largely responsible for the Factory Acts which, from 1833 onwards, began, however inadequately, to improve working conditions.

Utilitarianism was a purely rationalistic approach to the same problems. Originating in Jeremy Bentham's *Introduction to the Principles of Morals and Legislation* (1789), it was developed by James Mill and by his son, John Stuart Mill, whose *Utilitarianism* (1861) elaborated and somewhat humanized Bentham's original principle: 'It is the greatest happiness of the greatest number that is the measure of right and wrong.' This was the philosophy behind a long series of reforms during Tennyson's lifetime, which gradually transformed a social, political and legal system based on tradition and privilege into something like a democracy.

Through his mother, Evangelicalism was a strong early influence on

3

Tennyson's thought, though he came to reject the more literal-minded elements in its theology. He tended to base his own conclusions on emotion or intuition, rather than on logical calculations of the Utilitarian type. It was, however, J. S. Mill who published (1835) one of the first perceptive reviews of Tennyson's early volumes; and the poet certainly took to heart Mill's advice to 'cultivate, and with no half devotion, philosophy as well as poetry' (*London Review*, 1,402–24).

Until he went to Cambridge at eighteen, however, he knew hardly more of contemporary thought than of contemporary society: he was influenced mainly by the literature of the past. Much of his early reading was in classical and in eighteenth-century literature (his first attempt at English verse, written on a slate at about the age of six, was in the style of Thomson). Wordsworth, Shelley and Keats had written their best work before he was thirteen, but it was only at Cambridge that he seems to have had extensive access to their poetry. Meanwhile the living poets who made the greatest impact on him were Scott and Byron. At eleven he composed a lost epic of 6,000 lines in the style of *Marmion* (1808) but the dominant influence was that of Byron, and the day he heard the news of Byron's death (1824) was recalled by Tennyson as one on which 'the whole world seemed to be darkened for me' (*Memoir*, vol. 1, p. 4).

II

Going to Trinity College, Cambridge (1827) meant moving from a very secluded family environment to a much larger society of his contemporaries; and it also opened his eyes to what was going on in the country as a whole. In particular he was brought up against the urgent question of Parliamentary Reform. The system of representation had not been adapted to the recent shifts of population: 'rotten boroughs' like Old Sarum still had two MPs, nominated without election by wealthy landowners, while large new industrial towns like Manchester, Birmingham, Sheffield and Leeds were quite unrepresented.

The call for reform came first from the industrialists, who wanted to assert their right to political power against that of the landowners; but the cry was taken up by the working classes, who believed that justice would never be done to them until the franchise was widened. Riots broke out all over the country. Workers in the North started paramilitary training, in the South agricultural labourers began setting fire to ricks. Tennyson helped to extinguish some of these rick-fires near Cambridge, and acquired in the process a splendid image for a face turning red with rage, to be used in *The Princess* (iv, 564-7):

> the wrathful bloom
> As of some fire against a stormy cloud,
> When the wild peasant rights himself, the rick
> Flames, and his anger reddens in the heavens. . . .

On one occasion he was among the student volunteers who paraded, armed with clubs, to defend the university against a threatened invasion by rioters; but although he disliked their methods of 'righting' themselves, he felt great sympathy with them, and was very anxious that their wrongs should be righted. This, he was sure, could only be done by Parliamentary Reform, and when, after nearly fifteen months of violent agitation, the first Reform Act was passed (1832), abolishing rotten boroughs, giving representation to the large new towns, and extending the vote to householders with an annual property-value of £10, he celebrated the occasion by 'madly' ringing the bells of Somersby church in the middle of the night, to the annoyance of the new Rector.

Soon afterwards, however, he wrote some poems expressing what was to be his permanent attitude to Reform: that although it was long overdue, it must be carried out gradually, and by constitutional means. He had registered the sinister fact that, although the Act did practically nothing for the working classes, it was passed under the threat of mob violence.

These poems were not published at the time, and his first two volumes, *Poems, Chiefly Lyrical* (1830) and *Poems* (1833) showed no sign of interest in politics. They seemed strangely remote from the contemporary world, and this was one of the reasons for their poor reception. Readers and reviewers of poetry just then were seriously wondering whether poetry had any future. What was there for poets to say that had not been said already? And how could poetry be written in an age of science and machinery? The only answer, it seemed, was for poets to create a 'modern' type of poetry, by writing on modern themes. 'Is not the French Revolution as good as the siege of Troy?' asked one critic. From this point of view, Tennyson's poems appeared modern only in their style and versification, which were considered eccentric and affected: there was nothing modern about their subject-matter, unless this could be regarded as primarily psychological.

Another demand that was being made on poetry was that it should express and instil sympathy with ordinary humanity: it should deal, in simple language, with basic human experiences, familiar to everyone, and convey 'the transcendent and eternal grandeur of common-place and all-time truths'. And what kind of experience had Tennyson described in 'The Kraken'? That of a mythical monster, asleep (but still eating 'huge seaworms') at the bottom of the sea.

The events of the next few years gave him material more in line with current poetics. The sudden death of his Cambridge friend, Arthur Hallam, in 1833, set him writing short poems on the common human experience of love and bereavement, and when these were finally collected to form *In Memoriam* (1850), he could no longer be charged with lack of human sympathy. Meanwhile the state of the country threatened to provide him with a modern theme quite as dramatic as the French Revolution. The poorest classes, disappointed by the effects of the Reform Act, felt outraged by the Poor Law Amendment Act of 1834. This was the first important legislation inspired by the Utilitarians, and certainly rationalized the system of poor-relief; but it caused great hardship, first by the sudden withdrawal of outside relief from the able-bodied worker in distress, and second by the harshness with which the new workhouses ('Bastilles', as they came to be called) were administered. The principle of the Act was that the situation of the pauper 'must cease to be really or apparently so eligible as the situation of the independent labourers of the lowest class'; and this was implemented by such practices as separating married couples, whatever their age, and preventing parents from seeing their children in the same workhouse.

Continuing unrest among the working classes led to the rise of the Chartists (1838), who drew up a 'People's Charter' demanding a much more radical reform of the Parliamentary and electoral system. Though finally unsuccessful, this movement caused great public anxiety by organizing huge torchlight processions; and when their petition, with almost a million and a quarter signatures, was rejected by Parliament (1839), there was widespread rioting, and for a while civil war seemed imminent.

One factor that helped to save England from revolution was the mood of hopefulness created by sensational advances in technology. In 1830 the Liverpool and Manchester Railway had opened. Tennyson travelled on it one night, and, failing to see the wheels in the darkness, assumed that they ran in grooves. That was when he composed the line ('Locksley Hall', 1842): 'Let the great world spin for ever down the ringing grooves of change'.

The railway was an apt symbol for the astonishing progress that was being made. It suggested unprecedented speed (Tennyson later described the sensation of travelling in an open, third-class carriage as more like flying than anything else); and the very speed at which the railways were built (5,000 miles of line during the next twenty years) was a feat unequalled in previous human history. The symbol also included the idea of limitless change, for by accelerating commercial activity the railway was turning England into the richest country in the world; it was also transforming its landscape, and going far towards abolishing the distinction between town and country.

In many other ways technology was changing the character of everyday life. Better transport was followed by cheaper communication, with the introduction of the penny post (1840). Inventions of 1837 made the telegraph a commercial proposition, and in 1844 the first line was opened between Paddington and Slough, to be reproduced in miniature, as an educational toy, in the Prologue of *The Princess* (77-9). Gas lighting, which dated from 1812, was spreading rapidly. It appeared as a special luxury in 'The Palace of Art' (*Poems*, p. 412), but by the 1850s it was normal in middle-class houses. Photography was invented around 1839, to become one of Tennyson's special problems when Julia Cameron became his neighbour and kept badgering him to pose for pictures.

The accession of Queen Victoria (1837), with whom Tennyson was later to form a warm friendship, inaugurated a new social ethic, of respectability and domesticity. After her marriage to Prince Albert in 1840, the Royal Family came to epitomize that glorification of home, and that horror of sex, which are considered so typically Victorian. The cult of respectability may be regarded as a secularized version of the Evangelical emphasis on moral behaviour. As for the devaluation of sex, it may, perhaps, best be seen as a desperate effort to build a stable society in circumstances which constantly threatened a relapse into barbarism and chaos; and also as a response to Malthus's highly influential *Essay on Population* (1797). This attributed most social evils to the tendency of human beings to reproduce faster than food supplies could be increased. Contraception he rejected as 'vice'; so the only solution was 'moral restraint'.

Tennyson never seems to have doubted the soundness of this ethic, which he expressed with full conviction in his poetry. His longest work,

Idylls of the King (1859–85), shows a sexual irregularity (the adultery of Lancelot and Guinevere) leading to the downfall of a civilization; and the gospel of domesticity is so prominent in the very popular *Enoch Arden* volume (1864) that he first thought of calling it *Idylls of the Hearth*.

III

Poems (1842) showed Tennyson's increased concern with the modern world by a number of political poems, and by explicit references to the Reform Act and to Chartists ('Walking to the Mail', 59–68). In 'Locksley Hall', besides celebrating the achievements of science, he commented gloomily on the social situation:

> Slowly comes a hungry people, as a lion, creeping
>   nigher,
> Glares at one that nods and winks behind a
>   slowly-dying fire.   (135–6)

But most of the new poems, like those reprinted from the earlier volumes, had more to do with the poet's inner life, or with past literature, than with the world around him. Although friends, reviewers and his own inclinations impelled him to tackle a contemporary theme, he had not yet found one that suited him.

Meanwhile the 'condition of England', a phrase much used at that period, became more and more threatening. Working-class distress was increased by an economic depression, which reduced wages still further and caused widespread unemployment. A potato famine in Ireland (1845–6) increased the flow of Irish immigrants. The ghastly living and working conditions of the industrial poor were revealed in a series of government reports, and Friedrich Engels described them even more vividly in *The Condition of the Working Class in England in 1844* (1845). In *The Communist Manifesto* (printed in London, 1848) his friend Karl Marx prescribed revolution as the only cure.

Revolutions duly took place in France, Germany, Austria and Italy. The Chartists held a general convention, prepared a new petition to Parliament, and planned to call a national assembly to enforce their demand for the Charter. Troops were called into London, and this second attempt at revolution fizzled out.

A milder form of revolution took place that year in art. The Pre-Raphaelite Brotherhood was formed by Millais, Holman Hunt and Dante Gabriel Rossetti to overthrow the current artistic ortho-doxy. The movement was partly inspired by Tennyson's 1842 poems, and expressed itself in new forms of mediaevalism, of social realism, and of moral didacticism. Members of the group were later responsible for an illustrated edition of Tennyson's poetry (1857).

The year 1848 saw one of the first significant gains in the long, slow revolt of women against the legal, social, professional and educational handicaps imposed on them by men. Queen's College was founded for the higher education of women by F. D. Maurice, who later became one of Tennyson's friends. The previous year, while Maurice was organiz-ing the 'lectures for Ladies' which were the germ of the College, Tennyson published *The Princess,* on the subject of women's rights and education. It was his first large-scale attempt to treat a contempor-ary theme. Today, the line he took on this question seems rather re-actionary; but the poem was published more than twenty years before the first serious statement of the feminist case by an established male writer (J. S. Mill's *The Subjection of Women,* 1869). When this is re-membered, it seems remarkable how progressive this far from established poet dared to be. The climate of opinion on the subject at the time may be gauged from the fact that in 1848 the Bishop of London expressly forbade women to attend lectures at King's College on electricity.

In a revolutionary decade, the most subversive publication was not, perhaps, after all *The Communist Manifesto,* but *Vestiges of Creation* (1844). This was a scientifically inaccurate, but immensely readable argument for a theory of 'Progressive Development', i.e. evolution. It went into twelve editions and, as Darwin said in *The Origin of Species* (1859), did 'excellent service in calling attention to the subject, in removing prejudice, and in thus preparing the ground for the reception of analogous views'. Realizing from reviews that the book fitted in with his own ideas, Tennyson immediately sent for a copy; and although 'the sections of "In Memoriam" about Evolution had been read by his friends some years before' (*Memoir,* vol. 1, p. 223), *Vestiges* appears to have had some influence on the Epilogue to that poem.

Tennyson had always been interested in science, and had studied Lyell's *Principles of Geology* (1830-3), which made it impossible to take literally the account of the Creation in *Genesis,* or to believe that the world had come into existence as recently as 4004 BC (a calculation that had been printed in many Bibles). Reflecting on the death of Arthur Hallam, he had already been faced by one of the period's greatest problems: how to retain faith in a personal God, and in an after-life, in spite of the scientific evidence to the contrary. *In Memoriam* suggested, by way of a solution, that subjective religious feelings were also evidence, and of a more conclusive kind. To many readers, then as now, this solution seemed inadequate; but the honesty with which he had tackled the fundamental dilemma gave the poem a wide appeal, and led, the same year (1850), to his appointment as Poet Laureate.

IV

The new decade opened with an event which marked the triumph of technology, and introduced a relatively placid period, during which administrative reforms and a rising standard of living temporarily appeased social discontent. This was the Great Exhibition (1851), an enormously successful project largely promoted by Prince Albert. It attracted over six million visitors. The exhibits included such weird artefacts as a collapsible piano for use in yachts, and Gothic furniture made of cast bronze; but what Tennyson liked best was the building that housed them, appropriately an example of new techniques applied to architecture. Built entirely of glass and iron, the Crystal Palace (as it was named by *Punch*) was a light, airy structure, big enough to roof over some Hyde Park trees more than ninety feet high.

Tennyson saw the Exhibition ('To the Queen', *Poems*, p. 991) as an emblem of peace:

> When Europe and the scattered ends
> Of our fierce world were mixt as friends
> And brethren in her halls of glass.

The death of the Duke of Wellington the following year (which Tennyson commemorated with a sonorous funeral ode) seemed to confirm the close of an epoch of war; but in 1854 the Crimean War began, for the defence of Turkey against Russia. In retrospect, this war seems a fearful example of diplomatic and military incompetence, memorable only for the ghastly sufferings of the troops, and Florence Nightingale's victory over chaos at Scutari; but to Tennyson and most of his contemporaries it seemed at the time entirely just and necessary. In 'The Charge of the Light Brigade' he expressed his instinctive feeling that courage was a glorious thing, even in a context of sheer inefficiency; and in *Maud* (1855) he put into the mouth of a mentally unbalanced young lover a positive enthusiasm for the war, together with a condemnation of the horrible social conditions that had long prevailed in peacetime.

This ingenious treatment of two modern themes, the 'Condition of England' question and the Crimean War, was at first badly received, partly because its form (a story told indirectly through a series of dramatic lyrics) was novel enough to seem obscure, and partly because enlightened readers, including his friend Gladstone, were disgusted by the apparent implication of the poem: that war was preferable to peace.

Immediately after the Crimean War came the news of the Indian Mutiny (1857). The atrocities committed by the rebels hardened many English hearts, Tennyson's among them, towards the native populations of the Empire. In 1859 there was a war-scare: Napoleon III was thought to be planning an invasion of England. One hundred and eighty thousand men joined a Volunteer Force – some, no doubt, in response to Tennyson's recruiting poem, 'Riflemen Form!', which had been written in 1852, under the threat of another French invasion, but was now published in *The Times* (9 May).

Among the peaceful events of the decade were the foundation of the Working Men's College (1854) by F. D. Maurice and Tom Hughes (a friend, and a future friend of Tennyson's); and the publication of the first penny newspaper, the *Daily Telegraph* (1855). Both events were symptomatic of an expanding reading public. Dickens was the first major author to cater successfully for the new lower-class reader; but now Tennyson, too, was able to achieve his childhood ambition to be 'a *popular* poet' (*Memoir*, vol. 2, p. 79). The first four *Idylls of the King* (1859) were simple and slightly repetitive in style; and their subject-matter (love, jealousy, adultery, infatuation) was not too far removed from that of the popular magazine-story. Their moral scheme was equally familiar: a parabolic contrast between two good women (Enid, Elaine) and two bad ones (Vivien, Guinevere). The result was a sale of 10,000 copies. Tennyson became the poet, not merely of the intelligentsia, but of the whole community.

V

Vestiges of Creation had been the production of an amateur (Robert Chambers, part-publisher of *Chambers's Encyclopaedia*); and it had suggested no plausible mechanism by which evolution could take place. Darwin's *The Origin of Species* (1859) came out with the authority of a professional scientist; it was packed with corroborative evidence, and it supplied the missing mechanism, Natural Selection, or the reproduction of chance variations which had survival value in the 'struggle for existence'. It had to be taken seriously, and it immediately started the debate between religion and science that Tennyson had anticipated in *In Memoriam*.

To the orthodox believer, the idea of Natural Selection was blasphemous, since it replaced Providence by a series of accidents. Although, according to his autobiography, Darwin had lost his faith long before, he politely agreed when Tennyson told him in 1868: 'Your theory of Evolution does not make against Christianity' (*Memoir*, vol. 2, p. 57). But Samuel Wilberforce, the Bishop of Oxford, took a different view, and at a meeting of the British Association for the Advancement of Science, held on 30 June 1860, he undertook to 'smash Darwin' in the interests of true religion. Darwin was ill and could not attend, but his theory was defended by Thomas Huxley, whose obvious integrity and scientific reputation effectively pricked the balloon of Wilberforce's rhetoric, and made his facetious question, whether Huxley claimed descent from the apes on his grandfather's or his grandmother's side, seem as silly as it was.

The science-versus-religion controversy was further inflamed by the publication in the same year of *Essays and Reviews*, an attempt by seven thoughtful members of the Church of England to bring Church doctrine more into line with the findings of science and of scientific criticism of the Bible. The 'seven against Christ', as they were promptly nicknamed, included Tennyson's friend Benjamin Jowett, the future Master of Balliol. Eleven thousand clergymen signed a protest against the book, the Bishops condemned it, and action was taken against two of the authors in an ecclesiastical court. A similar outcry was raised against Bishop Colenso's *Critical Examination of the Pentateuch* (1862-79), which, by calculating such things as the number of tents that two million Israelites would have needed in *Exodus*, concluded that these books were post-Exile forgeries.

Tennyson's interest in the controversy, which continued throughout his life, led to the formation (1869) of the Metaphysical Society, a group of theological and scientific experts, including Huxley, whose terms of reference were 'to submit to searching criticism the intellectual foundation of the spreading positivism and agnosticism'. Tennyson's contribution to the first meeting was 'The Higher Pantheism', which was duly read aloud, but not thought suitable for formal discussion.

In 1865 another controversy had arisen about E. J. Eyre, the Governor of Jamaica, who had savagely suppressed a small Negro rebellion, hanging nearly 600 people, and flogging many more. Gladstone angrily denounced his behaviour, and other friends of Tennyson's, Thomas Hughes and Huxley, formed a committee to press for Eyre's prosecution for murder. Tennyson, recalling the Indian Mutiny, thought that Eyre's action had probably been justified, as the only method of saving English lives; and he even subscribed to a fund for Eyre's defence. To Gladstone's passionate counter-arguments he is said to have replied only with a growl: 'Niggers are tigers, niggers are tigers' (Sir Charles Tennyson, *Alfred Tennyson*, 1968, p. 359).

In 1867 England moved further towards democracy with a Reform Act which gave the vote to the working classes in towns. To Tennyson's old friend, Thomas Carlyle, this was equivalent to 'shooting Niagara'; and Matthew Arnold took a less hysterical, but no less anxious view in *Culture and Anarchy* (1869). The fear of anarchy was increased by the riot in Hyde Park (1866), which virtually forced the Bill through Parliament: a crowd of people, estimated at between one and two hundred thousand, were demonstrating for Reform, and when forbidden to enter the park, they simply pushed down the railings for about 1,400 yards, and held their meeting. Karl Marx, whose *Das Kapital*, written in the Reading Room of the British Museum, was published a year later, regretted that the railings had not been used as weapons against the police: 'Then there would have been some fun.'

Tennyson had long before picked out, as one of the 'two great social questions impending in England', 'the housing and education of the poor man before making him our master' (*Memoir*, vol. 1, p. 249); and he felt deeply apprehensive at the transfer of political power to an uneducated 'Populace', whose main interests (as defined by Arnold) were 'bawling, hustling, smashing' and 'beer'. The decade closed with an Education Act (1870) which at least ensured some elementary instruction for the children of the poor; but the dangers of democracy continued to worry him.

His own appeal, however, to the literate working classes was growing steadily; and after the extraordinary success of the *Enoch Arden* volume (1864), of which 40,000 copies were rapidly sold, he decided to earn the title which some reviewers had given him ('Poet of the People'), by publishing a special popular selection of his poems, to be sold in sixpenny parts. It came out the following year, with a dedication to the 'Working Men of England'.

As his reputation grew with the general public, it began to decline

13

with his original supporters, the intelligentsia. Swinburne's *Poems and Ballads* (1866) put a rival in the field, whose talent for versification was comparable with Tennyson's, and whose subject-matter, which included the aspects of sex which Tennyson had carefully avoided, was far more sensational. Critics were coming to expect a more complex view of life than Tennyson's poetry presented, and the intellectual and psychological subtlety of Browning's *The Ring and the Book* (1868-9) were welcomed as a refreshing change from what one reviewer called 'the graceful presentation of the Arthurian legend for drawing rooms... the little ethics of the rectory parlour set to sweet music'. Rejected by the critics of his youth for writing on subjects insufficiently commonplace, Tennyson was now being disparaged for precisely the opposite reason.

Intelligent women, too, were now less likely to approve of the poet who wrote *The Princess*. Since the foundation of *The Englishwoman's Journal* (1857) the feminist movement had at last begun to make progress. In 1865 J. S. Mill became the MP for Westminster, and two years later raised in Parliament the question of votes for women. In 1869 he published *The Subjection of Women,* and in 1870 his Women's Suffrage Bill was carried at its first reading by a majority of thirty. In the same year a Married Women's Property Act gave married women, for the first time, the right to some of their own earnings. The pioneers of feminism in the 1860s must have thought *The Princess* rather outdated. Emily Davies, for instance, the first Principal of Girton, made delightful fun in her pamphlet, *The Higher Education of Women* (1866), of Tennyson's 'bisexual theory of the human ideal', i.e. that woman's function in life is to complement man's personality.

Against any decline, however, in his English reputation must be set his growing fame in America, which had been brought much closer by the laying of the Atlantic cable in 1866. Arnold called it 'that great rope, with a Philistine at each end of it talking inutilities!' But Americans were not all Philistines: in 1871 Tennyson received an offer from New York of £1,000 for any poem of three stanzas.

VI

Since 1853 he had been living at Farringford, a country house near Freshwater in the Isle of Wight. He had first approached it by horse-bus and an open rowing-boat, and one of its great attractions for him was its seclusion. By 1869 improvements in all kinds of transport had made it a target for tourists and sightseers. He once looked up from his work to see a man staring at him from a branch of a tree on a level with his study window; and he was forced to have a bridge (which may still be seen) constructed across the deep lane that separates the garden from a field in which he liked to compose, to avoid being waylaid by autograph-hunters.

He therefore had another house built (Aldworth) on a much more inaccessible site three miles from Haslemere in Surrey. Here he got the best of both worlds: protection from the tiresome aspects of the machine age, and enjoyment of its benefits, such as a bath with hot and cold water laid on, which particularly pleased him, and which he used three times a day (Memoir, vol. 2, p. 81).

At Aldworth, as at Farringford, he was visited by a steady stream of guests, including nearly all the most important figures in Victorian literature, art, music and politics. He made frequent trips to London, and kept closely in touch with current affairs. When Dickens died in 1870, Tennyson's presence at the funeral in Westminster Abbey caused great excitement. Women climbed on the seats to catch a glimpse of him, and the service in honour of the dead novelist ended with the living poet sitting in state, surrounded by a dense crowd of his admirers.

He was deeply perturbed by the outbreak of the Franco-Prussian War (1871), and was so reluctant to publish his very light-weight song cycle, The Window, with music by Arthur Sullivan, 'in the dark shadow of these days' (Poems, p. 1197), that he is said to have offered Sullivan £500 to cancel the whole arrangement. He feared that England was not in a position to defend herself against a possible attack from the Continent, and for that reason stressed the need to keep on good terms with British territories overseas. He was therefore indignant when The Times suggested that it was 'too costly' to maintain the connection between Canada and England. In 'To the Queen' (1873) he protested passionately against this unworthy thought, and insisted upon the importance of preserving 'our ocean-empire with her boundless homes/For ever-broadening England' (29-30). For this he was duly thanked by the Governor General of Canada.

The development that affected Tennyson most at this time was the revival of the theatre. This dated back to 1843, when Covent Garden and Drury Lane lost their statutory monopoly. There were now more than forty theatres in London and, patronized by the Queen, the theatre had become respectable. The success of Henry Irving's Hamlet in 1874 (it ran for 200 nights) and profitable Shakespearian productions at three other theatres gave new hopes for poetic drama; so Tennyson, who knew Irving, and had written a quasi-Elizabethan comedy at the age of fourteen, decided, at sixty-five, to try his hand as a playwright. He began with a historical trilogy, intended to supplement Shakespeare's history plays. The subject of the first, *Queen Mary* (produced 1875), related to contemporary indignation against the Pope, who had formally rejected the idea of coming to terms with 'progress, liberalism and modern civilization' (1864), and reaffirmed the doctrine of Papal Infallibility (1870).

Tennyson wrote four more plays which were produced, with varying success, during his lifetime. The last, *The Promise of May* (1882), was a melodrama with a villain who epitomized such current ideas as socialism, atheism and sexual freedom, and whose philosophy seemed to be based on the Conclusion to Walter Pater's *The Renaissance* (1873): 'What can a man, then, live for but sensations,/Pleasant ones?' *(Oxford,* p. 726). This play was a theatrical failure; but *Becket,* produced after Tennyson's death by Henry Irving (1893), ran for 112 nights.

VII

In 1884 Gladstone's Reform Act gave the vote to the working classes in rural districts, and increased the electorate from three millions to five. Tennyson was now a close friend of Gladstone's, and on his advice had accepted a peerage (1883); but in the House of Lords he supported the Bill only with great reluctance, thinking that further delay might lead to a revolution, which would become world-wide. 'May I not live to see it' *(Memoir,* vol. 2, p. 303). In 'Freedom' (1884) he implicitly warned Gladstone not to give in to 'brass mouths and iron lungs' demanding 'all things in an hour' (39-40).

In this category of political extremists a notable figure was the poet turned Socialist, William Morris, who that year, with other members of the Social Democratic Federation, formed the Socialist League, and started publishing *Chants for Socialists.* Tennyson was prepared to agree to 'the heavy taxing of large incomes'; but his comment on a Socialist paper was that it made him 'vomit mentally'*(Diary,* 1907, p. 330).

He was equally nauseated by talk of disestablishing the Church, and must have been appalled when the militant atheist, Charles Bradlaugh, was finally allowed to take his seat in Parliament (1886), in spite of having refused to swear on the Bible.

At the end of his long life, Tennyson was living in a world that horrified him. Young girls were reading Zola. Irish peasants were burning horses and cattle alive: 'Couldn't they blow up that horrible island with dynamite,' he once asked, 'and carry it off in pieces – a long way off?' (*Diary*, p. 297). In 'Locksley Hall Sixty Years After' (1886), a sequel to 'Locksley Hall' (1842), this horror of the contemporary world is expressed by an old man of eighty from whom Tennyson always insisted on dissociating himself. In his 'On the Jubilee of Queen Victoria' (1887) he voiced, although with a mention of 'spectres moving in the darkness' (67), a much more positive attitude to the history of his period:

> Fifty years of ever-broadening Commerce!
> Fifty years of ever-brightening Science!
> Fifty years of ever-widening Empire! (52-4)

Perhaps Science should have the last word. Two years before the poet's death, Thomas Edison sent him a phonograph (invented 1877), into which he recited some of his poems. In recordings made from the original wax cylinders, his voice still manages to emerge from a barrage of background noise. It is not, as he described the sound from the 'mouth' of the machine, like 'the squeak of a dying mouse' (*Materials*, vol. 4, p. 329), but strong enough to show his personal style of reading poetry: a passionate kind of intoning, which stressed rhythm more than meaning. It seems somehow typical of that fabulously inventive age to have enabled its greatest poet to make himself heard in ours.

2

The Poet

Alfred Tennyson was the fourth son of Dr George Tennyson, the Rector of Somersby in Lincolnshire. Dr Tennyson was the elder son of a wealthy landowner, but had been disinherited in favour of his younger brother, Charles; so while Charles became the heir to the large estate of Bayons Manor, near Tealby, George was reduced to the status of a country clergyman. This unfair treatment by his father embittered his whole life, and the poet grew up in an atmosphere of resentment against his grandfather, and his favoured uncle Charles.

Dr Tennyson, who had married the Rector's daughter at Louth, combined powerful intellect with an irritable and depressive temperament. At Cambridge he had not been a model student (he once fired a pistol through a window of Trinity College chapel); but he became widely read in Greek, Latin and English literature, and acquired some knowledge of Syriac, Hebrew and modern languages. His large library formed the basis of Alfred's early education, and his practice of music and poetry (he played the harp and wrote some satirical poems) must have encouraged the poet's development. It may even be possible to see the germ of Tennyson's later religious thought in this extract from one of his father's sermons: 'The benevolent genius of Christianity affords the strongest presumption of its verity' (*Materials*, vol. 1, p. 32).

Latin poetry seems at first to have been a stronger influence than English. Before sending him to Louth Grammar School at the age of eight, Dr Tennyson made Alfred learn the four books of Horace's *Odes* by heart. The school, which he had expected to be 'a kind of paradise', turned out to be more like hell, with bullying boys and a sadistic headmaster. 'The only good I ever got from it', he said, 'was the memory of the words "*sonus desilientis aquae*" and of an old wall covered with wild weeds opposite the school windows' (*Materials*, vol. 1, pp. 23–5). The Latin words, an onomatopoeic fragment of a pentameter ('the sound of water leaping down') were evidently derived partly from Ovid's *Fasti*, and partly from the first Horace *Ode* he ever learned, the one addressed to a fountain.

He left school after five years, to be taught at home by his father, and perhaps indirectly by his elder brothers. Among the children's amusements were staging Arthurian tournaments in the garden, and composing serial stories, to be read aloud after dinner. Alfred's stories, some humorous and some 'savagely dramatic', were reckoned the most exciting; and he had already started writing English poetry. For an ode on his grandmother's death, his grandfather gave him half a guinea, adding, with a singular lack of prescience, that he would never earn any more money by poetry; but the young poet was quite sure he would be famous.

At this period he wrote a Miltonic fragment, 'Armageddon', and an unfinished pseudo-Elizabethan comedy, *The Devil and the Lady*. Though mostly flippant in tone, this sometimes suggests a mood of deep despondency, like that of some fictional prose, of roughly the same date, preserved in a manuscript at Harvard:

> No, Athanasius, there is not a hope which I feel not annihilated within me, not a joy which has not withered. The world holds out no beacon which can allure me over the waste of life. ... O that it were not a crime to snap the vital thread! Shall I not find peace in the tomb?

In such a mood Tennyson more than once threw himself down on a grave in the churchyard at night, and prayed for death. The main cause of his distress seems to have been the mental deterioration of his father, who was becoming an alcoholic, and whose chronic depression now often expressed itself in outbursts of terrifying violence.

Byron, however, had shown him how personal misery could be used as material for poetry, and Tennyson exploited his own unhappiness in several of his first published poems. Among his contributions to *Poems by Two Brothers* (1827) was 'The Grave of a Suicide'. The volume was published anonymously by a Louth bookseller, who paid the two brothers, Alfred and Charles (though Frederick had also participated), ten pounds in cash and ten in books for it. Part of the cash was spent on a celebration trip to the sea at Mablethorpe.

II

Tennyson was shy all his life, and the initial shock of immersion in student life (November 1827) must have been quite traumatic. The first glimpse of the crowded Hall at dinner was enough to send him and Charles scurrying back to their lodgings; but published poets of such striking appearance were bound to arouse curiosity. Tall, dark-skinned and handsome, with long, dark, wavy hair, in which his wife would detect 'a pervading shade of gold', Alfred looked exactly as a poet should; and the effect was enhanced by the far-away look in his eyes which was actually a symptom of myopia. He soon made a number of friends, in whose society his shyness disappeared, and Thackeray before long was moved to say: 'My dear Alfred, you do talk damned well.' He became noted for his epigrams, for example his comment on the portrait of an elderly politician: 'It looks rather like a retired panther' (*Memoir*, vol. 1, p. 37); for his story-telling, and for his mimes of George IV, and of the sun coming out of a cloud. He also distinguished himself as a Shakespearian actor, especially in the part of Malvolio. Frederick, however, was not doing quite so well at Trinity. In December 1828 he was rusticated for insubordination, throwing Dr Tennyson (whose own behaviour at Cambridge had been rather similar) into a rage in which he threatened to kill his son with a large knife, and tried to duplicate a previous exploit by firing a gun through the kitchen window.

Meanwhile another student had come up to Trinity from Eton, of whom Tennyson was to say 'he was as near perfection as mortal man could be' (*Materials*, vol. 1, p. 51). Arthur Hallam was the son of Henry Hallam, the historian. Of his brilliance and charm there seems to be no doubt, though neither quality is obvious in his writings. By the age of nine he was an expert in French and Latin, and had written several tragedies in prose and verse. Since he was just then convalescing from a hopeless love affair, he was perhaps ripe for some new emotional bond; and he was exactly the sort of friend that Tennyson needed - someone who suffered from depression, but could rise above it; who wrote poetry, but found Alfred's poems more exciting than his own.

In May 1829 Arthur Hallam and Tennyson became members of a debating society satirically nicknamed 'The Apostles'. It met every Saturday night during term to discuss, over coffee and anchovy sandwiches, serious questions of religion, literature and society. From two founder-members, John Sterling and F. D. Maurice, it inherited a tradition of reforming zeal and liberal theology, and its members included many eminent Victorians in embryo, such as R. C. Trench, the originator of the *Oxford English Dictionary*, R. M. Milnes, the first authority on Keats and the rejected suitor of Florence Nightingale, James Spedding, the editor of Bacon, and the Greek scholar, Edmund Lushington.

That June Tennyson won the Chancellor's Medal with 'Timbuctoo', the first blank-verse poem to receive the award. He had not wished to compete, but to satisfy his father had hastily cannibalized 'Armageddon', adding as an epigraph a couplet attributed to Chapman, but probably composed by himself.

After visiting Somersby during the Christmas vacation, and falling in love with Tennyson's sister, Emily, Arthur went on writing poems and encouraging Alfred to do so too, with a view to a joint publication; but finally he decided that his friend's productions, which their whole circle greatly admired, were too good to be published with his own; so Tennyson prepared to publish by himself, and in spite of a last-minute loss of the manuscript from an overcoat pocket, *Poems, Chiefly Lyrical* came out in June 1830.

In the summer vacation John Sterling involved some of the Apostles in supporting a revolution against the tyranny of King Ferdinand VII of Spain, which was being planned in London by General Torrijos; and Tennyson and Hallam set off on a secret mission to take money and coded instructions to the General's confederates in the Pyrenees. The Rector's son was not greatly attracted to their leader, whose motto was *'couper le gorge à tous les curés'*; but he enjoyed the scenery which, with memories of Arthur Hallam, inspired 'In the Valley of Cauteretz' thirty-one years later. They were quite lucky to get back alive: Sterling's cousin, Robert Boyd, was captured and executed by the Spanish authorities, together with Torrijos and his whole party.

Meanwhile Dr Tennyson had returned from a European trip of his own, telling stories of adventures so fantastic as to suggest incipient mental breakdown. His physical condition was certainly much worse, and in February 1831 he went down with an illness diagnosed as typhus. Alfred was called home, and on 16 March his father died. That night Tennyson slept in his bed, 'earnestly desiring to see his ghost, but no ghost came. "You see," he said, "ghosts do not come to imaginative people"' (*Materials*, vol. 1, p. 88).

He needed all his imagination to cope with the family's practical problems at this time. Frederick, Charles and Alfred had all run up debts at Cambridge, and it seemed uneconomical for Alfred to go back and take his degree, unless he meant to do what his grandfather wished, and become a clergyman; but Tennyson was determined to make poetry his career, and to publish another volume. Arthur Hallam tried to help by writing an enthusiastic article on the 1830 volume for the *Englishman's Magazine* (August 1831), and introducing him to a new publisher, Edward Moxon; but the new publication was delayed by a discouraging notice of the first one in *Blackwood's* (May 1832). Written by 'Christopher North' (John Wilson) it made fun of Hallam's article and of 'the not unfrequent silliness' of Tennyson's poems ('Alfred is greatest as an Owl.... All that he wants is to be shot, stuffed, and stuck into a glass-case, to be made immortal in a museum'). The notice ended on a much more positive note: 'Alfred Tennyson is a poet'; but Tennyson, always sensitive to criticism, deeply resented the jocular treatment of his poems and of his friend.

After an enjoyable tour of the Rhine with Arthur in July, he continued work on the new volume, in spite of distracting anxiety about his family. First, there were long wranglings between Arthur's father and Emily's grandfather over a marriage settlement for them, which for the moment made their marriage impossible. Then Alfred's younger brother Edward had a mental breakdown, which ended in life-long insanity; and finally his favourite brother, Charles, was showing signs of psychological trouble, and had become an opium addict.

Thanks largely to Arthur's support and practical help (he saw the manuscript through the press, and read all the proofs) Tennyson's second volume was published in December 1832 (dated 1833 on the title page). Though clearly better than its predecessor, it was less well received. There was only one good review (by W. J. Fox, the first critic to recognize the genius of Browning); and in April 1833 a long, spiteful and heavily sarcastic notice appeared in the highly influential *Quarterly Review*. The writer, J. W. Croker, alluded complacently to his notorious attack on Keats in 1818, and set out to do an equally effective hatchet-job on Tennyson. He succeeded in restricting the book's sales over the next two years to 200 copies out of 450 printed, and in seriously damaging Tennyson's morale. He admitted later that the article had 'almost crushed' him (*Materials*, vol. 1, p. 116).

He persevered, however, writing new poems and revising and improving his old ones. Arthur, whose engagement to Emily had now been recognized by his family, spent several weeks at Somersby, and then went off on a continental trip with his father. Two months later (1

October) the news reached Somersby that Arthur Hallam had been found dead in Vienna.

III

Arthur had long before shown 'symptoms of deranged circulation', and his death from cerebral haemorrhage was, according to one of his friends, 'always feared by us as likely to occur'; but Tennyson seems to have been utterly unprepared for it. The sudden withdrawal of a support on which he, his sister, and his whole family had relied in so many ways, was a paralysing shock. He made determined efforts, however, as a friend reported, 'to divert his thoughts from gloomy brooding, and keep his mind in activity'. He went to dinner-parties, danced, wrote facetious letters, and helped to eat a barrel of oysters; he also worked out a weekly timetable for educating himself in 'History, German, Chemistry, Botany, Electricity, Animal Physiology, Mechanics, Theology and Italian'. Above all he concentrated on rewriting some of his published poems, and composing new ones, including 'Ulysses', 'The Two Voices' (started some months before), 'Morte d'Arthur', the first instalment of his life-work, *Idylls of the King*, and the earliest sections of *In Memoriam*. Section ix was written five days after hearing of Hallam's death.

Increasingly aware of defects in his previous work, the rapidly maturing poet resolved not to publish until he could produce something relatively critic-proof; and he even tried to discourage the appearance of J. S. Mill's favourable review (*London Review*, July 1835), explaining '*I do not wish to be dragged forward again in any shape before the reading public at present*, particularly on the score of my old poems' (*Memoir*, vol.1, p. 145).

In 1834 he had fallen in love with Rosa Baring, an extremely rich girl living at Harrington Hall, two miles from Somersby; but she apparently agreed with her family that Tennyson's worldly prospects were inadequate, and married someone better off (1838). The disillusioning experience served to suggest the theme of several later poems, notably 'Locksley Hall' and *Maud*.

By selling his Chancellor's Medal for £15 he was able (1835) to visit James Spedding in Cumberland, where he enjoyed the scenery, read Wordsworth but refused to go and see him, and acquired a life-long friend, Edward FitzGerald, the translator of Omar Khayyám. The following year he became attracted to his future wife, Emily Sellwood, the daughter of a solicitor in Horncastle (six miles from Somersby), when she was bridesmaid at the wedding of her sister Louisa to Alfred's brother Charles; but Tennyson himself was in no position to marry, with no source of income but a property worth about £3,000 inherited from his grandfather (1835). The bulk of the estate had gone to his uncle Charles, who was spending his new wealth on the conversion of Bayons Manor into a pseudo-Gothic castle, complete with moat, drawbridge and portcullis.

In 1837 the Tennysons were asked to vacate Somersby Rectory, and made their new home at Beech Hill House, High Beech, Epping. Alfred organized every detail of the move, buying all the furniture, and the kitchen and garden equipment. He found the place dreary at first, 'with nothing but that muddy pond in prospect, and those two little sharp-barking dogs' (*Memoir*, vol. 1, p. 168), and pictured all the hurrying crowds of London as they would be in a few years' time, horizontal in their coffins; but he came to like London, thought the Strand and Fleet Street pleasant places to live, and made frequent use of some rooms rented by the family in Mornington Place (later Hampstead Road) in order to see FitzGerald, Spedding and Thackeray.

That year he published 'Oh! that 'twere possible', started after Hallam's death, and now hastily completed and contributed, to please his friend Milnes, to Lord Northampton's *The Tribute*. His own view was that 'To write for people with prefixes to their names is to milk he-goats; there is neither honour nor profit' (*Memoir*, vol. 1, p. 158); but the poem was quite profitable in 1855, when developed into *Maud*.

He made many new friends in London, including Gladstone (who had been Hallam's best friend at Eton), Forster, the biographer of Dickens, Macready the actor, Landor, Rogers and, most congenial of all, Carlyle, who gave this account of the poet (5 September 1840):

A fine, large-featured, dim-eyed, bronze-coloured shaggy-headed man is Alfred; dusty, smoky, free and easy; who swims, outwardly and inwardly, with great composure in an articulate element as of tranquil chaos and tobacco-smoke; great now and then when he does emerge; a most restful, brotherly, solid-hearted man.

The chaos was not always tranquil. Some time that year his engagement to Emily Sellwood, which had been recognized by her family in 1838, was broken off, and her father forbade further correspondence between them. In his view Tennyson was just a layabout, and the lovers seem not to have questioned parental authority. 'In ourselves', wrote Emily, 'there was no change. Whether I did rightly in yielding I cannot tell. My Father's love I never doubted but was divided between two duties. And years of great misery were consequent on my decision.' Tennyson, who expressed the misery of the separation in 'Love and Duty', had another conflict, between love and poetry, since he could doubtless have satisfied Emily's father by giving up full-time writing and taking a steady job. Instead, he staked everything on becoming a successful poet.

This gamble finally paid off, but another did not. He invested his whole capital in a scheme promoted by Dr Matthew Allen, a neighbour at High Beech, for carving wood by machinery (the products to be sold as 'pyroglyphs'). By 1843 the project had collapsed, and Tennyson lost all his money. His mother would have lost hers too, had he not threatened Allen with instant exposure if he did not cancel the agreement that he had got her to sign.

Having long resisted his friends' impatience for another publication, Tennyson had at last decided to publish, when he received a letter from America, 'threatening, tho' in the civilest terms, that, if I will not publish in England, they will do it for me in that land of free men' (*Memoir,* vol. 1, p. 178). This would have meant no guarantee of royalties, since English copyright was not then recognized in America. *Poems* (1842) came out in two volumes, the first containing a selection from the earlier published poems, greatly revised and improved, with seven new poems added, and the second consisting entirely of new poems. Although this publication included much of Tennyson's finest work, it was received at first without much enthusiasm. However, the *Quarterly* virtually recanted by printing a long and friendly, if rather insensitive review by John Sterling (September 1842); and a much more perceptive notice by James Spedding appeared in the *Edinburgh Review* (April 1843), although Spedding's original conclusion, that 'Powers are displayed in these volumes, adequate . . . to the production of a very great work' was weakened by the editor's deletion of *very*.

Though now taken seriously by the critics, and highly valued by small groups of intelligent readers, especially in Cambridge and Oxford, Tennyson seemed as far as ever from success, or even from earning a living by poetry. The frustration of his position after the wood-carving fiasco precipitated him into such a deep depression that his friends actually feared for his life. In the winter of 1843, when his family moved to Cheltenham, he had treatment in a hydropathic hospital near the town which, though intensely uncomfortable and boring, seemed to make him feel rather better.

His convalescence was probably accelerated by a gradual improvement in his finances. Dr Allen, whose life Edmund Lushington had insured in Tennyson's favour, for a large part of the sum that he had lost, had the grace to die of a heart attack in 1845. In September of that year, through the efforts of Henry Hallam and Gladstone, Tennyson was awarded a Civil List pension of £200 per annum. It led to an attack on 'School-Miss Alfred' in Bulwer Lytton's satirical poem, *The New Timon* (1846); but Tennyson neatly turned the charge of effeminacy back on 'The padded man – that wears the stays' in 'The New Timon and the Poets' (8), published in *Punch* on 28 February 1846, and Lytton removed the offensive passage from his next edition.

Tennyson refused an invitation from a new friend, Dickens, to share a house with him in Switzerland, but visited him there on a touring holiday with his publisher, Edward Moxon (August 1846). He disliked sev_ral things on the journey: the food, the sound of coughing from the room upstairs in one hotel, the flea-infested beds. He was also upset when Moxon told him that he was going bald; but he enjoyed the Alps, and in the neighbourhood of the Jungfrau composed the lyric, 'Come down, O maid, from yonder mountain height', which he incorporated in *The Princess*.

He had been working on this poem, his first long one to be published, since about 1839, and surviving drafts show what great efforts he made to perfect it. On publication, however (November 1847), it met a good deal of criticism, especially on the score of its heterogeneous subject-matter. FitzGerald thought it a waste of Tennyson's powers. But on the whole the reviews were favourable, and the sales were good: 60,000 copies were sold within a few months.

Encouraged by this first taste of success, and perhaps provoked by the news that Lytton was planning to publish a poem on King Arthur, Tennyson began thinking seriously about the long Arthurian work that he had envisaged writing as early as 1833, but had abandoned when Sterling's review of *Poems* (1842) had dismissed 'Morte d'Arthur' as lacking 'human interest'. He decided to visit Cornwall in search of local colour, but was diverted by a friend into a trip to Ireland, where after hearing the echoes at Killarney, he wrote (1848) the song 'The splendour falls on castle walls', published in the 1850 edition of *The Princess*. When he finally got to Cornwall, he started by dropping six feet on to some shingle at Bude in his eagerness to see the sea; but as soon as his leg was usable again, he duly inspected Tintagel, and extracted much useful information, and many books and manuscripts, from an Arthurian expert at Morwenstowe, the Rev. Stephen Hawker.

'But how', asked FitzGerald in a letter of November, 1848, 'are we to expect heroic poems from a valetudinary?'

> Tennyson is emerged half-cured, or half-destroyed, from a water establishment: has gone to a new Doctor who gives him iron pills; and altogether this really great man thinks more about his bowels and nerves than about the Laureate wreath he was born to inherit.

He had better tonics the following year: first, a dose of hero-worship from young Francis Palgrave, future editor of *The Golden Treasury* (1861), and then renewed correspondence with Emily Sellwood. His financial prospects were now more likely to satisfy her father; his brother Charles, whose opium addiction had caused a breakdown in his marriage to Louisa Sellwood, appeared to be cured, and proving that a Tennyson could make a good husband after all; and any lingering fears that Alfred was insufficiently religious were finally set at rest when Emily was able to read (April 1850) a manuscript of the poems for which she suggested the title of *In Memoriam*.

He had decided in November to publish them, and Moxon offered an advance of £300; but he still seems to have felt uneasy about exposing to the public the record of such an intensely personal experience. In February 1850 (perhaps through some sort of unconscious escape-mechanism) he lost the 'long butcher-ledger-like book' in which the poems were written (*Memoir*, vol. 1, p. 197). Appropriately, it was Coventry Patmore, the poet of domesticity, who found the book in a cupboard where Tennyson had kept his tea, bread and butter.

In May 1850 *In Memoriam* was published, and on 13 June Alfred and Emily were married. On their honeymoon they visited Arthur Hallam's grave at Clevedon, and lunched in a Refectory built by a member of Emily's father's family. It seemed to her 'a very pleasant coincidence that he, the last Abbot but one, should have been the only Abbot buried in the chancel near the real or reported grave of King Arthur'.

Although *In Memoriam* was published anonymously, Tennyson was soon known to have written it, and its immediate success, both with the critics and with the public (5,000 copies were sold in a few weeks), transformed him quite suddenly into 'the greatest living poet', as one reviewer called him (22 June 1850). Wordsworth, the Poet Laureate, had died that April; Samuel Rogers had declined, on grounds of age, to succeed him; Prince Albert greatly admired *In Memoriam,* and so in November the Laureateship was offered to Tennyson. The official letter arrived without warning, except for a dream the previous night, in which Prince Albert kissed him on the cheek, and he commented, 'Very kind, but very German' (*Memoir,* vol. 1, p. 335).

Tennyson drafted two replies, one accepting and one refusing the offer, and left the final decision to the oracle that he consulted on such occasions, his after-dinner bottle of port. It advised him to send off the letter of acceptance. When the appointment became known, it received general approval; but at Bayons Manor his uncle Charles was disgusted that 'British taste and poetry should have such a representative before the nations of the Earth and Posterity'.

IV

Alfred and Emily made their first home at Warninglid, Sussex. 'But alas!' wrote Emily, 'a storm came and made a great hole in the wall of our bedroom.' They patched it with a plate of zinc; but the house proved to have many other drawbacks, and they left it after a fortnight. They settled next at Chapel House, Twickenham, where they were visited by a young poet called William Allingham. He described Tennyson (28 June 1851) as

> a tall, broad-shouldered swarthy man, slightly stooping, with loose dark hair and beard. He wore spectacles, and was obviously very near-sighted. Hollow cheeks and the dark pallor of his skin gave him an unhealthy appearance . . . . He was then about forty-one, but looked much older, from his bulk, his short-sight, stooping shoulders, and loose careless dress. He looked tired, and said he had been asleep and was suffering from hay-fever.

Two months before, Emily's first child had been still-born, and the constant stream of callers on the new Poet Laureate was not assisting in her recovery; so they went off to Italy in July, visiting Frederick Tennyson in Florence, and meeting the Brownings in Paris. On 11 August 1852 their first son Hallam was born, to become the poet's first biographer. Henry Hallam concealed his pleasure at the choice of Christian name by remarking: 'They would not name him Alfred lest he should turn out a fool, and so they named him Hallam.'

In September the Duke of Wellington died, and Tennyson's *Ode* was printed in 10,000 pamphlets to be sold on the day of the funeral. In this poem he was not merely doing his job as Poet Laureate, but expressing his own real feelings about the Duke; but the critics did not like it and, fearing that Moxon might lose on the deal, Tennyson offered to reduce the sum (£200) that he was to be paid for it.

Life at Twickenham became increasingly uncomfortable, especially when a woman in Richmond started spreading a rumour that Tennyson had married her in Cheltenham; so in search of peace and privacy the Tennysons moved (November 1853) to Farringford in the Isle of Wight. They decided to lease this house, which stands in a small park near some high downs overlooking the sea, largely because of the splendid view from the drawing-room windows; and Tennyson had a special platform built on the roof, so that he could watch the stars.

Allingham came to live at Lymington, the nearest town on the mainland, and was one of their many visitors, who included Benjamin Jowett, Arthur Hugh Clough, Edward Lear and Millais. Tennyson also got to know a neighbour, Sir John Simeon of Swainston Hall, whom he later associated with Arthur Hallam and Henry Lushington as one of the 'three dead men' that he had loved ('In the Garden at Swainston').

A second son was born in March 1854, named Lionel because when Tennyson heard of the birth he was watching the planet Mars 'As he glowed like a ruddy shield on the Lion's breast' (*Maud*, iii, 14). This he connected with the fact that the British Lion was just about to engage in the Crimean War, for which the Navy could be heard preparing with gunnery practice in the Solent. He was already at work on *Maud*, which was published in July 1855, and at first generally abused. 'Poor "Maud"', said Tennyson, 'has been beaten as black and blue by the penny-a-liners as the "trampled wife" by the drunken ruffian in the opening poem' (*Materials*, vol. 2, pp. 136–7). The chief complaints were that it was morbid and obscure; and Tennyson was attacked, not only by the critics, but also by anonymous letter-writers, one of whom fulminated: 'SIR, I used to worship you, but now I hate you. I loathe and detest you. You beast! So you've taken to imitating Longfellow. Yours in aversion ***'(*Memoir*, vol. 1, p. 400).

Sales, however, were good; the first edition of 10,000 copies was sold, and a second issued within a year. On the proceeds of *Maud* and his previous publications Tennyson was able to buy the freehold of Farringford for £9,000 (1856).

Since about the end of 1855 he had been busy on his Arthurian epic, which he now planned to publish by instalments, in a series of short poems like the epic *Idylls* of Theocritus. The first four *Idylls of the King* ('Enid', 'Vivien', 'Elaine' and 'Guinevere') came out in 1859. 'Vivien' had been written first, 'Elaine' last. The first two lines that Tennyson composed of 'Guinevere' were his birthday present to Emily in 1857, perhaps in token of her utter unlikeness to Arthur's wife, who ruined her husband's life work. Emily sacrificed herself completely to Tennyson's poetry, protecting him from every kind of disturbance, and answering all his letters. In her diary for 14 April 1858 she wrote: 'If it were not faithless, I should be afraid of so much happiness as I have'; but the strain of combining the roles of wife, mother, housekeeper, hostess and private secretary (especially when she had to compose tactful replies to the countless unsuccessful poets who sent their poems for Tennyson to read) finally reduced her to a semi-invalid.

The huge sales of *Idylls of the King* (10,000 copies in the first week) enabled Tennyson from then on to take frequent holidays abroad. During the first, a trip to Portugal with Palgrave in 1859, he suffered badly from mosquitoes, and said he 'wished that he had a little baby in bed with him, as a whiter and more tempting morsel to the insect world' (*Materials*, vol. 2, p. 232). Other holidays were spent in the Pyrenees with Clough (1861), in Brittany (1864), in Belgium and Germany (1865) and in Switzerland (1869).

On the death of Prince Albert (1861), who had dropped in on the Tennysons, rather too casually for comfort, in 1856, Alfred inserted a tribute to him ('Dedication') in the 1862 edition of the *Idylls*. This led to a friendship with the Queen, who had found *In Memoriam* a great comfort in her bereavement. This relationship, rather touching on a human level, was satirically immortalized by Max Beerbohm in his caricature, 'Mr Tennyson reading *In Memoriam* to his sovereign'. Meanwhile the poet himself was giving quasi-royal audiences at Farringford to a long series of distinguished visitors, including Garibaldi, Ellen Terry, G. F. Watts the painter, and the inventor of the London Underground.

His fame was vastly increased by the phenomenal popularity of the *Enoch Arden* volume (1864). Forty thousand copies were sold in an incredibly short time: the critics were generally enthusiastic, and *Blackwood's*, which had published Wilson's patronizing notice in 1832, solemnly declared 'we have reason to render thanks that we have lived to hear such a poet sing'.

His personal life at this time was not untroubled. In 1865 his mother died, and in 1867 his son Hallam was dangerously ill at Marlborough. Tennyson was deeply distressed, but tried to prepare himself for Hallam's death by thinking, 'Surely it will be better for him than to grow up such a one as I am' (*Memoir*, vol. 2, p. 42).

He was cheered by Hallam's recovery, and by the prospect of escaping from the Freshwater tourists to a new summer-home outside Haslemere, then accessible only by a cart-track. What was first planned as a small cottage developed (partly through the collusion of Emily with his architect-friend Knowles) into a large pseudo-Gothic mansion named Aldworth, after a Berkshire village from which some of Emily's family had come. They moved in during August 1869, and in December four more *Idylls* came out in *The Holy Grail and Other Poems* (1870): 'The Coming of Arthur', 'The Holy Grail', 'Pelleas and Ettarre' and 'The Passing of Arthur' (incorporating 'Morte d'Arthur', 1842). The volume, which also contained 'Lucretius', was welcomed by the critics; and Knowles, having created Tennyson's new home, helped to build up his reputation by a letter to the *Spectator* (January 1870) explaining the design of the *Idylls*, and comparing its growth to that of a Gothic cathedral. Only Alfred Austin, a rightly forgotten poet who succeeded Tennyson as Poet Laureate, argued at length in *The Poetry of the Period* (1870) 'that Mr Tennyson is not a great a poet'.

V

Tennyson was now beginning to suffer from one of the penalties of old age described by Juvenal, the death of close friends and relations: Sir John Simeon (1870), his brother Charles (1879), W. G. Ward, a neighbour at Farringford (1882), FitzGerald (1883), his sister Emily (1887), Lear (1888), Browning (1889), and, worst of all, his younger son Lionel, from jungle-fever contracted in India (1886). These deaths, and the serious illness of Emily in 1874 (which made it necessary for Hallam to return from Cambridge and succeed her as the poet's private secretary), progressively lowered his spirits, and affected his health. He refused, however, to let depression or physical ailments interfere with the production of his poetry. After an attack of gout and madly irritating eczema (1870), in which he scratched 'till I could have shrieked with glory' (*Memoir*, vol. 2, p. 99), he resumed work on the *Idylls*, finishing 'The Last Tournament' and 'Gareth and Lynette' by 1872. They were published together that year, and the Imperial Library

Edition of his works (1872–3) included the complete *Idylls of the King*, except for 'Balin and Balan' (written 1872–4, published 1885).

In 1874 Tennyson set to work as a playwright. *Queen Mary* (published 1875) was cut down to less than half its length, and produced by Henry Irving at the Lyceum (1876); but it ran for only about five weeks. *Harold* (1877) was not produced until 1928. Irving was not at first prepared to produce *Becket* (printed 1879, published 1884); but *The Falcon* (published 1884) was produced by the Kendals at the St James's Theatre (1879), and ran for sixty-seven nights. *The Cup* (1884) was Tennyson's first stage success, when produced by Irving at the Lyceum (1881) with Ellen Terry playing the heroine: it ran, with crowded houses, for 127 nights. Encouraged by this, Tennyson wrote his only theatrical flop, *The Promise of May* (Globe Theatre, 1882). *The Foresters* (printed 1881, published 1892) also failed on the London stage (1893), but had been a great success in New York (1892). His real triumph in the theatre, however, was unfortunately posthumous (*Becket*, 1893).

Plays had not stopped his output of poems. *Ballads and Other Poems* (1880) included 'Rizpah', hyperbolically praised by Swinburne, in the course of an attack, begun in 1872, on 'the Morte d'Albert, or Idylls of the Prince Consort'. *Tiresias and Other Poems* (1885), *Locksley Hall Sixty Years After* (1886), and *Demeter and Other Poems* (1889) all contained important new pieces, the last volume ending with 'Crossing the Bar', composed while returning across the Solent to the Isle of Wight (October 1889). In 1883 Queen Victoria thought him 'grown very old – his eyesight much impaired *and he is very shaky on his legs* ... I asked him to sit down'. The next month he went with Gladstone to Denmark, where he met the Czar and Czarina of Russia, and patted the Czarina affectionately on the back, not being able to see who she was. That year he rather reluctantly accepted a barony, and the following March took his seat in the House of Lords.

He fought stubbornly against old age, climbing a 7,000-foot mountain at sixty-seven, taking up sketching in water-colours, though almost blind with cataract, when over eighty, and looking, according to Allingham, more like seventy. The year before he died he was waltzing, and defying his friends to imitate him in getting up quickly twenty times from a low chair, without touching it with his hands.

He was right, however, when he told the Queen, in a letter of 1889, after a severe rheumatic illness, 'possibly I shall never be quite the same man again' (*Memoir*, vol. 2, p. 451). On 23 September 1892 he came down to dinner for the last time at Aldworth. Emily wrote: 'He was very gentle and bright.' On 6 October he died.

VI

In physique and character Tennyson was remarkably tough. As a young man he performed such feats of strength as throwing an iron crowbar over a haystack, and carrying a pony round the dinner-table.Longevity was part of his family inheritance, and his constitution stood up surprisingly well to his life-long habit of pipe-smoking, and consuming a daily pint of port (he particularly enjoyed drinking it duty-free, on a voyage to Lisbon in 1859, while most of his fellow-passengers were being sea-sick). His only physical weaknesses were extremely short sight (which made him look as if he was smelling any object that he was looking at) and a tendency to hay-fever, especially when travelling by train.

Psychologically, he was predisposed to fits of depression and neurotic ailments; but he generally overcame this handicap by courage and will-power. To a friend staying at Farringford who talked of committing suicide, his first response was: 'Don't do it here. Go to Yarmouth and do it decently.' More seriously, he advised him: 'Just go grimly on' (*Materials*, vol. 2, p. 386). That was his own policy when he felt suicidal.

He had a genius for making friends, many of whom mentioned as part of his charm his utter naturalness and freedom from convention. A habit of saying the first thing that came into his head made some of his conversation sound rather zany, as when he solemnly remarked to Allingham (*Diary*, p. 133): 'I am told that a viper-bite may make a woman silly for life, or deprive a man of his virility.' He could also be childishly rude, or foolishly dogmatic; but Thackeray was far from alone in thinking Tennyson the wisest man he knew; and Jowett confirmed another friend's report of the poet's 'plain sledgehammer common sense'.

Having suffered so much disparagement in his youth, he certainly enjoyed the atmosphere of adulation that later surrounded him; but he never made the mistake of taking it seriously. When told by one gushing admirer of another: 'His soul is at your feet!' Tennyson replied: 'I hope his soles are at his own feet' (*Diary*, p. 189). His usual reply to exaggerated compliment was: 'Don't talk such damned nonsense!' (*Materials*, vol. 2, p. 342). He fobbed off a persistent autograph-hunter with the quotation (*Poems*, p. 829): 'Ask me no more' (*Diary*, p. 315), and told a correspondent who posed questions about life after death: 'I am not a God or disembodied spirit that I should answer them' (*Materials*, vol. 2, p. 409). After many years of fame and flattery he wrote: 'I feel sometimes as if my life had been a very useless life' (*Memoir*, vol. 2, p. 337).

One feature of Tennyson's personality, stressed by all his friends, but now often forgotten, is his humour. His son's tutor described it as 'far deeper and wilder … than most people would have guessed, Rabelaisian even'. Tennyson himself recalled reading Rabelais aloud to his friends at Cambridge, until 'they all nearly tumbled off their chairs with laughing' (*Diary*, p. 345). He was always telling funny stories, many of the type that suggested his late dialect poems, such as the one about the Lincolnshire clergyman's prayer: 'O God, send us rain, and especially for John Stubbs' field in the middle marsh, and if Thou dost not know it … it has a big thorn-tree in the middle of it' (*Materials*, vol. 3, p. 107). Queen Victoria was proverbially not easy to amuse; but even she, according to Emily, 'laughed heartily at A.T.'s jokes'.

3

Early Poems

From the start, Tennyson's poetry showed a special gift for adapting previous literature to purposes of self-expression. His earliest surviving work, a free translation of Claudian's *Rape of Proserpine* (i, 1–93), is not merely an exercise in the style of Pope's *Iliad*. It describes something closely resembling Somersby Rectory at its worst: a Hell dominated by a gloomy tyrant, Pluto, bitterly resentful of his unjustly privileged brother, Jove. The translation stops just before the text of an angry message to the god of heaven, containing a complaint that might almost have been addressed by Dr Tennyson to his brother Charles at Bayons Manor: 'Cruel brother, is it not enough that I should have to endure this hideous darkness, while you enjoy the light of the stars?'

Tennyson's next production, written at fourteen, was *The Devil and the Lady*, founded on a mediaeval anecdote mentioned in the *Quarterly Review*, about a jealous husband who told a Puck-like devil called Hoodekin to keep an eye on his wife while he was away. It ended with the exhausted devil saying: 'Never set me such a task again: sooner would I tend all the swine in the woods of Westphalia, than undertake to keep one woman constant against her will.' This the young poet developed into a rollicking pastiche of an Elizabethan comedy. The husband becomes an octogenarian Necromancer called Magus, the wife a twenty-year-old at first called Jessica (from the young daughter of Shylock in *The Merchant of Venice*, who is locked up by her father with 'a merry devil', Launcelot, but still manages to elope with Lorenzo), and later called Amoret (from the unhappy lady in Spenser's *Faerie Queene* who is imprisoned and cruelly tormented by the magician Busirane). Both names suggest sympathy with the wife, who seems to express some of Tennyson's own adolescent frustrations, like several

35

other enclosed and frustrated females who figure in his early poems; but Magus is also allowed some sympathy, when he speaks like Othello (e.g. III, ii, 157f), and he partly prefigures the pathos of the magician Merlin, when outwitted by Vivien in *Idylls of the King*. The amoral gusto with which the sexual theme is treated may owe something to Byron's *Don Juan;* and there are hints that Tennyson's unfinished play might have ended with the surprise discovery of Amoret (as of Julia in the first Canto of that poem) in bed, but not asleep and not alone.

The dialogue is often very funny, and the diction extraordinarily accomplished, especially where Amoret's various lovers (entertained by the devil, disguised as Amoret) are made to use imagery appropriate to their professions. At first reading, the work seems un-Tennysonian in its constant facetiousness, and in the vigour of its abusive speeches, like this of Amoret's to her husband:

> Go thy ways!
> Thou yellowest leaf on Autumn's withered tree!
> Thou sickliest ear of all the sheaf! thou clod!
> Thou fireless mixture of Earth's coldest clay!
> Thou crazy dotard, crusted o'er with age
> As thick as ice upon a standing pool!
> Thou shrunken, sapless, wizen Grasshopper,
> Consuming the green promise of my youth! . . .
> He bears a charmèd life and will outlast me
> In mustiness of dry longevity,
> Like some tough Mummy withered, not decayed -
> His years are countless as the dusty race
> That people an old Cheese and flourish only
> In the unsoundest parts on't.   (I, iv, 117-38)

There are many signs, however, of the later Tennyson. A scientific world-view is first suggested by an adaptation of the prelude to Lucretius' *De Rerum Natura* in Magus's opening speech (I, i, 14f) and confirmed by technical references, as when the Devil tells Amoret to lie as still 'As the dull yolk within its parent shell, Ere yet the *punctum saliens* vivify it' (I, v, 156-7), or informs the angry Antonio: 'Why, thou art 80, man, by Réaumur's scale, And more than twice as much by Fahrenheit' (II, iv, 58-9).

Closer to Tennyson's mature thought are the Devil's reflections on man's insignificance in astronomical space and time, and on the

difficulties of scientific materialism (II, i, 8f). In a context of slapstick
and verbal buffoonery, the Devil sometimes speaks in a key of true
Tennysonian melancholy. Immediately after threatening to 'stalemate'
Amoret ('My mate is stale enough', she replies), he comments sadly on
the superficiality of her beauty:

> Gaze on the mirror of the silver lake
> In its clear picture deftly pencilling
> The soft inversion of the tremulous woods,
> But probe it not to the bottom: weeds, rank weeds,
> Darkness and swarming reptiles harbour there.　　(I, v, 177–81)

The blank-verse fragment, 'Armageddon', written at about fifteen,
describes a vision on the eve of the great battle which in *Revelation*
precedes the end of the world. Milton is the chief literary influence, but
Byron's 'Darkness' also seems to contribute to the powerful realization
of the Biblical statement that sea, fountains and rivers were turned to
blood, and the kingdom of 'the beast' was filled with darkness:

> Never set sun with such portentous glare . . .
> Strange figures thickly thronged his burning orb,
> Spirits of discord seemed to weave across
> His fiery disk a web of bloody haze,
> Through whose reticulations struggled forth
> His ineffectual, intercepted beams,
> Curtaining in one dark terrific pall
> Of dun-red light heaven's azure and earth's green.　　(i, 32–41)

Byron had mentioned volcanoes as the only source of natural light
when 'the bright sun was extinguished', so a reference to the 'red erup-
tion' of Cotopaxi, which Tennyson had seen described and illustrated in
a travel book, was added to the nightmarish picture (99–100).

The prophetic vision on a mountain, under the influence of a seraph,
had obvious analogies with a passage in *Paradise Lost* (xi, 411f) where
Michael opens Adam's eyes; but Tennyson was probably familiar with
Milton's precedents too, which included Aeneas' vision of unborn
Romans in the Underworld (*Aeneid* vi) and Scipio's view of the universe from the Milky Way in Cicero's *Somnium Scipionis*. The simultaneously telescopic and microscopic nature of the vision (29f)
might even suggest an acquaintance with an amusing work in Dr

Tennyson's library, Lucian's *Icaromenippus,* in which the hero, having flown to the moon, is enabled, by flapping an eagle's wing, to study life on earth in minute detail. Tennyson's familiarity with such classical treatments of the universal-vision theme may explain some resemblances between 'Armageddon' and Shelley's *Queen Mab,* which he is not believed to have seen at this time.

The personal element in 'Armageddon' can perhaps be found in its sense of imminent catastrophe. As a child living under the constant threat of Dr Tennyson's unpredictable black moods, the young poet must often have felt that the world might come to an end at any moment. As an adolescent in a very restricting environment, he must often have been bored, and he expressed the idea of endless monotony through the image of the Lincolnshire fens:

> Broad before me
> Lay a huge plain whereon the wandering eye,
> Weary with gazing, found no resting-place,
> Unbroken by the ridge of mound or hill,
> Or far-off cone of some aerial mount
> Varying the horizon's sameness. (i, 25-9)

The idea is repeated later:

> an icy veil
> Of pale, weak, lifeless, thin, unnatural blue
> Wrapt up the rich varieties of things
> In grim and ghastly sameness. (iv, 21-4)

Above all, Tennyson tried to find words for a curious trance-like state into which he could throw himself by thinking intently of his own name. He described it (1858) as 'no nebulous ecstasy, but a state of transcendent wonder, associated with absolute clearness of mind' (*Memoir,* vol. 2, pp. 473-4). This was his first attempt to convey it in verse:

> I wondered with deep wonder at myself:
> My mind seemed winged with knowledge and the strength
> Of holy musings and immense Ideas,
> Even to Infinitude. All sense of Time
> And Being and Place was swallowed up and lost

Within a victory of boundless thought.
I was a part of the Unchangeable,
A scintillation of Eternal Mind,
Remixed and burning with its parent fire.
Yea! in that hour I could have fallen down
Before my own strong soul and worshipped it.   (ii, 40–50)

Another unfinished poem, 'The Coach of Death', probably started at fourteen or fifteen, was a ballad influenced both by Milton and by Coleridge's 'Ancient Mariner'. It describes a dark and wintry hell 'Behind the burning Sun' (2), and traces the journey of the coach that carries the damned across the bridge built over the void by Sin and Death in *Paradise Lost*. The passengers are collected from an inn, which is a crude precursor of the one in 'The Vision of Sin' (1842). The landlord is 'no jolly host',

For his shanks were shrunken to willow wands
    And his name was Atrophy!   (54–6)

The coachman is no jollier:

His sockets were eyeless, but in them slept
    A red infernal glow;
As the cockroach crept, and the white fly leapt
    About his hairless brow.   (80–4)

In all this schoolboy Grand Guignol two stanzas are worth noticing. The first implies that Tennyson felt in hell himself:

But some have hearts that in them burn
With power and promise high,
    To draw strange comfort from the earth,
    Strange beauties from the sky.   (29–32)

The second points forward to 'The Ballad of Oriana' (1830) and tries out a type of poetic effect in which the poet would specialize at Cambridge:

They lifted their eyes to the dead, pale skies,
    And above the barkless trees

> They saw the green verge of the pleasant earth,
>   And heard the roar of her seas.   (61-4)

II

Tennyson's contributions to *Poems by Two Brothers* (1827) are much less individual than his earlier work, which was excluded from the book, 'being thought too much out of the common for the public taste' (*Memoir*). The public was evidently assumed to want imitations of Gray, Moore, Scott, and especially Byron. The Advertisement is modelled on the Preface to Byron's first volume, *Hours of Idleness* (1807), even down to the statement 'we have passed the Rubicon, and we leave the rest to fate'; and Tennyson's first poem, 'Memory', shares its theme with Byron's 'Childish Recollections' in that volume. This piece compares memory to a 'distant' sun that 'dimly twinkles o'er the watery plain' in the darkness of a storm. 'Memory' concludes:

> Thus, Memory, thus thy light
>   O'er this worn soul is gleaming,
> Like some far fire at night
>   Along the dun deep streaming.   (73-6)

Equally Byronic is the main burden, in more senses than one, of nearly all Tennyson's contributions: a lament for vanished happiness or glory, whether in the destruction of great empires, the partings of lovers, the thoughts of exiles, or simply the fact of death. The poems show the influence of *Childe Harold* in particular: an explicit imitation of *Don Juan*, written at the same period ('I dare not write an Ode for fear Pimplaea'), was omitted from the volume, possibly because it alluded to a slightly obscene epigram of Catullus (*Poems*, pp. 157-8).

Another pervasive influence was that of Burke's essay on 'the Sublime' (1756). Burke associated sublimity with ideas of pain, danger, terror, vacuity, darkness, solitude and silence. In his 'On Sublimity' Tennyson gave an illustrated catalogue of sublime themes, including 'headless spectres of St Mark' (69) and 'Kentucky's chambers of eternal gloom' (82); and many of his titles (e.g. 'I wander in darkness and sorrow', 'The Vale of Bones', 'Midnight', 'The Walk at Midnight', 'Come hither, canst thou tell me if this skull') suggest how seriously he took Burke's description. Among his better efforts in this line is 'Unhappy man, why wander there', about a man in a snow-storm at night,

40

whose refrain, '"Tis all the same to me', gives an extra twist to Lucretius' gloomy comment on human life, *'eadem sunt omnia semper'* (all things are always the same), and to Tennyson's own sense of monotony.

While submitting to such influences, he was expressing his own real unhappiness, and apparently a feeling of guilt in which, no doubt, 'puberty assisted' (Byron's phrase), but which must have been intensified by his Calvinist aunt, who one day said to him: 'Alfred, Alfred, when I look at you, I think of the words of Holy Scripture — "Depart from me, ye cursed, into everlasting fire."' This sense of guilt and of reprobation is vividly conveyed in 'Remorse':

> And I was cursèd from my birth,
> A reptile made to creep on earth,
> An hopeless outcast, born to die
> A living death eternally!
> With too much conscience to have rest,
> Too little to be ever blest ...   (19–24)

Something like the 'damnèd vacillating state' of 'Supposed Confessions' (1830) had already developed.

Poems by Two Brothers shows little evidence of Tennyson's real powers; but it contains, in 'The sun goes down in the dark blue main', a first attempt at a lyric pattern that he perfected in 'Break, break, break' (1842), just as 'No More' (*Poems*, p. 161), written in 1826, but not included in this volume, is an embryonic 'Tears, idle tears' (1847).

III

The subject of *Timbuctoo* (1829) had a topical interest, for A. G. Laing, the first European to enter the city, was murdered there in 1826. Tennyson probably consulted Hugh Murray's *Historical Account of Africa*, where he could have found the basic idea of the poem (though it also appeared in Wordsworth's *Excursion*, 1814), that glorious figments of human imagination were destroyed by geographical discovery. He gave deeper meaning to the idea by associating it with the prophetic vision from 'Armageddon', and identifying the Seraph as the Spirit of Fable, who plays an important part in man's spiritual education:

> There is no mightier Spirit than I to sway
> The heart of man: and teach him to attain

By shadowing forth the Unattainable . . .
I play about his heart a thousand ways,
Visit his eyes with visions, and his ears
With harmonies of wind and wave and wood . . .
I have raised thee nigher to the spheres of Heaven,
Man's first, last home: and thou with ravished sense
Listenest the lordly music flowing from
The illimitable years.   (191–215)

In making audible the music of the spheres, the Spirit resembles the elder
Scipio in the *Somnium Scipionis*; but in sending dreams and visions, in
style, and in the image of a city reflected on the surface of a river, he
shows his descent from Shelley's 'The Witch of Atlas':

Seest thou yon river, whose translucent wave
Forth issuing from the darkness, windeth through
The argent streets o' the city, imaging
The soft inversion of her tremulous Domes . . .
                    the time is well-nigh come
When I must render up this glorious home
To keen *Discovery*: soon yon brilliant towers
Shall darken with the waving of her wand;
Darken, and shrink and shiver into huts,
Black specks amid a waste of dreary sand. . .   (225–43)

Timbuctoo anticipates an aspect of Tennyson's later religious thought:
his willed belief in concepts which he realizes may be illusory. In
'Friendship' (1827), he had admitted that ideal friendship might be a
'fable', but concluded: 'I will deem thee Truth, so lovely is thy might!'
(27), just as Magus had said: 'Well, Amoret, I will believe thee true'
(*The Devil and the Lady*, I, iv, 87). In *Timbuctoo* the human tendency to
cling to illusions is explicitly connected with religion, in a description of
a priestess in an earthquake praying to 'the awful Genius of the place'
(28–40):

Nathless she ever clasps the marble knees,
Bathes the cold hand with tears, and gazeth on
Those eyes which wear no light but that wherewith
Her phantasy informs them.

Tennyson follows her example in *In Memoriam* (cxxiii) when, in defiance of all the geological evidence, he says:

> But in my spirit will I dwell,
>   And dream my dream, and hold it true;
>   For though my lips may breathe adieu,
> I cannot think the thing farewell.

IV

In *Poems, Chiefly Lyrical* (1830), as the title implies, the emphasis is on verbal music. The first poem, 'Claribel: A Melody', exploits the effect of alliteration with liquids:

> Where Claribel low-lieth,
>   The breezes pause and die,
>   Letting the rose-leaves fall:
> But the solemn oak-tree sigheth,
>   Thick-leaved, ambrosial,
>   With an ancient melody
>   Of an inward agony,
> Where Claribel low-lieth.   (1–8)

Some of the best pieces are 'Songs', and other titles include an 'Ode', a 'Chorus', a 'Dirge' and a 'Ballad'.

The versification is highly original. Tennyson invented new metrical patterns, with complex and often irregular rhyme-schemes, and free transitions between iambic, trochaic and anapaestic rhythms. Such novelties led Coleridge to comment (1835) 'Mr Tennyson...has begun to write without very well understanding what metre is', advising him to practise composing in such well-known metres as the heroic couplet, like a schoolboy learning to write 'good Latin verses by conning Ovid and Tibullus'. Tennyson had, of course, been doing that for many years, and also writing Greek and Latin quantitative verses, a far more rigid discipline than coping with English prosody. He had even combined the two prosodies in 'Leonine Elegiacs' (i.e. Ovidian couplets with internal rhymes added in each line).

The first three poems in the volume, 'Claribel', 'Lilian', 'Isabel', are often found an obstacle to further reading. They are not, however, mere pieces of sentimentality, but attempts at psychological description. Claribel is more than euphonious: she is a type of injured innocence from Spenser's *Faerie Queene,* where she is killed by a causelessly jealous lover. The 'melody' is a lament for a character misjudged. She remains, perhaps, too dead to have much individuality; but 'Lilian' gives a much more precise impression of a young girl (about twelve or thirteen in 1830) called Sophy Rawnsley. She lived near Somersby: Tennyson used to waltz with her, and his sister Emily described her as 'the lightest and most indefatigable dancer I ever saw', and 'so cheerful and happy, that it brings sunshine into one's heart, though it were gloomy before, to look at her'. Though it makes many people squirm, the poem is an interesting effort to convey, by words and rhythms, how the lightness, mobility and gaiety of this small person appeared to a beefy, rather melancholy six-foot-tall undergraduate.

'Isabel' is a portrait of Tennyson's mother. The name was probably suggested by the chaste and pious heroine of Shakespeare's *Measure for Measure,* and the character-traits listed are clearly influenced by the contemporary stereotype of the perfect wife and mother, pure, kind, intuitive and obedient; but the poem ceases to be conventional when it describes Mrs Tennyson, however euphemistically, as the victim of her husband's psychopathic personality:

> A mellowed reflex of a winter moon;
> A clear stream flowing with a muddy one,
> > Till in its onward current it absorbs
> > > With swifter movement and in purer light
> > > The vexèd eddies of its wayward brother:
> > > A leaning and upbearing parasite,
> > > Clothing the stem, which else had fallen quite
> With clustered flower-bells . . . .   (29-36)

Tennyson's note on his poems of this kind was: 'All these ladies were evolved, like the camel, from my own consciousness' (*Eversley*); but each probably had some external basis, especially 'Marion', written at the same period as the 1830 poems, but not published until 1897. This is an attempt, almost clinical in tone, to define the peculiar charm of a very ordinary person. Its conclusion is delicately balanced between compliment and insult:

> Thou art the soul of commonplace,
> > The body all mankind divide.   (*Poems*, p. 294)

The most scathing satire, however, in the volume was on a fellow-student called Sunderland, whom FitzGerald described as 'a very plausible, parliament-like, and self-satisfied speaker at the Union Debating Society':

> He spake of virtue: not the gods
> More purely, when they wish to charm
> Pallas and Juno sitting by:
> And with a sweeping of the arm,
> And a lack-lustre dead-blue eye,
> Devolved his rounded periods. ('A Character', 13–18)

V

This poem is not really Theophrastan, for it defines an individual rather than a type; but literary influences are strong throughout the volume. 'Chorus' is clearly modelled on one in the *Antigone* of Sophocles, beginning 'There are many strange things', though its first phrase is Lucretian, its refrain derived from Shelley's 'On Death', and its general theme expressive of the poet's interest in physical science.

The most important classical influence was Ovid. 'Leonine Elegiacs' (originally just 'Elegiacs') contains the words: 'she cometh not morning or even' (15). Read 'he' for 'she', and you have the *leit-motiv* of Ovid's *Heroides,* a series of verse letters from deserted females like Dido, Oenone, Ariadne. Penelope waits nearly twenty years for Ulysses, and warns him that she will be an old woman by the time he comes home; Phyllis resolves on suicide, listing several different methods, because Demophoon has failed to arrive on the promised day. The Ovidian 'heroine' offered Tennyson a perfect vehicle for expressing his moods of frustration and depression; and the 'dejected Mariana' in *Measure for Measure,* waiting 'at the moated grange' for her faithless fiancé, Angelo, exactly corresponded with Ovid's formula. In the play that Tennyson called 'the greatest creation in literature that I know of' (*Memoir*, vol. 2, p. 291) he could find appropriate imagery for expressing the moods in question, where Hamlet says:

> How weary, stale, flat, and unprofitable
> Seem to me all the uses of this world!
> Fie on't! O fie! 'tis an unweeded garden
> That grows to seed . . . .

The neglected-garden image is brilliantly elaborated in the opening lines of 'Mariana':

> With blackest moss the flower-pots
> Were thickly crusted, one and all:
> The rusted nails fell from the knots
> That held the peach to the garden-wall.
> The broken sheds looked sad and strange:
> Unlifted was the clinking latch;
> Weeded and worn the ancient thatch
> Upon the lonely moated grange. (1-8)

The flatness image (suggested by the Lincolnshire fens) he had already used in 'Armageddon', and it had acquired new meaning for him at Cambridge, where he wrote in 1828: 'I know not how it is, but I feel isolated here in the midst of society. The country is so disgustingly level . . .' (*Memoir*, vol. 1, p. 34). So Mariana is 'isolated' among 'flats' (20), whose level monotony is broken only by a single object, symbolic of Mariana's one obsessive thought:

> Hard by a poplar shook alway,
> All silver-green with gnarlèd bark:
> For leagues no other tree did mark
> The level waste, the rounding gray. (41-4)

The poplar, too, comes from Ovid: Oenone, deserted by Paris, addresses a poplar, with 'wrinkled bark', on which Paris has carved a promise never to desert her. Thus the tree representing Paris's breach of promise does the same for Angelo's, and enables Tennyson to hint delicately at Mariana's sexual frustration:

> But when the moon was very low,
> And wild winds bound within their cell,
> The shadow of the poplar fell
> Upon her bed, across her brow. (53-6)

In the last two passages quoted, the 'rounding' landscape and the endlessly repetitive nature of Mariana's existence are realized acoustically by the circular rhyme-scheme of what was to become the *In Memoriam* stanza; and the same function is performed by the dreary refrain, built around the Ovidian 'He cometh not', but possibly suggested by the refrain in Theocritus, *Idyll* ii (a monologue spoken by a woman using magic to bring back a faithless lover). There the repeated line, 'Wryneck, draw that man to my house', operates as an incantation. And this *Idyll* may have contributed to the atmosphere of bewitchment in which Mariana seems, like the Sleeping Beauty, to live:

> All day within the dreamy house
>   The doors upon their hinges creaked;
> The blue fly sung in the pane; the mouse
>   Behind the mouldering wainscot shrieked ....   (61–4)

Ovid was partly responsible for another of the volume's successes, 'The Dying Swan'. Dido begins her complaint to Aeneas in the *Heroides*, by comparing herself to a white swan, singing by the river Maeander, just before its death. Tennyson would have known the swan-song tradition from several other sources; but it is noticeable that he makes his swan female (28), and gives her a backcloth of snow-capped mountains, much more appropriate to the Maeander (overlooked by Mount Latmos) than to any English fen-country. Like the poets in hell ('The Coach of Death') who draw 'strange beauties' from a sky with 'never an inch of blue' (22), the swan seems to symbolize the power of poetry to make triumphant music in an utterly grey world:

> And the silvery marish-flowers that throng
> The desolate creeks and pools among
> Were flooded over with eddying song.   (40–2)

The world presented by 'Recollections of the Arabian Nights', Arthur Hallam's favourite poem in the volume, is contrastingly colourful: Tennyson is trying to recapture the vivid pictures projected on to his imagination by these stories in childhood. He alludes particularly to the tale of 'Noureddin and the Fair Persian', which explains the details and clarifies the feeling of the poem.

Noureddin is a handsome but irresponsible youth who, having squandered a fortune, arrives almost destitute in Baghdad with his wife, the Fair Persian, a miracle of beauty, virtue and intellectual accomplishment. They wander into a garden, which belongs to the Caliph Haroun Alraschid, and go to sleep on a sofa. By using their charm on the elderly caretaker, Ibrahim, they later contrive to have a gay party in the

Pavilion, making Ibrahim, who as a 'true Mussulman' (9) is not supposed to touch alcohol, so drunk that he lets them light all the candles, including those in 'The fourscore windows' (122). The brilliant illumination catches the Caliph's eye. Coming over to investigate, he plays such practical jokes as pretending to be a poor fisherman, and cooking the young couple some fish. He compliments Noureddin on his wife's lute-playing, and Noureddin, now as drunk as Ibrahim, returns the compliment with oriental courtesy by making a present of her to the supposed fisherman. The story ends happily, however, with Noureddin and his wife becoming King and Queen of Basra.

The poet, as an excited child reading the story, describes his imaginative approach through the garden to the brightly-lit Pavilion, and his final vision of the Persian girl and of the Caliph. The poem has been wrongly regarded, either as a tasteless exhibition of Tennyson's verbal extravagance, or as an elaborate build-up to a symbol of eroticism and injured womanhood. The Technicolour fantasy is meant to suggest an immature taste in fiction; the Fair Persian is no more erotic than the Princess in a pantomime; and her ill-treatment by her husband, played down in the original because of its generally playful atmosphere, is nowhere even hinted at in the poem. It is the Caliph, not the Fair Persian, who figures in the refrain, and it is his sense of humour that is finally celebrated:

> Thereon, his deep eye laughter-stirred
> With merriment of kingly pride,
>> Sole star of all that place and time,
>> I saw him – in his golden prime,
>> THE GOOD HAROUN ALRASCHID. (150–4)

In English literature the chief influences were the Elizabethans and the Romantics. Spenser, while contributing to verbal music, also encouraged allegory, with less happy results. In 'Love, Pride, and Forgetfulness' Pride smokes out the bee of Love, steals Love's honey, and feeds Memory only with gall, a diet which makes it 'wax' thin (12) and die. In 'Sense and Conscience', written at the same period but not then published, Conscience is drugged to sleep by Sense in a flowery forest reminiscent of Spenser's Bower of Bliss, and woken by Memory and Pain. In an access of guilt, Conscience cuts down all the flowers, and does penance by eating bitter roots dug up by Memory (*Poems*, pp. 273–6). Inspired, apparently, by an idle student's remorse at having wasted precious time, the poem expresses, like 'The Lotos-Eaters' (1833), a conflict between self-indulgence and purposeful effort, and defines, in the phrase 'wars of Spirit and Sense' (33), what was to be the theme of *Idylls of the King*.

Shakespeare's influence, always strong in Tennyson's work, is most obvious in the lyrical humour of 'Song – The Owl' (based on 'When icicles hang by the wall' in *Love's Labour's Lost*). Keats, whose poetry was being 'discovered' by the Apostles, contributed to the formation of Tennyson's rich and compressed imagery; and Shelley's view of the poet's special function and value, in *A Defence of Poetry* (1821), underlay both 'The Poet' and 'The Poet's Mind'. In 'Ode to the West Wind' Shelley had prayed: 'Drive my dead thoughts over the universe Like withered leaves to quicken a new birth.' In *Adonais* he had made one of the poet's Dreams, which used to wander 'from kindling brain to brain', feel like breaking 'Her bow and winged reeds'. These images seem to have combined in Tennyson's mind with memories, from Waterton's *Wanderings in South America (1825)*, of arrows shot from blowpipes by American Indians; with a passage in the *Aeneid* (v, 519f) where an arrow ('a reed'), shot high in the air, miraculously catches fire, and thus portends the firing of the Trojan fleet; and with his botanical knowledge of the dandelion:

> The viewless arrows of his thoughts were headed
>   And winged with flame,
> Like Indian reeds blown from his silver tongue,
>   And of so fierce a flight,
> From Calpe unto Caucasus they sung,
>   Filling with light
> And vagrant melodies the winds which bore
>   Them earthward till they lit;
> Then, like the arrow-seeds of the field flower,
>   The fruitful wit
> Cleaving, took root, and springing forth anew
>   Where'er they fell, behold,
> Like to the mother plant in semblance, grew
>   A flower all gold,
> And bravely furnished all abroad to fling
>   The wingèd shafts of truth . . . .   ('The Poet', 11–26)

'The Poet's Mind' is said to be Tennyson's reply to his friend

Blakesley's laughing criticisms of 'The Kraken'; but it seems to be almost as serious as Shelley's *Defence of Poetry*, provoked by his friend Peacock's satirical *The Four Ages of Poetry*. There may, perhaps, be a trace of mock-heroic in the orotund reworking of the epic formula warning the profane off the holy ground of poetry, familiar from Horace *Odes*, III, i, and from Claudian ('Translation of Claudian's "Rape of Proserpine"', 5-8). Solemnity, however, was encouraged by the precedent of Shelley (the source of the image of the poet as a bird singing in solitude), and of Keats, whose 'Lamia' allegorized the destruction of poetry by rationalism, embodied as a 'sophist' (8). Precedents apart, Tennyson was so sensitive to hostile criticism that he really meant it when he wrote:

> In the heart of the garden the merry bird chants.
> It would fall to the ground if you came in. (22-3)

VI

Of the poems whose inspiration was more personal than literary, two were suggested by the poet's childhood environment. 'Ode to Memory: Written Very Early in Life', which Tennyson thought one of his best early nature-poems, contains sharply focused descriptions of Somersby and the surrounding countryside, embedded in a framework of rather pompous allegory. The memory-pictures are treasured, as in Wordsworth, for their restorative power in after-life; but there is something more relevant to Tennyson's own poetic practice in the conception of Memory as an artist, who keeps returning to her earliest works (80-95), just as he was always incorporating in new poems lines or phrases written for other contexts many years before.

The garden at Somersby supplied both setting and theme for the best 'Song' in the volume:

> A spirit haunts the year's last hours
> Dwelling amid these yellowing bowers:
>   To himself he talks;
> For at eventide, listening earnestly,
> At his work you may hear him sob and sigh
>   In the walks;
> Earthward he boweth the heavy stalks
>   Of the mouldering flowers:
>   Heavily hangs the broad sunflower

> Over its grave i' the earth so chilly;
> Heavily hangs the hollyhock,
>> Heavily hangs the tiger-lily.   (1-12)

Tennyson's originality shows itself in a simultaneous allusion to, and departure from, his literary models. For Keats's picturesque female spirit of autumn he substitutes an invisible male, who, instead of tying up the drooping flowers, like Eve in *Paradise Lost* (ix), relentlessly forces them down. He is an anti-gardener, depressive in temperament, and presenting one of the traditional symptoms of mental derangement ('To himself he talks'). The refrain, with its repeated aspirates, simulates his 'sobs and sighs', and suggests, by the effort needed to pronounce it, his utter weariness.

The hint in the first stanza of 'grey hairs brought down in sorrow to the grave' leads to the death-bed image in the second, a transition superbly mediated by direct appeal to the physical sense of smell:

> The air is damp, and hushed, and close,
> As a sick man's room when he taketh repose
>> An hour before death;
> My very heart faints and my whole soul grieves
> At the moist rich smell of the rotting leaves,
>> And the breath
> Of the fading edges of box beneath,
>> And the year's last rose.   (13-20)

The depressive, slightly mad, destructive character in the garden, and the dying man upstairs, both suggest, not only autumn, but the quality of life at Somersby during Dr Tennyson's last years.

After *In Memoriam* Tennyson was regarded primarily as a philosophical poet, speculating on the nature of reality and the validity of religious experience. The 'honest doubt' of that poem (xcvi, 11) is variously expressed in the 1830 volume: flippantly at first, in 'The "How" and the "Why"', where he asks:

> Why the life goes when the blood is spilt?
>> What the life is? where the soul may lie?
> Why a church is with a steeple built;
> And a house with a chimney-pot?   (32-5)

51

A more serious uncertainty is suggested by three poems ('Nothing Will Die', 'All Things Will Die', 'οἱ ῥέοντες' i.e. 'the flowing people') which circle round the river-image of Heracleitus, 'All things flow', and a physical embodiment of it, presumably the Somersby rivulet, later the Halton River. Two views of reality are offered: that it is permanent, though in a state of constant flux, and that it is purely temporary. Both views are expressed with equal conviction; and the third poem, which ends the volume, makes only a tentative effort to solve the dilemma, by invoking Protagoras' 'Man is the measure of all things' and Berkeley's 'To be is to be perceived', thus reducing everything to subjectivity:

> There is no rest, no calm, no pause,
> Nor good nor ill, nor light nor shade,
> Nor essence nor eternal laws:
>   For nothing is, but all is made.
> But if I dream that all these are,
>   They are to me for that I dream;
> For all things are as they seem to all,
>   And all things flow like a stream.   (11–16)

Even this solution is undermined in a footnote: 'Argal – this very opinion is only true relatively to the flowing philosophers', an argument which is itself undermined by association ('Argal') with the clownish logic of the grave-diggers in *Hamlet*.

The most interesting 'doubt' poem is 'Supposed Confessions of a Second-Rate Sensitive Mind Not in Unity With Itself'. The cumbrous title was evidently meant to indicate that the piece was a dramatic monologue; but as in Browning's first publication, *Pauline*, on a somewhat similar theme, the autobiographical element is unmistakable. The conflict in the speaker's mind is between a nostalgic longing for his mother's type of unquestioning religious faith, and a sense that such faith is intellectually untenable. How much pressure Mrs Tennyson put on the poet in this matter may be guessed from a letter that she wrote him on 10 January 1860, after reading *Idylls of the King* (1859):

> O dearest Ally how fervently have I prayed for years that our
> merciful Redeemer would intercede with our Heavenly Father to
> grant thee His Holy Spirit to urge thee to employ the talents He has
> given thee in His service by taking every opportunity of
> endeavouring to impress the precepts of His Holy Word on the

minds of others. My beloved son, words are too feeble to express the joy of my heart in perceiving that thou art earnestly endeavouring to do so.

The chief intellectual difficulty was in reconciling a belief in an after-life with the facts of physiology and physics. 'How sweet', thinks the speaker (in a passage not reprinted) it would be

To stand beside a grave, and see
The red small atoms wherewith we
Are built, and smile in calm, and say –
'These little motes and grains shall be
'Clothed on with immortality
'More glorious than the noon of day.
  'All that is passed into the flowers,
'And into beasts, and other men,
  'And all the Norland whirlwind showers
'From open vaults, and all the sea
'O'erwashes with sharp salts, again
'Shall fleet together all, and be
'Indued with immortality'   (*Poems*, p. 198)

Recalling his youthful belief that 'It is man's privilege to doubt' (142), he supports it with cogent arguments. Animals may well enjoy a thoughtless happiness, the lamb may 'answer to his mother's calls' (159), but a human being should be prepared to ignore his mother's calls, analyse the situation rationally, and decide accordingly:

Shall we not look into the laws
Of life and death, and things that seem,
And things that be, and analyse
Our double nature, and compare
All creeds till we have found the one,
If one there be?   (172-7)

From this courageous attitude of scientific agnosticism he feels himself relapsing into one of compulsive self-delusion (for 'Idols' is used in the Baconian sense of false mental images):

> Ay me! I fear
> All may not doubt, but everywhere
> Some must clasp Idols.   (177-9)

The conflict is left unresolved; but the poem deserves more respect for its
honest formulation of the problem than is implied by Tennyson's later
comment, that if only the speaker had been less self-centred, 'he might
have been a happy man, though sensitive' (*Eversley*).

VII

The character of the volume results not only from its constituent
poems, but from their careful arrangement, and from certain unifying
themes and images. The arrangement seems designed to suggest a kind
of double vision, for the poems are often linked in complementary or
contrasting pairs. Thus the frivolous 'Lilian' is followed by the
matronly 'Isabel', the irresponsibly hedonistic 'Merman' by his female
counterpart, and she by the gloomy, guilt-ridden speaker of 'Supposed
Confessions'. Memories of a fairy-tale world in the *Arabian Nights* are
balanced by memories of real life ('Ode to Memory'); the poet's
beneficent effect on society ('The Poet') by society's potentially destructive effect on the poet ('The Poet's Mind'); 'A Dirge', pointing out
the advantages of being dead and buried, by 'The Grasshopper', celebrating the joys of life, in 'a short youth sunny and free' (29).

An important unifying theme is implied in the use of the word
'inward'. The 'agony' associated with Claribel is 'inward' (7); so is the
child's happiness in 'Supposed Confessions' (51). In the sonnet, 'Could I
outwear my present state of woe', the poet weeps 'inwardly' (11), and
the river that carries 'The Dying Swan' runs 'With an inner voice' (5).
There is a pervasive feeling, exemplified by Mariana's introverted
brooding, as by the bird singing 'in the heart of the garden' ('The Poet's
Mind') that the stuff of poetry is internal, subjective experience.

One image for such experience seems to be a submarine existence. For
the Merman, the Mermaid and the Kraken this means unrestricted
indulgence of one's basic instincts:

> Below the thunders of the upper deep;
> Far, far beneath in the abysmal sea,
> His ancient, dreamless, uninvaded sleep
> The Kraken sleepeth: faintest sunlights flee

About his shadowy sides: above him swell
Huge sponges of millennial growth and height;
And far away into the sickly light,
From many a wondrous grot and secret cell
Unnumbered and enormous polypi
Winnow with giant arms the slumbering green.   (1–10)

Tennyson seems to be using the deep sea (as Matthew Arnold also seems to use it in 'The Forsaken Merman') to represent what he later called (adapting a phrase of Arthur Hallam's) 'the abysmal deeps of personality' ('The Palace of Art', 223).

The Kraken preserves his 'inwardness' not only by his habitat, but also by his sleep; and in 'The Sleeping Beauty', the nucleus of 'The Day-Dream' (1842), sleep again appears to symbolize the attractions of the inner life:

She sleeps, nor dreams, but ever dwells
     A perfect form in perfect rest.   (22–3)

In 'Sense and Conscience', however, sleep is a regrettable form of self-indulgence, and the retreat into subjectivity is sometimes seen as a dereliction of duty. 'The Sea-Fairies' (the Sirens of the *Odyssey*) call temptingly to a life of pleasure, but they are the death of heroic effort, and their seductive song is immediately countered by a sonnet, 'To J.M.K.', encouraging Tennyson's friend Kemble to be 'a soldier-priest', 'spurred at heart with fieriest energy' (2,7). The two poems reflect conflicting aspects of the poet's personality, which found fullest expression in 'The Lotos-Eaters' and 'Ulysses'. The final predominance of the latter aspect was already foreshadowed in an adaptation of Odysseus's famous reflection (of which even Plato approved), 'Endure, my heart; you have endured worse things before':

Though Night hath climbed her peak of highest noon,
And bitter blasts the screaming autumn whirl,
All night through archways of the bridgèd pearl,
And portals of pure silver walks the moon.
Walk on, my soul, nor crouch to agony . . . .   ('Sonnet', 1–5)

4

Poems 1833

Arthur Hallam thought Tennyson 'point-blank mad' when he decided, after it was printed, not to publish 'The Lover's Tale' (i, ii) as the last
poem in his new volume. He explained to Moxon (20 November
1832): 'it is too full of faults and tho' I think it might conduce towards
making me popular, yet, to my eye, it spoils the completeness of the
book, and is better away' (*Memoir*, vol. 1, p. 90). He was right, but the
piece is interesting, both in itself and in its relation to the rest of the
volume.

'The Lover's Tale' is based on a story in Boccaccio's *Decameron* (Day
Ten, Novella Four) about a young Bolognese gentleman called Gentile
who falls in love with a married woman, Catalina. Hearing that she had
died, he visits her in her tomb, lies down beside her, and starts kissing
her. Then he thinks: 'Why don't I touch her breast a little, since I'm
here? I've never touched it before, and I'll never have another chance.'
Yielding to this desire, he finds that her heart is still beating, carries her
home, gets his mother to nurse her back to health, and in a final theatrical gesture restores her publicly to her husband.

There was a copy of the *Decameron* at Somersby, and Tennyson
taught himself Italian by writing 'a kind of private grammar' on the
sides of his bedroom mantelpiece, until the housemaid washed 'the
nasty dirty mess' off *(Memoir*, vol. 2, p. 51). His interest in Italian
literature was probably started by Arthur Hallam; and the story seems
to have attracted him, not by its aura of necrophily, but by Gentile's
final magnanimity. His version improves the hero's moral position by
making his love for the heroine start in childhood, and dwelling on his
despair (like that of Philip in *Enoch Arden*) when he finds that she is in
love with someone else.

Tennyson told both Palgrave and Mrs Bradley that 'The Lover's Tale' was written before he knew Shelley; but he must have been referring to some lost draft of 1827–8. Soon after that date he certainly read Shelley; he voted 'No' at a meeting of the Apostles to the question 'Have Shelley's poems an immoral tendency?' *(Memoir,* vol. 1, p. 44), and the 1832 version of parts i and ii is full of Shelleyan echoes. The husband, Niccoluccio in the *Decameron,* becomes Lionel, like the hero of Shelley's 'Rosalind and Helen' (the lover, in the text of 1879, becomes Julian, Shelley's name for himself in 'Julian and Maddalo'). Cadrilla (Boccaccio's Catalina) is made the lover's foster-sister, as Cythna is Laon's in Shelley's *The Revolt of Islam.* The lover and Cadrilla call each other 'brother' and 'sister', and the conflict between this relationship and the speaker's passionate love recalls the incestuous overtones in Laon and Cythna's intercourse (in an early version they were actually brother and sister). 'Rosalind and Helen' also contains two explicit references to brother-sister incest, in one case committed, in the other narrowly escaped.

A curious verbal parallel occurs in the dream with which the 1832 version ends:

> I wound my arms
> About her: we whirled giddily; the wind
> Sung; but I clasped her without fear: her weight
> Shrank in my grasp, and over my dim eyes,
> And parted lips which drank her breath, down-hung
> The jaws of Death: I, groaning, from my flung
> Her empty phantom: all the sway and whirl
> Of the storm dropped to windless calm, and I
> Down weltered through the dark ever and ever.   (ii, 197–205)

In *The Revolt of Islam* a sinister Ethiopian had 'wound his long arms around' Cythna, and plunged with her into the sea; and in *The Cenci* Lucrezia had feared that after death her father would 'wind' her 'in his hellish arms' and drag her 'down, down, down!'

In one respect Boccaccio's story was intensely relevant to the 1833 volume: its central idea of a live woman shut up in a tomb, but finally emerging into human society, was close to the volume's chief symbolic theme, one aspect of which was summed up in the poem's opening lines (a romanticized version of the well-known opening of Lucretius' second book):

Here far away, seen from the topmost cliff,
Filling with purple gloom the vacancies
Between the tufted hills, the sloping seas
Hung in mid-haven, and half-way down rare sails,
 White as white clouds, floated from sky to sky.
Oh! pleasant breast of waters, quiet bay,
Like to a quiet mind in the loud world,
Where the chafed breakers of the outer sea
Sank powerless, as anger falls aside
And withers on the breast of peaceful love.   (1-10)

These complementary conceptions of the inner world as a pleasant retreat from the outer, and as a living tomb, are fundamental to what Tennyson called, 'the completeness of the book'.

II

The notion of movement from the inner world to the outer is expressed in the first and last poems of the volume through the image of *influence*, in the literal sense of 'flowing into' something. The prefatory sonnet begins:

Mine be the strength of spirit, fierce and free,
Like some broad river rushing down alone . . .
Which with increasing might doth forward flee
By town, and tower, and hill, and cape, and isle,
And in the middle of the green salt sea
Keeps his blue waters fresh for many a mile.
Mine be the power which ever to its sway
Will win the wise at once, and by degrees
May into uncongenial spirits flow.   (1-11)

No longer content to sing in the heart of an empty garden, the young poet wishes to 'influence' a wider audience than that of his family and Cambridge friends, but fears a hostile reception. The final poem, 'To J.S.', aims to 'influence', not a public but an individual: to console James Spedding for the death of his brother. His friend, he suggests, is philosophical by temperament,

Or else I had not dared to flow
In these words toward you, and invade
    Even with a verse your holy woe.   (6–8)

The influence-image probably carries suggestions derived from
Shelley's *Alastor.* In this poem a young poet, growing dissatisfied with
the world of his own imagination, develops a yearning for human
contact which leads him to his death, after long wanderings by a stream
which 'images' his life. The stream finally falls over a precipice, which
seems 'to overhang the world', thus 'Scattering its waters to the passing
winds'. Tennyson's volume explores the same dilemma: the inner
world is not enough, but for a poet the attempt to escape from it may
be disastrous. His precious 'waters' may be lost in the 'immeasurable
void'.

The usual vehicle for the theme of the paradoxical relationship
between internal and external, subjective and objective, private and
public, poetry and life is a symbolic female. It was a vehicle suggested
not only by literary precedent, but also by social history. The early
nineteenth century saw the simultaneous growth of a code which
confined women rigidly to the home, and of protest against such
confinement. 'Woman's place', like the private world of the mind,
could be regarded both as a pleasant retreat from harsh reality, or as a
kind of tomb. Home, as the feminist writer, William Thompson,
observed in 1825, was for husbands 'the abode of calm bliss', but for
wives an 'eternal prison-house'. For unmarried women, as Florence
Nightingale's 'Cassandra' shows, it could be even more frustrating.

Militant feminism appears in 'Kate', a 'woman-soldier' (15) who
doubtless takes her name from the heroine of *The Taming of the Shrew,* as
well as from the Kate who 'would cry to a sailor, "Go hang!"' in *The
Tempest* (II, ii, 50); but the main emphasis is on female frustration. The
purely sexual variety is most prominent in 'Fatima', based on the fragment of Sappho ('He seems to me equal to the gods . . .') describing the
physical symptoms of unsatisfied homosexual desire. Tennyson makes
it heterosexual (as in another adaptation of the fragment, 'Eleanore',
122–44) and physically suggestive, though the poem's most vivid stanza
(like the title) did not appear until 1842:

Last night I wasted hateful hours
Below the city's eastern towers:
I thirsted for the brooks, the showers:

59

I rolled among the tender flowers:
I crushed them on my breast, my mouth;
I looked athwart the burning drouth
Of that long desert to the south. (8–14)

The flower-rolling sequence, which looks at first like the result of observing a cat on heat, was probably inspired by a passage in C.-E. Savary's *Letters of Egypt* about Gemilé, the teenage wife of an elderly Turk, who never allowed her out except into a walled garden guarded by sentries. She lies down 'to roll amongst the flowers' while waiting for a young lover who for nine months keeps failing to show up. Her situation is like Mariana's; and the 'burning drouth' image for Fatima's frustration is paralleled in 'Mariana in the South', where Tennyson uses the hot, dry, barren country that he had seen in 1830 between Narbonne and Perpignan to perform the symbolic function of the Lincolnshire fens in the original 'Mariana'. The 1833 version of the quasi-refrain, addressed to 'Madonna' (my lady), simultaneously suggests the local form of religion, and echoes the recurrent address to 'Lady Mòon' in Simaitha's story of her desertion (Theocritus, *Idyll* ii):

Madonna! lo! I am all alone,
Love-forgotten and love-forlorn.

The whole poem (especially the last stanza in 1833, which marks the passage of time by the appearance of the evening star and the moon) reads like an elaboration of another fragment once attributed to Sappho: 'The moon has gone down, and the Pleiades: it is midnight, and time is passing; but I lie in bed alone.'

'Oenone' uses material from many classical poets, but is chiefly modelled on *Heroides* v (Oenone to Paris), on the pastoral love-lament (Theocritus iii, xi) and on the deserted woman's incantation (Theocritus ii), in which the repeated line: 'Lady Moon, tell how my love came', combines with Homeric 'many-fountained Ida' to produce Oenone's refrain. Tennyson gave moral significance to this largely amoral subject-matter (for Lucian the Judgment of Paris was material for cynical comedy) by equating Paris's desertion of Oenone with his rejection of Here's true wisdom: 'Self-reverence, self-knowledge, self-control' (142). James Beattie, in 'The Judgment of Paris' (1765), had similarly condemned Paris's verdict as preferring 'Pleasure' to 'Virtue'; but he had confused the moral issue by also condemning Paris's initial surrender to 'soft Oenone's charms', whereas Tennyson firmly harnessed Oenone's pathos to didactic purpose. In thus elevating an otherwise humble fusion of Ovid and Theocritus, he added epic dignity by allusions to Homer and Virgil. The setting of the Judgment, especially where flowers spring up beneath the goddesses' feet (94f), carries tragic suggestions from its source in *Iliad* xiv, where Here, with the help of Aphrodite, interrupts Zeus' efforts to protect Troy from destruction by persuading him to go to bed with her (an aspect of Here's character which Tennyson has to suppress); and a similar effect is produced by echoes of the *Aeneid* which associate Oenone with Dido, as in the lines adapted from one of Dido's nightmares:

> I will not die alone,
> Lest their shrill happy laughter come to me
> Walking the cold and starless road of Death
> Uncomforted .... (253–6)

Dido, as an example of private feeling sacrificed to public expediency (the interests of the Roman Empire), was a fitting symbol (as in Matthew Arnold's 'The Scholar-Gipsy') for the destruction of the inner life by external reality.

The symbolism comes rather nearer to the surface in 'The Lady of Shalott', which is based on an early fourteenth-century Italian novella relating 'How the Damsel of Scalot died for love of Lancelot de Lac'. Tennyson changed the initial *Sc* into the 'softer sound' *Sh (Eversley)*, and faintly underlined the Damsel's sexual frustration by making Lancelot, at her first sight of him, sing 'Tirra lirra, tirra lirra' *(Poems*, p. 359), taken from a song in *The Winter's Tale* where Autolycus thinks of 'tumbling in the hay' with his 'aunts' (whores). He also added several details unconnected with love. He placed his Lady in solitary confinement, by-passed by the stream of human life:

> Willows whiten, aspens shiver,
> The sunbeam-showers break and quiver
> In the stream that runneth ever
> By the island in the river
>   Flowing down to Camelot.
> Four gray walls, and four gray towers
> Overlook a space of flowers,
> And the silent isle embowers
>   The Lady of Shalott. *(Poems*, p. 355)

He gave her two occupations, singing and weaving 'a charmèd web' (p. 356), in which she copies reflections of the outside world seen in a mirror; and put her under a curse if she ever looked directly down to Camelot. This she does when she sees Lancelot, a colourful contrast to her 'gray' environment, reflected in the mirror.

The meaning of these additions seems fairly clear. The invisible Lady's song relates her to Shelley's Skylark: 'Like a Poet hidden In the light of thought, Singing hymns unbidden ... Like a high-born maiden In a palace-tower, Soothing her love-laden Soul in secret hour With music . . . .' It relates her equally to Shelley's poet in *A Defence of Poetry*: 'a nightingale, who sits in darkness and sings to cheer its own solitude with sweet sounds; his auditors are as men entranced by the melody of an unseen musician . . .' The web is a form of art, and the mirror (which enables a tapestry-maker to see his work from the right side) also refers to Plato's *Republic* (x, 597), where Socrates introduces his definition of art and poetry as 'third in succession from reality' by comparing paint-ers and poets to a man who 'creates' a whole universe simply by turning a mirror in every direction. F. D. Maurice had alluded to the same passage (*Athenaeum*, 8 April 1828) when he called the poet's mind 'a mirror which catches and images the whole scheme and working of the world'.

The Lady's connection with art and poetry is confirmed by the symmetry of her home ('Four gray walls, and four gray towers'), echoed in the quadruple rhyme-scheme, and by its resemblance to the 'twice five miles of fertile ground With walls and towers . . . girdled round' in Coleridge's 'Kubla Khan', which is clearly concerned with poetic creation.

Tennyson's comment on 'The Lady of Shalott': 'The new-born love for something, for some one in the wide world from which she has been so long secluded, takes her out of the region of shadows into that of realities' (*Memoir*, vol. 1, p. 117) recalls Shelley's comment on *Alastor*: 'The Poet's self-centred seclusion was avenged by the furies of an irresistible passion pursuing him to speedy ruin.' Tennyson's poem seems to be expressing three things: his sense that it is morally wrong to be self-centred; his belief that, as a poet, he should look for subject-matter outside his own mind, and try to reach a larger public; and his fear that this might destroy his special magic, and ruin his reputation. When the Lady 'flows in' to the great world at Camelot, she does not influence, but merely puzzles her unimagin-ative readers:

They crossed themselves, their stars they blest,
Knight, minstrel, abbot, squire and guest.
There lay a parchment on her breast,
That puzzled more than all the rest,
    The wellfed wits at Camelot.
'The web was woven curiously
The charm is broken utterly,
Draw near and fear not – this is I,
    The Lady of Shalott.'   (1833; *Poems,* p. 361)

The Ovidian 'heroine' is still more explicitly allegorized in 'The
Palace of Art', where she represents, for moral condemnation, 'the
Poet's self-centred seclusion':

I built my soul a lordly pleasure-house,
    Wherein at ease for aye to dwell.
I said, 'O Soul, make merry and carouse,
    Dear soul, for all is well.'   (1–4)

The Palace, which resembles in its symmetry (21–2) the castle of 'The
Lady of Shalott', is built on 'A huge crag-platform' (5) and designed to
give every kind of aesthetic and intellectual pleasure. It is full of paint-
ings and sculptures, gas-lit at night (*Poems,* p. 402), acoustically
adapted for music, and equipped (in stanzas added in a note) with an
astronomical observatory. After enjoying herself for three years, the
Soul develops 'Deep dread and loathing of her solitude' (229) and falls
into a depression which is God's method of ensuring her salvation. In
this mood she decides to come down to earth and mix with ordinary
human beings:

'Make me a cottage in the vale,' she said,
    'Where I may mourn and pray.

'Yet pull not down my palace towers, that are
    So lightly, beautifully built:
Perchance I may return with others there
    When I have purged my guilt.'   (291–6)

The thought and the basic image come from Bacon, to whom Tennyson transfers Dante's title for Aristotle: 'The first of those who know'
(164). In *The Advancement of Learning* Bacon had said that one should
not seek in knowledge 'a tarrasse, for a wandering and variable mind to
walk up and down with a fair prospect; or a tower of state, for a proud

mind to raise itself upon', but 'a rich storehouse, for the glory of the Creator and the relief of man's estate'. The poem seems, however, to be also a reaction against the Epicurean ideal expressed in the opening lines of Lucretius' second book, which are quoted approvingly by Bacon a few pages later:

> It is a view of delight . . . to be in a fortified tower, and to see two battles join upon a pain; but it is a pleasure incomparable, for the mind of man to be settled, landed and fortified in the certainty of truth; and from thence to descry and behold the errors, perturbations, labours, and wanderings up and down of other men.

It is in this spirit that the Soul says:

> I dwell apart, holding no forms of creeds,
>   But contemplating all.   (1833; *Poems,* p. 409)

Like Shelley's poet, the Soul is compared to a nightingale, singing in solitude purely for her own satisfaction (160, 173–6), and she is, of course, the soul of the poet; but apart from her song, she is remarkably uncreative, a consumer rather than a producer of art. The poem is partly, perhaps, a protest against academic life at Cambridge, as a life in which one enjoyed the creative works of others, but created nothing oneself, and was also cut off from ordinary human beings. It was this moral aspect of 'The Palace of Art', relating to the whole social function of the educated classes, that Tennyson emphasized in his introductory sonnet to Trench, although he mentioned 'Its many lesser meanings' (1833; *Poems,* p. 399), which doubtless included the aesthetic problems expressed in 'The Lady of Shalott'.

Artistically, 'The Palace of Art' is not a complete success. The four-line stanza is appropriate enough for describing a four-year attempt to live in a four-courted mansion, and the shortened last line images the final descent from palace to cottage; but the epigrammatic verse-form does not contribute to the total structure, which is virtually formless. The poem is most enjoyable as an anthology of compressed word-pictures, such as a Botticellian Birth of Venus (1833; *Poems,* p. 406), a Rape of Europa based on Moschus, *Idyll* ii, 125–8, or a purely subjective landscape:

> Some were all dark and red, a glimmering land
>   Lit with a low round moon,
> Among brown rocks a man upon the sand
>   Went weeping all alone.   (1833; *Poems,* p. 404)

III

This male Mariana may serve to introduce two important poems in which the volume's recurrent theme is expressed otherwise than by the symbolic female figure considered hitherto. 'The Hesperides' is an enigmatic version of 'The Poet's Mind', concerned with the protection of the poet's inner world against the intrusion of 'wellfed wits' from the outer. It is based on *The Periplus of Hanno,* an account of an exploratory voyage round the north-west coast of Africa by a Carthaginian of the fifth century BC. Tennyson seems to have used the Greek text edited with an English translation by Thomas Falconer (1797), and probably also consulted an edition by I. P. Cory, Fellow of Caius College (1828).

Starting from the Pillars of Hercules (Gibraltar), Hanno sailed down the west coast of Africa, founding a city called Thymiaterion. Then, passing a promontory called Soloeis, and a river full of crocodiles, he reached a large bay, the Western Horn, containing an island, containing a lake, containing another island. Here they saw nothing but trees during the day, but at night saw many fires burning, and heard pipes, cymbals, drums and confused shouting. Sailing away in terror, they came to a country full of fire, with a great mountain, named 'The Chariot of the Gods', on top of which was a fire that seemed to touch the stars. They sailed on to another bay, the Southern Horn, which also contained an island, containing a lake, containing an island. This inner island was full of savage, hairy women, whom their interpreters called 'Gorillas'. They caught and flayed two of them, and took their skins back as evidence to Carthage.

The mysterious music and shouting heard from the first inner island must have reminded Tennyson of the story from Plutarch, told in a gloss to Spenser's *The Shepheardes Calender,* that a man sailing past an island heard a voice telling him to report, at Palodes, that the great Pan was dead. When he got there, and delivered his message, in a sudden calm, 'there was heard such piteous outcryes and dreadful shriking, as hath not been the like ... for at that time ... all Oracles surceased'. The association with the Hesperides came from the maps in Falconer's edition, which showed, near Hanno's route, some islands marked 'once the islands of the Hesperides'; and from one of his Dissertations, which discussed the location of the Hesperides, and said that Hesiod had placed them not far from the Gorgons (i.e. Hanno's 'Gorillas').

The poem was apparently suggested by this cluster of ideas: strange music and voices heard at sea, a calm, divine fire, two doubly insulated

65

sanctuaries, and oracles (the last idea possibly reinforced by the fact that Cory's edition of the *Periplus* was immediately preceded by 'The Oracles of Zoroaster'). A pictorial influence may have been J. M. W. Turner's 'The Goddess of Discord Choosing the Apple of Contention in the Garden of the Hesperides' (1806), which was relevant also to 'Oenone', and contained a dragon which Ruskin thought exactly like a pre-historic iguanodon, except for its pterodactyl-type wings.

The Hesperides were not traditionally connected with poetry; but Milton referred to their singing 'about the golden tree' (*Comus*, 983), Hesiod called them 'clear-voiced' (Theocritus' epithet for the nightingale), and Virgil mentioned a priestess who guarded the Hesperidean temple, fed the dragon, and preserved the sacred branches of the tree, 'scattering liquid honey and sleep-bringing poppy' (*Aeneid*, iv, 486), a line famous for its euphony, and also for its unusual prosody (no strong caesura in either the third or the fourth foot). This, combined with the knowledge that a special refinement of the hexameter, also occasionally used by Virgil, was called 'the golden line', could have made Tennyson associate the golden apples of the Hesperides not only with poetry in general, but particularly with verbal music and metrical technique.

He may also have thought of the Golden Rule (or Rule of Three) in mathematics, which would partly explain the cryptic references to 'number', e. g. 'Five and three (Let it not be preached abroad) make an awful mystery' (28-9). This statement may have come from Jacob Bryant, who saw all myths as oblique references to the Deluge, and wrote that the number eight was 'held sacred and esteemed mysterious' because it stood for the eight passengers in Noah's Ark; but 'numbers' are probably emphasized chiefly in their Latin and Miltonic sense of 'metre': 'If ye sing not, if ye make false measure, We shall lose eternal pleasure' (23-4). When the singers call themselves, Hesper and the dragon 'Five links, a golden chain' (65, 106), it is hard not to think of the iambic pentameter, or of the metrical 'jewels five-words-long' in *The Princess* (ii, 355).

The details of the 'Song' are evidently meant to baffle the outsider who dares to invade the holy precinct of poetry. In the myth the expected intruder is Heracles, who steals the golden apples: in the poem he becomes 'one from the East' (42) and the apples represent 'the wisdom of the west' (26), i. e. of evening, autumn, old age, an 'ancient secret' (72) guarded by a dragon not merely pre-historic, like Turner's, but 'older than the world' (58). Tennyson seems to imply that for him poetry is connected, not with raw modernity, but with the ripeness of the antique:

> But when the fullfaced sunset yellowly
> Stays on the flowering arch of the bough,
> The luscious fruitage clustereth mellowly,
> Goldenkernelled, goldencored,
> Sunset-ripened above on the tree.
> The world is wasted with fire and sword,
> But the apple of gold hangs over the sea. (99-105)

The image resembles one in 'The Lotos-Eaters' (76-8), a poem similar in tone, but antithetical in feeling. Instead of the Hesperides' positive vigilance, we have a drowsy apathy; instead of guarding a 'treasure' (26), the Lotos-Eaters deny value to everything but relaxation. Their condition is just like that described in a passage (quoted in Falconer's edition of the *Periplus*) on the effects of equatorial heat:

> An universal relaxation, a kind of irresistible languor, and aversion to all action, takes possession of both man and beast; the appetite fails, and sleep and quiet are the only things the mind is capable of desiring, or the body of enduring.

The poem is based on the *Odyssey* (ix, 82-104), and the note of heroism sounds in the first word, ' "Courage!" ', which refers to the fact that the 'mariners' have been driven about in a storm for the last nine days, and corresponds with Aeneas' call for endurance in similar circumstances (*Aeneid*, i, 198f), where Virgil adapts the thought of Odysseus ('Endure, my heart; you have endured worse things before') which Tennyson adapted in his sonnet of 1830. It is important to realize that Tennyson's 'Lotos-Eaters' (who are not natives of the country, but members of Odysseus' crew who became addicted to the lotos) in no way represent an ideal: they are merely backsliders from the heroic ideal, whom Odysseus punishes by forcing them back to the boats, shoving them under the benches, and tying them up.

It was the way Tennyson dealt with his own suicidal tendencies, and the suicidal aspect of 'The Lotos-Eaters' is indicated by two of its literary sources. 'A land where all things always seemed the same' (24) is another echo of Lucretius' 'eadem sunt omnia semper', a phrase used by Nature in a prolonged attempt (iii, 931-62) to make death seem acceptable, and life seem not worth living. This Lucretian 'sameness' (echoed in the identical rhymes of lines 1 and 3) is combined with the uniformly dreamy movement of the Spenserian stanza (1-45), and with reminiscences of Despayre's arguments for suicide (*The Faerie Queene*, I, ix, 40-7):

> Is not short paine well borne, that brings long ease,
> And layes the soule to sleepe in quiet grave?
> Sleepe after toyle, port after stormie seas,
> Ease after warre, death after life does greatly please . . .
> Death is the end of woes: die soone, O faeries sonne.

So, too, the Lotos-Eaters (86-98):

> Death is the end of life; ah, why
> Should life all labour be? . . .
> Let us alone. What pleasure can we have
> To war with evil? Is there any peace
> In ever climbing up the climbing wave?
> All things have rest, and ripen toward the grave
> In silence; ripen, fall and cease:
> Give us long rest or death, dark death or dreamful ease.

In their wish to live permanently in a subjective world, 'Falling asleep in a half-dream!' (101), they certainly relate to the volume's central theme; but it is wrong to see them as directly symbolizing poetic creation. They are as uncreative as the Kraken, and their Choric Song is merely an automatic group-response ('And all at once they sang', 44) to a drug-induced sense of exhaustion. Tennyson's enormous success in conveying their state of mind is no reason for supposing that he thought it the right state for composing poetry. He probably considered his Lotos-Eaters, as Matthew Arnold considered his Strayed Reveller, imaginatively akin to poets, but incapacitated for poetry by their refusal to suffer 'pain' or 'labour' ('The Strayed Reveller', 207-11, 270-4).

IV

The abstract idea of movement from the subjective to the objective, symbolized by the Lady of Shalott's emergence from her island-castle, and the Soul's descent from her crag-platform, begins to be implemented in two poems about females who are not primarily symbolic.

Alice, 'The Miller's Daughter', is a Lady of Shalott with a difference. She lives beside a stream, which at one point suggests an image of human life: 'There's somewhat flows to us in life, But more is taken quite away' (21-2). It has, however, the purely mundane function of turning the wheel of the mill. 'No particular mill,' wrote Tennyson, 'but if I thought at all of any mill it was that of Trumpington, near Cambridge' (*Eversley*). She sits, and spins, and sings (121-3), and she has a 'mirror where her sight she feeds' (1833, *Poems*, p. 377); but she uses it for normal narcissistic purposes, and her reflection in the stream is a vision of substantial flesh and blood:

> A water-rat from off the bank
>   Plunged in the stream. With idle care,
> Downlooking through the sedges rank,
>   I saw your troubled image there.
> Upon the dark and dimpled beck
>   It wandered like a floating light,
> A full fair form, a warm white neck,
>   And two white arms – how rosy white! (1833; *Poems*, p. 375)

Instead of living in a world of shadows, and becoming 'half sick' of them ('The Lady of Shalott', 71), she makes a young man love-sick with watching her shadow in 'the blind' (124).

He, too, is a real-life version of a literary formula. The pastoral lover of Amaryllis (Theocritus, *Idyll* iii) wishes he were a bee, so that he could fly into her cave, and Alice's lover has similar fantasies (*Poems*, pp. 379-80), paralleled in Anacreon and Catullus; but unlike the pastoral lover's, his passion is far from hopeless: the poem is spoken by Alice's husband, after years of happy marriage. Instead of threatening to hang himself, he hopes that he and his wife will die 'the self-same day' (24), and in the meantime seems anxious not to contract rheumatism:

> On the chalk-hill the bearded grass
>   Is dry and dewless. Let us go. (245-6)

With its realistic adaptation of pastoral convention, its precisely localized setting, and its easy, near-humorous tone, 'The Miller's Daughter' initiated a new genre, the 'English Idyll'.

A parallel movement from literature to life can be seen in 'A Dream of Fair Women'. Suggested by Chaucer's 'The Legend of Good

69

Women' (which was largely based on Ovid's *Heroides*), it owes to
Chaucer its dream-form, and one of its 'Women', Cleopatra. Tennyson
presents them more dramatically: where Chaucer had merely seen a
group of 'ladyes nyntene', and then told their stories, Tennyson inter-
viewed his ladies one by one, making them speak for themselves. He also
mentioned historical figures (e.g. Joan of Arc and the daughter of Sir
Thomas More) as well as mythological ones; and where Chaucer's
women were chosen merely to exemplify dedication to the Religion of
Love, Tennyson's related to a much larger question, the position of
women in a patriarchal society. His reaction to the stories in 'The
Legend' was explicitly feminist:

> In every land I thought that, more or less,
>   The stronger sterner nature overbore
> The softer, uncontrolled by gentleness
>   And selfish evermore . . . .   (1833; *Poems*, p. 442)

Besides anticipating the theme of *The Princess*, the poem is also concerned with the relation between such a theme and poetry. Chaucer's
art holds the reader for a while 'above the subject' (9–10), that is, delays
emotional realization of the human problem described. On the other
hand, some degree of artistic detachment seems to be necessary for the
effective treatment in poetry of this real-life theme, and the need for
distancing the subject is implied by three different images, the balloon,
the dream, and the wood.

In the 1840s Tennyson expressed a great wish to see the earth from a
balloon, but missed an opportunity of doing so, for fear of upsetting his
mother and sisters (*Materials*, vol. 1, p. 343). His friend Milnes,
however, had gone up in a balloon from Cambridge in 1829, and had
written during the flight to Arthur Hallam: 'Oh, if the spirit of Adonais
would sail with me in my little boat, my very crescent moon!' He was
alluding to Shelley's name for Keats, and to Wordsworth, who in the
Prologue to *Peter Bell* had pictured himself travelling, not on 'a flying
horse' or in a 'huge balloon', but in an aerial boat. Tennyson adapted the
image for the poetic imagination in the first four stanzas (1833) of his
poem, comparing the poet's detached view of the world to that of a
balloonist, who 'Lets the great world flit from him seeing all . . .' (*Poems*,
p. 441).

The dream image, derived from Chaucer, also has the effect of
distancing the experience of 'Beauty and anguish walking hand in hand

The downward slope to death' (15-16), especially when, on waking, the poet feels the content of his dream as remote and inaccessible as a moment of happiness that is 'mingled with past years' (281-2). In the third image of the 'old wood', doubtless suggested by Dante's 'selva oscura', the Past itself is expressed (53f). The dawn of time is presented paradoxically in a landscape of death, which Tennyson thought Turner should have painted (*Eversley*):

> The dim red morn had died, her journey done,
> And with red lips smiled at the twilight plain,
> Half-fallen across the threshold of the sun,
> Never to rise again.
>
> There was no motion in the dumb dead air,
> Nor any song of bird or sound of rill;
> Gross darkness of the inner sepulchre
> Is not so deadly still
>
> As that wide forest. (61-9)

And yet Tennyson realized that this region of the past was pre-eminently his own poetic sphere: 'Pass freely through,' says an inner voice, 'the wood is all thine own' (83). Distance, whether in space or in time, was what stirred his imagination. 'To me,' he wrote in 1839, 'often that far-off world seems nearer than the present. The present is always something unreal and indistinct, but the other seems a good solid planet, rolling round its green hills and paradises to the harmony of more steadfast laws' (*Memoir*, vol. 1, pp. 171-2).

V

The 'completeness of the book' was evidently meant to emerge, not only from the unifying themes, but also from the links of similarity or contrast between consecutive poems. The image of lovers waiting hand in hand for death while a 'deluge' roars past them ('If I were loved, as I desire to be') introduces 'The Lady of Shalott', past whom a peaceful river flows, on which she dies of unrequited love. The alien landscape of 'Mariana in the South' leads to a comparison between the influences of English and foreign scenery ('Eleanore'). This poem ends with a passage of swooning sentiment, in which 'the amorous, odorous wind Breathes low between the sunset and the moon' (123-4): an excess immediately corrected by a comic vision of the miller's 'mealy face, Like the moon in an ivytod' (1833; *Poems*, p. 372). Fatima's sexual frustration is accentuated by the picture of contented, middle-aged affection which precedes it. 'Oenone' concludes with vague threats of revenge ('I will not die alone'); 'The Sisters' makes revenge explicit ('Three times I stabbed him through and through'); and the introductory sonnet to 'The Palace of Art' replaces the image of bitter sororal rivalry by that of 'three sisters That doat upon each other, friends to man' (10-11).

The Soul in 'The Palace of Art' finally decides to 'mourn and pray' in 'a cottage in the vale' (291-2): her change of status is paralleled by the cottage-dwelling 'May Queen', who is brought down from that village eminence to the prospect of lying 'low i' the mould' ('New Year's Eve', 4). She asks her mother not to mourn for her, but mourns her own death, thinking of 'the chancel-casement' (21) and of her grave in the church yard.

The drowsy inertia of 'The Lotos-Eaters' sets off the boundless energy of 'Rosalind', the 'frolic falcon, with bright eyes', an image of flight taken up in the balloon-stanzas of 'A Dream of Fair Women'. This poem ends with the thought of the irrecoverable past, and the next ('Song') asks why the past can be recalled by the smell of a violet. 'Margaret', who keeps well out of 'the fight' (26), precedes the 'woman-soldier', 'Kate', who introduces a sonnet calling the Poles to battle.

Two unhappy efforts, 'O Darling Room' and 'To Christopher North', are linked by the fact that both are flippant exercises in the use of John Walker's *Rhyming Dictionary* (1801), which had specifically listed as 'allowable' a rhyme satirically italicized in Croker's review (*right, exquisite*). The epithets for Christopher North ('crusty, rusty, musty, fusty') were intended to suggest that such a critic was a thing of the past; and in 'The Death of the Old Year' North merges into the image of the dying year, who was also 'full of joke and jest' (28). His semi-comic demise is hastened in the last stanza because 'There's . . . a new face at the door, my friend'. 'To J.S.', which replaced 'The Lover's Tale' as the final poem in the volume, seems almost to identify the new friend as James Spedding, and the demise as that of Spedding's brother. This gradual shifting of identities between the last two poems is paralleled by a shift of imagery. 'The Death of the Old Year' begins with a mention of 'winter winds' (2), which become metaphorical in the first lines of 'To J.S.', modelled on Horace (*Odes*, II, x, 9-12):

The wind, that beats the mountain, blows
  More softly round the open wold,
And gently comes the world to those
  That are cast in gentle mould.   (1-4)

The poem justifies its position as epilogue by lightly recapitulating several of the volume's themes. Lines 1-2 touch on the relation between the outer world and the inner, through a reversal of the 'influence' image. Frustrated love is summed up in 'love is left alone' (16), the idea of the past in 'This is the curse of time' (17). The consolation concludes with an emphasis on the 'peace' of the grave which recalls 'The Lotos-Eaters', and the Lucretian aspect of the 'land where all things always seemed the same' reappears in the last stanza. Lucretius had asked (iii, 977): 'Is death not more free from care (*securius*) than any sleep?' Tennyson, using the English word in the Latin sense, congratulates the dead man on his escape from the fear of innovation:

Sleep till the end, true soul and sweet.
  Nothing comes to thee new or strange.
Sleep full of rest from head to feet;
  Lie still, dry dust, secure of change.   (73-6)

5

Poems 1842

I

The revised versions of previously published poems, in volume 1 of the new collection, were much better than their originals, and are the forms generally known today. Apart from stylistic and metrical improvements (in which Tennyson clearly relied on his own judgment rather than that of his critics), the most important changes were the replacement of the final stanza of 'The Lady of Shalott' (which J. S. Mill had called a 'lame and impotent conclusion'); the rewriting of the end of 'The Lotos-Eaters'; and the addition of a 'Conclusion' to 'The May Queen'.

The chief effect of the new sections in 'The Lotos-Eaters' (vi, viii) was to stress the Homeric context of the poem, and its heroic implications. The mariners have nearly forgotten their past 'great deeds' (123), and describe as not worth attempting the great deed which Odysseus is actually going to accomplish: the restoration of 'order' (127) in Ithaca. Their wish to behave 'like Gods', smiling 'in secret' over their nectar, and showing callous indifference to the prayers and sufferings of mankind (154–70), is designed to increase the reader's disapproval of their attitude. Hallam Tennyson obscured the issue by comparing this passage to Lucretius (v, 83, vi, 58), since the idea is perfectly Homeric also (cf. *Iliad*, xxiv, 525–6). In Homer all the heroic and moral excellence is displayed by human beings: the gods merely enjoy themselves in their 'golden houses' (158), taking sides in the Trojan War like dinner-jacketed spectators at a prize-fight. The additions serve to underline the poem's purpose: to recommend, by contrast, the heroic ideal.

In the 'Conclusion' to 'The May Queen' Alice becomes impatient instead of reluctant to die, and looks forward to 'a blessèd home' where 'the wicked cease from troubling and the weary are at rest' (57–60).

The poem may express Tennyson's increased suicidal feelings after the death of Arthur Hallam; but certain parallels suggest the influence of Robert Southey's 'English Eclogue', 'The Funeral'. This tells how 'a village girl' called Hannah wasted away with a 'strange illness' for eighteen months, until 'the hour of death Came welcome to her', and she comforted her mother with the same text from *Job* as Alice used to comfort hers.

The other new poems in volume one, written around 1833, deal directly or indirectly with the political and social questions raised by the 1832 Reform Act. 'You ask me, why, though ill at ease' (in the *In Memoriam* metre) celebrates England as the home of liberty and peaceful democratization:

A land of settled government,
A land of just and old renown,
Where Freedom slowly broadens down
From precedent to precedent. . . .   (9–12)

'Of old sat Freedom on the heights' treats the same theme allegorically, ending with a protest against 'The falsehood of extremes!' (24). 'Love thou thy land, with love far brought.' (*In Memoriam* metre) is another sermon in favour of progressive reform, and against violent revolution, the product of 'Raw Haste, half-sister to Delay' (96).

'The Goose' is a satirical ballad probably based on Sir Thomas More's use of an Aesop fable in his *Dialogue of Comfort against Tribulation*, while arguing against the equal distribution of wealth:

For surely the rich man's substance is the wellspring of the poor man's living. And therefore here would it fare by the poor man, as it fared by the woman in one of Aesop's fables, which had an hen that laid her every day a golden egg; till on a day she thought she would have a great many eggs at once, and therefore she killed her hen. . . .

Like More, Tennyson makes Aesop's man a woman. He also makes the goose the present of a kindly and reasonable 'stranger', who finally saves the goose from being strangled; and he changes the woman's reason for wanting to kill it. Wealth has made her first idle and then proud: she condemns the goose to death merely because its cackling annoys her. Tennyson seems to imply that the poor would not benefit morally from a large increase in their income, and that radical agitation for the dispossession of the rich is caused by irrational prejudice against them, not by economic 'rhyme and reason' (6). The storm that follows the sensible stranger's departure is presumably a comic metaphor for revolution:

> The wild wind rang from park and plain,
>   And round the attics rumbled,
> Till all the tables danced again,
>   And half the chimneys tumbled.
>
> The glass blew in, the fire blew out,
>   The blast was hard and harder.
> Her cap blew off, her gown blew up,
>   And a whirlwind cleared the larder.   (45–52)

'The Blackbird' is reproached for similar ingratitude. Though left free (like Adam and Eve) to eat all the other fruit in the garden, he insists on eating the poet's apples, and has also stopped singing so well:

> Plenty corrupts the melody
> That made thee famous once, when young . . .
> Take warning! he that will not sing
>   While yon sun prospers in the blue,
>   Shall sing for want, ere leaves are new,
> Caught in the frozen palms of Spring.   (15–24)

The social comment concealed in this garden-poem is quite in the spirit of the Poor Law Reform Act (1834): Tennyson's 'outdoor relief' had evidently made the blackbird's non-working conditions too 'eligible'.

The last poem of the group, 'Lady Clara Vere de Vere', is a tirade against snobbery addressed to 'The daughter of a hundred Earls' (7), who has toyed with the affections of a simple yeoman, causing him to commit suicide. Its absurdity must be explained partly by the poet's bitter feelings about Rosa Baring (and perhaps about the aristocratic pretensions of his uncle, Charles Tennyson d'Eyncourt); and partly by the relevance of the theme to the contemporary political climate: if Freedom was to broaden slowly down, and English society to become more democratic, it needed pointing out that 'Kind hearts are more than coronets, And simple faith than Norman blood' (55–6).

II

The political and social views expressed in the first volume lay special emphasis on time:

> Love thou thy land, with love far-brought
>> From out the storied Past, and used
>> Within the Present, but transfused
> Through future time by power of thought.   (1–4)

The concept of time is what unifies the rich variety of volume two. Tennyson saw time destroying traditional beliefs, but bringing new knowledge; giving nostalgic retrospects, but also prospects of progress. For the individual the passage of time seemed equally ambivalent: as Horace said in an *Epistle*, 'Each year that passes robs us of something', but as Theocritus had said (*Idyll* xv), 'The dear Hours are the slowest of the gods, but we long for their coming, because they bring something to everyone'. In 'Love and Duty', thinking of his parting from Emily, but also of the possibilities that became realities in 1850, he combined the two statements:

> The slow sweet hours that bring us all things good,
> The slow sad hours that bring us all things ill,
> And all good things from evil. . . .   (56–8)

Apart from the gains or losses caused by time, Tennyson had always had what he called 'the passion of the past', an acute sense of the sadness and strangeness of time gone by. 'And it is so always with me now'; he told Knowles (after 1867), 'it is the distance that charms me in the landscape, the picture and the past, and not the immediate to-day in which I move' (*The Nineteenth Century*, vol. 33, p. 170).

This idiosyncrasy, coupled with the fact that his earliest experience of poetry had been mostly in classical literature, presented him, as a poet, with a special problem: how could the traditions of classical poetry be adapted to the modern age?

III

The second volume opened with 'The Epic', of which an early draft began:

> you ask – if any writer now
> he style of some heroic age
> he mastodon – nay, why should he
> models rather than the life?   (*Poems*, p. 584)

The question is discussed in a Christmas Eve conversation between a poet, a parson, a narrator, and their host, about various departures from tradition. Christmas, they say, is no longer taken seriously, and the parson goes on to lament 'the general decay of faith', encouraged by 'geology and schism', and exemplified in the passing of an act for church reform. The host laughingly implies (as Matthew Arnold was to suggest more solemnly) that poetry might serve as a substitute for religion. The poet has written a twelve-book epic on King Arthur, but thinking it anachronistic and derivative ('faint Homeric echoes, nothing worth') decided to burn it. The host, however, has saved the eleventh book from the flames, and the poet is persuaded to read it aloud. Having thus anticipated likely objections to 'Morte d'Arthur', Tennyson begins to answer them in the second part of the framing poem, when the narrator says: 'Perhaps some modern touches here and there Redeemed it from the charge of nothingness' (278–9). This hint is spelled out in the narrator's dream, when Arthur becomes 'a modern gentleman' (294) who, merging with the sound of Christmas bells, develops religious associations, and heralds the return of all the 'good things' (300) that time has taken away.

'Morte d'Arthur' is based on Malory (xxi, 4–5) and the 'faint Homeric echoes' consist of a paratactic style and a few semi-allusions to passages in Homer. When Bedivere imagines living 'three lives of mortal men' (155) he recalls lines about Nestor (*Iliad*, i, 250–2, *Odyssey*, iii, 245). Arthur, 'reclining on his arm' (168), shares his posture with Nestor, when woken up at night (*Iliad*, x, 80). An early draft (*Poems*, p. 586) describes Gawain's appearance in a dream, using words adapted from Patroclus' appearance to Achilles (*Iliad*, xxiii, 60). The description of Avilion (260–3) is modelled on that of the Elysian Fields (*Odyssey*, iv, 565–8).

Virgilian echoes are rather less faint. When Bedivere wonders whether or not to throw Excalibur into the lake, 'This way and that dividing the swift mind' (60), the phrase associates him with Aeneas, when in doubt whether to obey the gods and throw over Dido (*Aeneid*, iv, 285). The connection is significant, since both men are torn between obedience to a higher power and attraction to physical beauty (Aeneas is actually wearing a sword, adorned like Excalibur with jewels, which Dido has given him). There is another obvious parallel between the lines on Arthur's sadly changed appearance (222-5), and the passage (*Aeneid*, ii, 274f) where the dead Hector appears to Aeneas in a dream, just before the fall of Troy.

The general effect, however, is neither Homeric nor Virgilian, but purely Tennysonian:

>   and from them rose
> A cry that shivered to the tingling stars,
> And, as it were one voice, an agony
> Of lamentation, like a wind, that shrills
> All night in a waste land, where no one comes,
> Or hath come, since the making of the world. (198-203)

The 'modern touches', then, result from Tennyson's peculiar sensibility to ideas of isolation, desolation, and emptiness, and his despair at the death of Arthur Hallam (the poem was written 1833-4):

> 'Ah! my Lord Arthur, whither shall I go?
> Where shall I hide my forehead and my eyes?
> For now I see the true old days are dead . . .
> And I, the last, go forth companionless,
> And the days darken round me, and the years,
> Among new men, strange faces, other minds.' (227-38)

Tennyson contrived to convert his own predicament (the loss of Arthur) into a symbol for the spiritual plight of his age, especially its 'general decay of faith', imaged in the chapel to which Arthur is carried: 'A broken chancel with a broken cross' (9). This chapel, which is not ruined in Malory, refers more to the nineteenth than to the sixth century; and the Excalibur incident is also given a 'modern' meaning. Throwing it away meant, for the poet himself, accepting the loss of his friend; for his age it meant accepting the loss of 'the true old days', whether in religious or in social matters, as a condition of progress to something better. Hope for the future depended on willingness to reject the past. The poem gives a religious turn to a statement by the antireligious Lucretius (iii, 964-5): 'Antiquity is always pushed out by novelty; one thing must be destroyed to create another.'

> The old order changeth, yielding place to new,
> And God fulfils himself in many ways,
> Lest one good custom should corrupt the world.   (240–2)

The next four poems in the volume are modernizations of another classical form, the pastoral. The transition from epic to pastoral is subtly prepared for in the last few lines of 'The Epic':

> and all the people cried,
> 'Arthur is come again: he cannot die.'
> Then those that stood upon the hills behind
> Repeated – 'Come again; and thrice as fair;'
> And, further inland, voices echoed – 'Come
>   With all good things, and war shall be no more.'   (295–300)

This is the formula for ending pastoral elegy, as in Virgil's *Eclogue* v, which concludes a lament for Daphnis' death with an account of his peace-bringing deification. Pan, shepherds and Dryads express delight; the mountains 'fling joyful voices to the stars' and the rocks and trees re-echo: 'He is a god, a god!'

'The Gardener's Daughter', like 'The Miller's Daughter', is an old man's account of a successful love affair in youth. The sub-title, 'The Pictures', refers to the portraits painted by two friends of the girls they love; but it also suggests the idyll, which means 'a little picture'. The poem resembles *Idyll* vii of Theocritus in its lush descriptions of summer, but the scenery is unmistakably English. In that *Idyll* Theocritus walks from the city into the country with a friend, and meets another friend called Lycidas: both friends have always been assumed to represent real contemporary poets. The narrator of 'The Gardener's Daughter' makes a similar excursion with a friend called Eustace, who clearly represents Arthur Hallam (the poem was started before, and finished after, Arthur's death, certain drafts being written in the notebook which contains the earliest sections of *In Memoriam*). The Gardener's Daughter is called Rose, presumably after Rosa Baring, and is described in one draft (*Poems*, p. 514) with a physical suggestiveness unusual in Tennyson:

> An unforgotten vision! The clear heat
> Bathing the ripe anemones, that kissed
> Each other in her lips, deepened the blush

Below her violet eyes and underneath
Glowed on one polished shoulder, – basking warm
Between the halfseen swell of maiden breasts
Moulded in smoothest curves. ...

The sadness of the conclusion, in which this fleshly creature survives only as a picture and a memory, may reflect both Rosa's defection and the loss of Arthur Hallam.

This poem, which Tennyson called 'full and rich ... to a fault, especially the descriptions of nature, for the lover is an artist' (*Eversley*), is followed by one contrastingly bare in style. 'Dora' is a Wordsworthian type of pastoral, like 'Michael'; but its story, which comes from Mary Mitford's *Our Village* (vol. 3, 1828), is there compared to 'the Arcadian peasants of Poussin' and to the classical myth of Demeter and Proserpine, as well as to 'the finest pastoral of the world, the far lovelier Ruth'. Tennyson brought it still nearer to classical pastoral by imitating Theocritus' habit of incorporating phrases from Homer to the extent of twice adapting a formulaic line of the *Odyssey* to mark the passage of time: 'And the sun fell, and all the land was dark' (77,107).

The story describes the effects of parental tyranny. A farmer orders his son William to marry his cousin Dora. William refuses, is turned out of the house, and marries Mary Morrison (her original surname was Hay, which doubtless seemed almost too pastoral, so, with a little help from Burns, Tennyson found her another). William dies in poverty, and Dora finally engineers a reconciliation between the old man and his daughter-in-law. The original story ends ambiguously, with Dora crying, ostensibly with joy, and saying 'How very strange it is ... that I should be so foolish as to cry!' Tennyson removes the ambiguity, by making Dora in love with William from the start, so that there is no happy ending for her. The change not only turned Dora, who 'lived unmarried till her death' (167) into a standard Ovidian 'Heroine', but also stressed the political aspect of the time-theme: if the old are too reactionary, and the young too radical, the result will be generally disastrous.

The central scene of 'Dora' (as of *Ruth*) is a cornfield at harvest time; the next poem, 'Audley Court', is again based on Theocritus, *Idyll* vii, which centres on a harvest festival. On the way there the poet-narrator and his friend Lycidas both sing songs. The first, by Lycidas, wishes his boy-friend a safe voyage to Mytilene: 'Audley Court' ('partially suggested', wrote Tennyson, 'by Abbey Park at Torquay') begins with the

81

narrator's friend, Francis Hale, 'just alighted from the boat, And breathing of the sea' (6–7). The homosexual element has gone, and the voyager was probably associated in Tennyson's mind with his own 'Lycidas', Arthur Hallam, who had died five years before the date of the poem (1838). The first section that Tennyson wrote of *In Memoriam* (ix) belonged to the same genre as Lycidas' song, i.e. the *propemptikon* (prayer for a safe voyage). There is also some similarity between this greeting of Francis on the quay, and the fantasy of seeing the dead Arthur 'stepping lightly down the plank' (*In Memoriam* xiv).

The narrator and his friend sing songs, as in the *Idyll*, and have a picnic; a draft passage describing the abundance of fruit in the orchard (*Poems*, p. 707) closely follows lines 144–6 in Theocritus. More ingenious are the modernizations and Anglicizations of details in the original. The harvest festival becomes 'Audley Feast'; the hotels, given such pastoral names as 'The Bull' and 'The Fleece', are consequently 'crammed'; and the crowd on the quay originally included a curious figure playing what looks more like a shepherd's pipe than bagpipes: '. . . over hollowed tubes Purse-lipt the swarthy piper moved his beard' (*Poems*, p. 705). The harvest featured in the *Idyll* is translated into a subject of picnic conversation, the Corn Law agitation of 1837 (33–4); and Sicilian wine and fruit change to Devon cider and a pie provoking a geological allusion, not only topical but also highly relevant to the theme of time:

> a pasty costly-made
> Where quail and pigeon, lark and leveret lay,
> Like fossils of the rock, with golden yolks
> Imbedded and injellied . . . .   (22–5)

Idyll vii ends with a reference to the one-eyed Polyphemus, 'who pelted ships with rocks', and a picture of the corn-goddess 'laughing' with joy. The monster's winking eye becomes the 'one green sparkle' of a 'little buoy appearing and disappearing in the dark sea' (Tennyson, *Eversley*), and the descending rocks become a natural stairway. The happy goddess merges with the 'Shepherd' in the famous conclusion to *Iliad* viii, who, gazing at 'the stars about the moon' on a windless night, 'gladdens in his heart' (Tennyson's later translation of the Homeric phrases):

> but ere the night we rose
> And sauntered home beneath a moon, that, just

In crescent, dimly rained about the leaf
Twilights of airy silver, till we reached
The limit of the hills; and as we sank
From rock to rock upon the glooming quay,
The town was hushed beneath us: lower down
The bay was oily calm; the harbour-buoy,
Sole star of phosphorescence in the calm,
With one green sparkle ever and anon
Dipt by itself, and we were glad at heart.   (78–88)

'I'm glad I walked', begins the next poem, announcing the more colloquial and pedestrian style of Theocritus' dialogue-poems, which Southey had imitated in his 'English Eclogues'. The first of these, 'The Old Mansion', anticipated Tennyson's time theme: it was a conversation between an old man, nostalgic for 'old times', and a young squire who has been 'improving' the old house, and replies: 'But sure all changes are not needs for the worse.' Tennyson, however, comes much closer than Southey to Theocritus: 'Walking to the Mail' is a highly inventive variation on *Idyll* iv, a rambling conversation between Battus, a goatherd, and Corydon, a cowherd. 'Whose cows are those?' asks Battus. They belong to Aegon, who has gone off to box in the Olympic Games, after displaying his strength by dragging a bull down a hill by its hoof and presenting it to Amaryllis. 'Oh, lovely Amaryllis,' exclaims Battus, 'I'll never forget you, even now you're dead. Why, I loved you as much as one of my own goats!' Battus then runs off to stop a cow eating some olives, gets a thorn in his foot, and, following some obscure train of thought, suddenly asks: 'Is the old man still working away at that girl he's so fond of?' 'Oh yes', says Corydon, 'I came across them the other day behind the cowshed, when he was hard at it.' 'Dirty old man!' comments Battus, and there the *Idyll* ends.

Battus and Corydon become James and John, walking to catch the mail-coach. Their conversation is at first utterly flat and prosaic. 'Whose house is that I see?' asks John. It is Sir Edward Head's, so named, it seems, because instead of having Aegon's bodily strength, he is slightly weak in the head:

Vexed with a morbid devil in his blood,
That veiled the world with jaundice, [he] hid his face
From all men, and commercing with himself,
He lost the sense that handles daily life –

That keeps us all in order more or less –
And sick of home went overseas for change. (14–18)

'His devil goes with him', says James, and then, perhaps remembering Horace's 'Black Care sits behind the horseman', tells a funny story of a man who packed all his possessions, including his wife, into a cart and drove away from a haunted house, only to find that the 'jolly ghost' was in the cart too. The mention of a wife leads on to Sir Edward Head's: a 'lovely Amaryllis' who, though not dead, has become fat and sour through an unfortunate inter-class marriage. This return to the 'Lady Clara' question brings up politics: Sir Edward was frightened away by the Reform Act and by the Chartist movement. James then reduces the political issue to the inevitable conflict between the Haves and the Have Nots, illustrating his argument with another anecdote: when at school, he had stolen a farmer's pig, and dragged it up a spiral staircase on to the roof (Aegon's feat with the bull in reverse). His secret crime was never discovered, and John, reverting to Sir Edward, comments:

What know we of the secret of a man?
His nerves were wrong. What ails us, who are sound,
That we should mimic this raw fool the world,
Which charts us all in its coarse blacks or whites,
As ruthless as a baby with a worm,
As cruel as a schoolboy ere he grows
To Pity – more from ignorance than will. (94–100)

The absurdity of calling people simply black or white is subtly reaffirmed when the coach finally arrives, drawn by 'three pyebalds and a roan' (104).

The last point in the poem, reached circuitously by a free association of ideas, was clearly suggested by Battus' harsh judgment of the old man, comparable to the schoolboy's callous treatment of the farmer (and his pig); but with the notion of growth to knowledge through time it develops wider significance in the thought of the whole book.

IV

The thought of judging more humanely, by realizing the complexity of human nature, is put into practice in the next poem, 'St Simeon Stylites', the first of two poems primarily concerned with the past, not in literature but in history. St Simeon, who lived on pillars for thirty-six years (the last three feet in diameter and sixty feet high), was clearly 'vexed by a morbid devil', which isolated him as effectively as the Soul's 'crag-platform' or the pig's aerial prison. The visual image of his psychological condition was vividly presented in an illustration to William Hone's *Every-Day Book* (1825), which was Tennyson's main source (pp. 35–9). The saint appears as a grotesque, bald, wildly bearded figure crouched on the top of a pillar scarcely wider than his knee to toe base-line. In the fields below stand tiny people with upstretched hands, and above his head is a cloud: he is indeed 'A sign betwixt the meadow and the cloud' (14).

His relevance to the time-theme, hinted at by his own comparison of his pillar to a sun-dial (94), is that he represents a religious attitude which time has made us see to be ridiculous: the tempering of ridicule with sympathy is the balancing-feat of the poem. The ridicule was probably encouraged by Gibbon, who mentioned St Simeon (*Decline and Fall of the Roman Empire*, chapter 37) to illustrate his thesis that 'the extravagant penance of the Hermits was stimulated by applause and emulation', and quoted 'a piece of ancient scandal' which attributed the ulcer on the saint's thigh to his haste in accepting a lift from the Devil in a fiery chariot apparently bound for heaven. He also made the serious point: 'This voluntary martyrdom must have gradually destroyed the sensibility both of the mind and body; nor can it be presumed that the fanatics, who torment themselves, are susceptible of any lively affection for the rest of mankind.'

If he read Hone's source, Alban Butler's *Lives* of the saints, he would have found encouragement for sympathy in the statement that, for all his apparent pride, St Simeon was a humble man who 'spoke to all with the most engaging sweetness and charity'. Ridicule, however, is uppermost in the poem. The first line, as spoken by a man sixty feet above ground level, has a certain deadpan humour: 'Although I be the basest of mankind ...', and according to FitzGerald, Tennyson used to read the poem aloud 'with grotesque grimness', especially when the saint catalogues his ailments (13), 'laughing aloud at times'.

Sympathy is expressed chiefly by stressing the pathetic irony of his situation. This revolting bundle of self-inflicted disease and filth can finally only 'trust' that he is 'whole, and clean, and meet for Heaven'; at the end of a miserable life he realizes that he may have been 'fooled' (209–10), though he still prays for 'this foolish people' to follow his example (219–20). W. E. H. Lecky recalled (*Memoir*, vol. 2, p. 201) 'the terrible force' with which Tennyson, in his old age, read aloud Rochester's lines about the man who gets more and more deluded by his own ideas.

> Till Old Age and Experience hand in hand
> Lead him to Death, and *make* him understand,
> After a search so painful and so long,
> That *all* his life he has been in the wrong.

The compassion that tinges the black humour of 'St Simeon Stylites' appears in its presentment of a man on the brink of just such a realization.

For a monologue spoken by a character at once repulsive, ridiculous and pathetic Tennyson again had a precedent in Theocritus, *Idyll* xi, where the ugly monster Polyphemus (who devours human beings in the *Odyssey*) sits on 'a high rock' and tries to recommend himself to a creature from another element, the sea-nymph Galatea. He complains of his physical ailments (head and feet throbbing), offers to let her burn out his one eye, and says that on land he too is thought 'somebody', just as St Simeon boasts that on earth people think that he is 'somewhat' (124). Polyphemus finally decides he is a fool to suffer so much for a person who rejects him.

The light-hearted companion-poem to 'St Simeon Stylites' reviews the history of the last five hundred years as seen from a height approximately equal to that of the saint's pillar. The title and the idea come from Aeschylus' *Prometheus Vinctus* (832), which refers to an oak-oracle; but when Walter, the narrator, consults this one, he learns only what he knew already: that times are always changing, and that the girl he loves is more beautiful than anyone who has come near the oak in half a millennium. The poem (written 1837 or 1838) may have an autobiographical reference. When Tennyson first met Emily Sellwood in Holywell glen, near Somersby (1830), he politely enquired whether she was a 'Dryad' (an oak-nymph) or an 'Oread' (H. D. Rawnsley, *Memories of the Tennysons*, 1912 edn., p. 71); so when Walter decides that his bride must look 'Dryad-like' at the wedding (286), the poet was possibly thinking of Emily, with whom he had contemplated marriage since 1836. The next poem, 'Love and Duty', certainly refers to the breaking-off of their engagement, and shows the personal significance of the time-theme for Tennyson:

The Sun will run his orbit, and the Moon
Her circle. Wait, and Love himself will bring
The drooping flower of knowledge changed to fruit
Of wisdom. Wait: my faith is large in Time,
And that which shapes it to some perfect end.   (22–6)

'Love and Duty' introduces a group of poems expressing faith in the future. 'Ulysses' presents an old man's determination to make the most of what little future remains to him. The main sources are the *Odyssey* (xi, 119–37) and Dante's *Inferno* (xxvi, 90–142). In the first, Odysseus is told by Teiresias that, when he has dealt with the suitors, he must set off again with an oar; and that 'a gentle death' will come to him 'from the sea', when the people round him are prosperous, and he is 'worn out with a comfortable old age'. This paradoxical phrase apparently suggested Tennyson's picture of a man used to danger and excitement, who finds a comfortable, normal life extremely boring.

Dante puts Ulysses in hell for the sin of fraud (e.g. inventing the Trojan Horse), where he relates the story of his death at sea on a last voyage, undertaken because his passion for exploration overcame his feelings for son, father and wife. He recalls how he urged his few faithful companions 'not to refuse experience of the uninhabited world behind the sun', but to employ the brief possession of their faculties, as a human being should, in 'following manly virtue and knowledge'.

Tennyson clearly sides with Homer, who thinks Odysseus admirable, rather than with Dante, who thinks him wicked; but he takes from Dante's version the doctrine of forever seeking new experience, just as he takes from Homer's the perceptive characterization of a man of action 'worn out' by domestic comfort in a 'prosperous' society:

It little profits that an idle king,
By this still hearth, among these barren crags,
Matched with an agèd wife, I mete and dole
Unequal laws unto a savage race.
That hoard, and sleep, and feed, and know not me.   (1–5)

Hamlet says that to do nothing but 'sleep and feed' is to be 'a beast, no more' (IV, iv, 35); but Shakespeare's phrase is used to express the thought of Dante, whose Ulysses had told his men: 'You were not made to live like brutes.'

The second paragraph expresses the hero's zest for life in words that stress the Homeric aspect of his character, by paraphrasing the opening lines of the *Odyssey*, and incorporating two phrases from the *Iliad* ('delight of battle', a literal translation of *charme*, and 'windy Troy'). The third begins by adapting Aeneas' remark, when asked to relate the fall of Troy, that he himself played a large part in this passage of history (*Aeneid*, ii, 6); and then conveys Dante's idea of 'experience' by a startlingly modern image:

> I am a part of all that I have met;
> Yet all experience is an arch wherethrough
> Gleams that untravelled world, whose margin fades
> For ever and for ever when I move.   (18–21)

The kind of 'arch' that Tennyson was thinking of may be seen in the third illustration to J. F. C. Harrison's *The Early Victorians* (1971), a print of the entrance to the tunnel at Edgehill, on the Liverpool and Manchester Railway, on which Tennyson had travelled three years before writing the poem. Although the precise reference of this 'modern touch' is delicately concealed, since the classical Ulysses could never have travelled through such a tunnel, the image works best from the viewpoint of a passenger in an open, third-class carriage, watching the semicircle of 'untravelled world' that appears through the end of the tunnel ahead, its 'margin' constantly 'fading', i.e. disappearing outwards as the angle of vision widens. The claustrophobic suggestions of seeing present experience as a tunnel leading to a distant 'gleam' are appropriate both to Ulysses' present sense of frustration, and to Tennyson's habitual attitude: 'It is the distance that charms me . . not the immediate to-day in which I move.' The veiled allusion to the railway, his favourite symbol for scientific progress, also fits in with Ulysses' desire (derived from Dante) 'To follow knowledge like a sinking star Beyond the utmost bound of human thought' (31–2).

The next paragraph describes Telemachus as ideally qualified to implement the kind of political policy in which Tennyson believed: the gradual civilization of 'a rugged people' (36–8), i.e. the 'education of the poor man before making him our master' (*Memoir*, vol. 1, p. 249). The point of the passage in its context is that Ulysses is now free to leave home, without fear of precipitating the anarchy that prevailed on the island during his previous absence. He does not try to carry out the programme himself, because he is temperamentally unsuited to it, and also because he has no time left to him for such a slow process. He is not depreciating Telemachus, as some critics have imagined, but being realistic about their difference in age and personality. 'Common duties' means duties to the community; 'decent' means behaving properly (with a memory of Horace's praise of a young barrister as 'nobilis et decens', *Odes*, IV, i, 13); and 'blameless', far from implying contempt, is a regular Homeric epithet for heroes, here recalling Nestor's phrase: 'my dear son, mighty and blameless' (*amumon*) in the *Odyssey* (iii, 111).

The conclusion creates a deliberate contrast between the vigorous sentiments and the enervated rhythms:

> The lights begin to twinkle from the rocks:
> The long day wanes: the slow moon climbs: the deep
> Moans round with many voices. Come, my friends,
> 'Tis not too late to seek a newer world.   (54-7)

The contrast beautifully conveys Ulysses' age: the spirit is willing, but the flesh is weak:

> Though much is taken, much abides; and though
> We are not now that strength which in old days
> Moved earth and heaven; that which we are, we are:
> One equal temper of heroic hearts,
> Made weak by time and fate, but strong in will
> To strive, to seek, to find, and not to yield.   (65-70)

The last three words allude to Nestor, who 'did not yield to wretched old age' (*Iliad*, x, 79), and who first appears in that poem 'leaping up' from his seat (i, 248), just as the aged Tennyson kept jumping up from his low chair. 'There is more of myself in *Ulysses*,' he told Knowles, 'which was written under the sense of loss and that all had gone by, but that still life must be fought out to the end' (*Nineteenth Century*, vol. 33, p. 182).

'Locksley Hall' dramatizes an attempt to forget about a gloomy personal past, and look forward to the exciting world-future promised by scientific progress, again symbolized by the railway: 'Not in vain the distance beacons. Forward, forward let us range. Let the great world spin for ever down the ringing grooves of change' (181-2). The young speaker has had a disillusioning experience with Amy, comparable to Tennyson's with Rosa Baring. The poem has been conjecturally dated within the period 1837 to 1841. In the absence of conclusive evidence to the contrary, I suggest that it was written after May 1839, when W. E. Aytoun published in *Blackwood's* (vol. 45, pp. 634–42) a translation of *Iliad* xxii in the 'Locksley Hall' metre (eight-foot trochaic couplets). Tennyson said that he chose the metre because Henry Hallam said 'that the English people liked verse in trochaics' (*Eversley*), and this advice was possibly reinforced by the frequent trochaic rhythms in the narrative source (Sir William Jones's prose translation of the Arabic *Moâllakât*); but neither of these influences suggested the rhyming couplet. Tennyson doubtless kept an eye on the magazine in which Christopher North had reviewed him, and his own Homeric interests would have turned his attention to Aytoun's piece, which interpolated into Achilles' speech about his dead friend Patroclus a line which came close to Tennyson's feeling about Arthur Hallam (and to the wording of the penultimate line of 'Vastness'): 'He whom I have loved so dearly, and whom I shall ever love.' Thus Aytoun probably inspired the poem's final metrical form.

The disappointed lover accuses his age of being obsessed with money, in a passage modelled, both in theme and in tone, on Juvenal, *Satire* iii, which includes the question: 'What young man is ever thought an eligible son-in-law if he is short of cash and cannot rival his girl's money-bags?' 'Every door is barred with gold and opens but to golden keys' (99–100). Juvenal had asked: 'What should I do at Rome? I cannot lie . . . .' Tennyson's speaker imitates Juvenal's 'verse-making indignation' (*Satire* i, 79): 'I have but an angry fancy: what is that which I should do?' (102). The shrill, hysterical manner is not Tennyson's, but a traditional feature of the Juvenal-type satire (as, for instance, in Marston's *The Scourge of Villanie*, 1598).

Amy herself is denounced in equally literary terms. The imagined scene where she is haunted by her lover's memory 'In the dead unhappy night', when her husband is asleep beside her is a reworking of Donne's 'The Apparition'; the idea that the husband will be still hunting, 'Like a dog', in his dreams comes from Lucretius' discussion of dreams which immediately precedes his disparagement of love (iv); and the thought that she will be tormented by 'remembering happier things' is an explicit allusion to Francesca's words in the *Inferno* (v, 121–3) when asked to tell the story of her love affair with Paolo (75–86).

'Locksley Hall' is often regarded as an artless overflow of Tennyson's immature feelings: it is actually a cleverly contrived, if finally unsatisfactory, translation of past resentment into two literary modes (Juvenalian satire and the metaphysical love-poem), combined with a celebration of contemporary science.

'Godiva' links scientific with political progress, and discourages complacency by pointing out that modern political reform is merely a stage in a process that has been going on for at least a thousand years:

> *I waited for the train at Coventry;*
> *I hung with grooms and porters on the bridge,*
> *To watch the three tall spires; and there I shaped*
> *The city's ancient legend into this:–*
> Not only we, the latest seed of Time,
> New men, that in the flying of a wheel
> Cry down the past, not only we, that prate
> Of rights and wrongs, have loved the people well,
> And loathed to see them overtaxed; but she
> Did more, and underwent, and overcame,
> The woman of a thousand summers back,
> Godiva . . . . (1–12)

Leigh Hunt missed the point when he took the italicized lines to imply the casual ease with which Tennyson composed the poem. They are there to mark the contrast between the present (the railway) and the past (the mediaeval cathedral).

The lines that follow are modelled on the introduction to the story of Hylas in Theocritus, *Idyll* xiii, which is told to prove that love is not a purely modern invention. This *Idyll* was one of Tennyson's special favourites: he told Palgrave that he would be 'content to die' if he had written anything equal to one passage in it (*Memoir*, vol. 2, p. 495), and his version of the Godiva legend seems to have been an attempt to imitate Theocritus' poetic narrative. There was a certain analogy between the two stories: Heracles' beautiful boy-friend, going off alone to be drowned by amorous water-nymphs, was not unlike the 'grim' Earl's beautiful wife, exposed naked to the potentially amorous citizens. The Earl is made preternaturally shaggy ('His beard a foot before him and his hair A yard behind', 18–19), partly, no doubt, to conform to the pattern of Beauty and the Beast, but also because Heracles regularly wore a lion-skin, and is compared in the *Idyll* to a 'raw-flesh-eating mountain-lion'.

The best passage in the poem is the description of the empty street, as experienced by Godiva, in which the very buildings are partially anthropomorphized:

> ... the blind walls
> 'ere full of chinks and holes: and overhead
> rantastic gables, crowding, stared ...   (59-61)

'Godiva' ends with a glance towards the future, when the heroine 'built herself an everlasting name' (79), and 'The Day-Dream' uses the story of the Sleeping Beauty to point forward impatiently to future scientific, poetic, political and international developments ('L'envoi', 1-20). This section includes a paraphrase of Bacon's epigram: '*Antiquitas saeculi juventus mundi*': 'For we are Ancients of the earth, And in the morning of the times.' In *The Advancement of Learning* the epigram immediately follows a statement of the attitude towards past and future which 'Godiva' suggested: 'Antiquity deserveth that reverence, that men should make *a* stand thereupon and discover what is the best way; but when the discovery is well taken, then to make progression.'

V

'The Two Voices', placed between 'Godiva' and 'The Day-Dream', discusses, and finally answers in the affirmative, the question whether the future is worth having at all; it introduces a new group of poems with an autobiographical reference. Though clearly expressing the depressive side of the poet's own temperament (when started, around June 1833, it was called 'Thoughts of a Suicide'), the theme of the poem was probably suggested by Hamlet's 'To be or not to be' soliloquy, and the form and title by Wordsworth's sonnet beginning 'There are two voices . . .'. Tennyson's voices, however, are both internal. The first puts the case for suicide:

> A still small voice spake unto me,
> 'Thou art so full of misery,
> Were it not better not to be?'   (1-3)

In the Bible (1 *Kings*, xix, 12) 'a still small voice' is the voice of God, comforting Elijah when he is 'weary of life', wishes to die, and feels much as Bedivere feels in 'Morte d'Arthur': 'The children of Israel have forsaken thy covenant . . . and slain thy prophets with the sword; and I, even I only am left.' The voice assures him that the priests of Baal will not finally prevail. Tennyson (seeing himself, perhaps, as a true prophet of poetry left at the mercy of Baalite reviewers) opposes to this voice of

God a voice of Lucretian Nature, urging him to 'put an end to life and misery' (iii, 943), thus anticipating the conflict of *In Memoriam* (lv, 5): 'Are God and Nature then at strife?'

At first the argument is carried on between the suicidal voice and the poet himself. Since the process of thought is being represented, the sequence of ideas is often elliptical and so momentarily obscure: a characteristic amusingly exaggerated by Lewis Carroll in his parody, 'The Three Voices'. The suicidal voice easily demolishes all the poet's counter-arguments, telling him that he is expendable: in a 'boundless universe' (26) there is nothing special about a human being, and even if he is unique as an individual, 'Who'll weep for thy deficiency?' There is no point in staying around to see the triumphs of human thought, because the time-scale is infinite, so a thousand years would show him no appreciable progress (88–93).

He is finally reduced to positing some objective reality to account for the subjective human feeling that death is not the end, something divine exists, and the universe is not pointless. Here he virtually makes Plato's theory of Ideas answer Lucretius:

> That type of Perfect in his mind
> In Nature can he nowhere find.
> He sows himself on every wind.
> He seems to hear a Heavenly Friend,
> And through thick veils to apprehend
> A labour working to an end. (292–7)

With this counter-argument the original poem ended after line 309.

The conclusion, first heard by Edmund Lushington in 1837 or 1838, introduces the second voice, which cheers him by vague suggestions of 'a hidden hope' (441). The poet finds himself wondering why on earth he should have chosen to 'commune with that barren voice' rather than 'him that said, "Rejoice! Rejoice!" ' (458–62). So far it is a perfectly realistic account of a change of mood brought about, not by argument, but by something quite non-specific and unpredictable. The positive mood is then reinforced by the sight of a married couple and their child going to church.

This passage, though much weaker than the rest of the poem, has been excessively depreciated. Tennyson is not propagandizing for the nuclear family or for the Church of England: he is merely recording the truth that what keeps most people out of the Slough of Despond is a sense of human solidarity. His depressive tendencies had been effectively counteracted by his relationship with Arthur Hallam; and now the best prescription seemed to be marriage with Emily Sellwood.

In 'The Two Voices' Tennyson is seen trying to talk himself out of a depression. 'Amphion' shows him in an up-phase, cheerfully resolving to cultivate his natural gift for poetry:

> And I must work through months of toil,
>   And years of cultivation,
> Upon my proper patch of soil
>   To grow my own plantation.   (97–100)

'Will Waterproof's Lyrical Monologue' records another down-phase, in which Tennyson tries to raise his spirits by alcohol and wry humour, but continues to see himself as a faintly ridiculous failure:

> For I had hope, by something rare,
>   To prove myself a poet:
> But, while I plan and plan, my hair
>   Is gray before I know it.   (165–8)

The picture is not seriously distorted by the natural tendency to see this pathetic caricature of Will Shakespeare at the Mermaid Tavern as a seedy figure in a raincoat; but the surname probably alludes to two current uses of the adjective, 'pickled in alcohol', and 'proof against tears', like Mr Bumble in the contemporaneous *Oliver Twist*: 'Tears were not the things to find their way to Mr Bumble's soul: his heart was waterproof.' While trying to fight off his own sense of *lacrimae rerum* with port, Tennyson-Waterproof parodies his own practice of modernizing classical literature by making 'The violet of a legend blow Among the chops and steaks!' (147–8). In this he casts the 'plump head-waiter at The Cock' (1) in the role of Ganymede, snatched up to heaven by an eagle because of his extreme beauty. He ends by making the waiter a symbol of permanence in a changing world, like Keats's nightingale, for ever

> Returning like the pewit,
> And watched by silent gentlemen,
>   That trifle with the cruet.   (230–2)

The victim of this immortalization rather resented it. 'Had Mr Tennyson dined oftener there,' he said, 'he would not have minded it so much.'

To Keats St Agnes suggested a poem about sexual fulfilment: Tennyson's 'St Agnes' Eve' is a celebration of virginity, spoken by a nun whose only idea of marriage is to a 'Heavenly Bridegroom' (31). The companion-poem, 'Sir Galahad', presents the Arthurian knight as a kind of monk:

> I never felt the kiss of love,
>   Nor maiden's hand in mine.
> More bounteous aspects on me beam,
>   Me mightier transports move and thrill;
> So keep I fair through faith and prayer
>   A virgin heart in work and will.   (19–24)

No doubt the theme of these poems expresses Tennyson's sense of dedication to poetry, as when Keats wrote to Shelley 'My imagination is a monastery, and I am its monk', but it must also be taken literally. As Carlyle once said, 'Tennyson means what he says, poor fellow!' Seeing no prospect of marriage until he could earn a living by poetry, he also shared Malthus's rigid ethic: 'By moral restraint I would be understood to mean a restraint from marriage from prudential motives, with a conduct strictly moral during the period of this restraint.' The difficulty that a vigorous young man like Tennyson must have had in adhering to this programme is reflected in these poems, where he was evidently preaching to himself, as he was in 'The Vision of Sin' also.

This poem, which Tennyson described in a letter as one of his favourites (*Poems*, p. 718), allegorizes the fearful consequences of sexual indulgence in a form influenced by Plato, Homer, Euripides, and a picture by Turner:

> I had a vision when the night was late:
> A youth came riding toward a palace-gate.
> He rode a horse with wings, that would have flown,
> But that his heavy rider kept him down.   (1–4)

In Plato's *Phaedrus* the soul is a chariot (with Reason as charioteer) drawn around heaven by two winged horses, one good and one bad. The weight of the bad horse brings the soul down to earth, where it loses its wings and enters a human body. At the sight of a beautiful person, the good component is reminded of heavenly beauty, and begins to sprout new wings; but the bad horse thinks of nothing but sex, and

95

keeps making ugly rushes at the beloved object, to the good horse's disgust and embarrassment.

The notion of riding, rather than driving, one's good horse seems to come from the *Iliad* (vi, 155f), where the 'blameless' Bellerophon, the rider of the winged horse, Pegasus, refuses to go to bed with a married woman who falls 'madly' in love with him. To ride Pegasus (the symbol of poetry) one evidently had to be equally self-controlled.

A 'child of sin' introduces the youth to 'a company' who sit 'with heated eyes, Expecting when a fountain should arise' (5-8). Why on earth should it? The answer is in the *Bacchae* of Euripides (which Tennyson probably read in connection with his 'Semele'), where one Bacchant produces a spring of water by sticking a thyrsus into a rock, and another creates a fountain of wine by planting her thyrsus in the earth.

Tennyson's Bacchanals begin to dance to 'Low voluptuous music',

> Till the fountain spouted, showering wide
> Sleet of diamond-drift and pearly hail . . . .   (14-22)

It is now like a fountain of water, but as the music grows louder and more exciting, the water seems to become tinged with wine, and 'Purple gauzes' and a 'torrent rainbow' are 'flung' around (31-2). This is the climax of the orgy:

> Then they started from their places,
> Moved with violence, changed in hue,
> Caught each other with wild grimaces,
> Half-invisible to the view,
> Wheeling with precipitate paces
> To the melody, till they flew,
> Hair, and eyes, and limbs, and faces,
> Twisted hard in fierce embraces,
> Like to Furies, like to Graces,
> Dashed together in blinding dew,
> Till, killed with some luxurious agony,
> The nerve-dissolving melody
> Fluttered headlong from the sky.   (33-45)

This powerful image for sexual intercourse, considered as a frightening kind of compulsive behaviour, is followed by a vision of dawn among the mountains: 'God made Himself an awful rose of dawn' (50). Tennyson told Palgrave that the fountain 'was partly suggested by "Turner's Fountain of Fallacy" ' (*Poems*, p. 718), and the dawn scene possibly had the same origin. Turner's picture was exhibited (1839) with a quotation from the artist's fragmentary poem, 'The Fallacie_ of Hope', beginning:

> Its rainbow-dew diffused fell on each anxious lip
> Working wild fantasy, imagining . . . .

The picture has unfortunately disappeared; but Ruskin described it in *Modern Painters* as 'a piece of rich Northern Italy, with some fairy water-works', and complained in a letter of its deterioration: 'the sky entirely gone – but a nobler picture than even I had imagined.' Its original state is described in the *Literary Gazette* (1839): 'The rainbow tints that play in prismatic order about the fountain (which occupies the centre of the piece) are quite enchanting . . . and, with the Claude-like distance, and classical arrangement, render it one of Mr. Turner's most captivating pictures.' As for the extract from Turner's poem, the reviewer assigned it 'to that order of composition – the unintelligible'.

A scene of northern Italy in the manner of Claude would probably contain mountains in the 'distance'; the sky was evidently colourful enough for Ruskin to regret its disappearance; and that it was red may be guessed from Tennyson's comment on the 'dim red morn' in 'A Dream of Fair Women': 'How magnificently old Turner would have painted it' (*Eversley*). It is also likely to have been misty, an effect that Turner had always been fond of, since his 'Sun Rising Through Vapour' (1807):

> . . . and detaching, fold by fold
> From those still heights, and, slowly drawing near,
> A vapour heavy, hueless, formless, cold,
> Came floating on for many a month and year,
> Unheeded.   (51-5)

Tennyson's vapour (as in 'Oenone' 3-5, 234) signifies the approach of death; and the next section shows the youth transformed by a life of sin into 'A gray and gap-toothed man as lean as death' (60), whose dental condition associates him with the promiscuous Wife of Bath. In a humorously macabre monologue, spoken in 'a ruined inn' (62) recalling that of 'The Coach of Death', he displays the cynicism that now

his whole view of life, making him despise all the things that
men care about, fame, friendship, virtue, political ideals, and
even sex:

> 'Death is king, and Vivat Rex!
>   Tread a measure on the stones,
> Madam – if I know your sex,
>   From the fashion of your bones . . . .
>
> 'Lo! God's likeness – the ground-plan –
>   Neither modelled, glazed, nor framed:
> Buss me, thou rough sketch of man,
>   Far too naked to be shamed!'   (179–90)

Thus the orgiastic dance of the first scene is finally parodied by a dance
of skeletons. The sinner's moral deterioration is then emphasized by an
image of putrefaction, of evolution in reverse:

> Below were men and horses pierced with worms,
> And slowly quickening into lower forms . . . .   (209–10)

An anonymous interpreter explains: 'Behold! it was a crime Of sense
avenged by sense that wore with time.' Another voice asks: 'Is there any
hope?' The reviewer's comment on Turner's oracular poetry might
almost seem to have suggested the reply:

> To which an answer pealed from that high land,
> But in a tongue no man could understand;
> And on the glimmering limit far withdrawn
> God made himself an awful rose of dawn.   (221–4)

Tennyson's statement (*Poems*, p. 718) that the landscape symbolizes
'God, Law and the future life' reminds us how the poem contributes to
the general theme of time. It looks towards the future, like the dawn-
image that concludes 'Morte d'Arthur' (271).

So does the epithalamion (written either to celebrate his brother
Charles's wedding in 1836, or his own engagement in 1838) which
begins:

> Move eastward, happy earth, and leave
>   Yon orange sunset waning slow,

where the sunset is appropriately given the colour of the bridal veil (*flammeum*) in Catullus' epithalamion (lxi). The autobiographical poems also include two splendid lyrics, 'A Farewell' expressing Tennyson's regret for his childhood home, when the family left Somersby (1837), and 'Break, break, break' (probably 1834), a lament for Arthur Hallam, which subtly combines the hint of a breaking heart with the chronometrical suggestions of perpetually breaking waves, each carrying the poet further away from the irrecoverable past:

> Break, break, break,
> At the foot of thy crags, O Sea!
> But the tender grace of a day that is dead
> Will never come back to me.   (13–16)

Wishing, presumably, to show that he did not take himself too seriously, Tennyson preceded his epithalamion by another self-deriding show of reliance on his rhyming dictionary, 'The Skipping-Rope'. This anti-romantic dialogue between a sentimental lover, who seems to parody the author of 'Lilian' ('How fairy-like you fly!'), and his exasperated loved-one ends with her saying:

> There, take it, take my skipping-rope,
> And hang yourself thereby.   (11–12)

The lines reflect satirically on the following epithalamion, by alluding to the opening of Juvenal's satire on women (vi), where he asks a friend, who has just become engaged: 'Can you really bear to become a woman's slave when there are so many ropes available?' After thus showing a willingness to make fun of his own poems, Tennyson ends the collection with 'The Poet's Song', which defiantly reasserts the Shelleyan view of the poet that he had expressed in his first volume. Shelley's poet-bird has the last word on the relation between poetry and the future:

> And the nightingale thought, 'I have sung many songs,
> But never a one so gay,
> For he sings of what the world will be
> When the years have died away.'   (13–16)

6

The Princess; A Medley

Tennyson's feminist sympathies, first aroused by his mother's marriage predicament, encouraged by Ovid, implied in 'Kate' and made explicit in 'A Dream of Fair Women', were strengthened by feminist writers whose views were discussed by the Apostles. On both sides of the Channel socialists advocated the emancipation of women, and criticized the institution of marriage. Fourier wished to replace it by a less rigid system of sex control, Enfantin (the co-founder of the Saint-Simonian movement) by a quasi-religious ethic of free love, and Robert Owen by a form of civil marriage without oaths, and with easy arrangements for divorce.

By 1831 the education of women had become a highly controversial topic, which, according to an article in the *Westminster Review* (vol. 15, p. 70), excited so much 'Passion, prejudice, and selfishness', and such 'bitter' and 'rooted hostility', that 'a calm investigation of the important subject in dispute' was 'rendered almost impossible'. It was this impossibility that Tennyson attempted in *The Princess*.

Tennyson's attitude to 'the woman question' was not unlike that of a young economist, Arianna Stassinopoulos, who has recently made a distinction (*The Female Woman*, 1974) between 'emancipation', which 'insists on equal status for distinctively female roles', and 'liberation', which demands their total abolition. Her 'female woman will assert her right to be free, but will refuse' to be forced to become 'an *ersatz* man. The frenetic extremism of Women's Lib seeks not to emancipate women, but to destroy society.' Thus Tennyson's hero tells the Princess that they will raise the status of woman,

> Will clear away the parasitic forms

That seem to keep her up but drag her down -
Will leave her space to burgeon out of all
Within her - let her make herself her own
To give or keep, to live and learn to be
All that not harms distinctive womanhood.
For woman is not undevelopt man,
But diverse . . . .   (vii, 253-60)

In the words of Miss Stassinopoulos, 'We are different from men -
different but equal.'

Tennyson wanted 'emancipation' but not 'liberation'. He was
against feminist extremists who tried to foment a sex war, and against
the abolition of marriage, which he considered the foundation of
society. He sympathized with his heroine, Ida, but thought her
mistaken in trying to become 'an *ersatz* man'.

His belief in 'emancipation' is obliquely suggested by the poem's
recurrent image of 'losing the child', a tacit allusion to the first reduction
of women's legal disabilities, the Custody of Infants Act (1839). This
Act, passed in the year that he probably started writing the poem, at last
gave mothers a limited right of access to their own children after a
campaign had publicized the story of how Caroline Norton's separated
husband had taken away her three children (all below the age of six)
and let one of them die of neglect.

II

Tennyson needed a form in which to plead for 'emancipation', while
satirizing both sets of extremists, the 'Libbers' and the 'male chauvinist
pigs'. In devising one, he combined many literary sources. The central
idea of the poem (at first called 'The New University') seems to have
come from a novel that he 'dipped into' in 1834, F. D. Maurice's *Eustace
Conway*, which shares many features with the poem's Prologue: a
country house owned by a squire called 'Vivyan', a touchy maiden-
aunt, undergraduate son, and a daughter of independent character, who
replies to her brother's grumbles about university life: 'Well, Eustace, I
think as universities are so mischievous to men, you must make them
over to us.' Eustace gives his 'full consent to the transfer'.

Aristophanes and Juvenal suggested a comic treatment of woman-
power. In the *Lysistrata* the women stop a war by refusing to sleep with
their husbands until they make peace. In the *Ecclesiazusae* (women in

101

parliament) they take over government, by dressing up as their husbands. On a visit to Park House, Maidstone (the setting of the Prologue) about 1841-2, Tennyson's attention was drawn to this play by a punning application of its title to the church-going ladies of the party, a joke that he remembered fifty years later. Juvenal's *Satire* vi contains a caricature of a female intellectual, and refers to the intrusion of Clodius, disguised as a girl-musician, into the all-female rites of the Bona Dea, 'from which even the buck-mouse runs away, concious of its testicles', a phrase bowdlerized by the Prince, when describing his intrusion into the women's College: 'we, consious of ourselves, Perused the matting' (ii, 53-4); and also by the inn-keeper's *aposiopesis*: 'all the swine were sows, And all the dogs – ' (i, 190-1).

Aristophanes and Juvenal showed how to please the reactionary male; Froissart's *Chronicle* (in which the heroine of *Eustace Conway* 'delighted') suggested a method of approach to the progressive female. Froissart describes (Lord Berners's translation, chapter 80) how 'the countesse of Mountfort', besieged in 'Hanybont', led a sortie from the town, riding in armour on horseback, and set fire to the enemy's 'lodgings'. Hence the extract from 'a chronicle' read in the Prologue about

> a lady, one that armed
> Her own fair head, and sallying through the gate,
> Had beat her foes with slaughter from her walls.   (27-34)

The lady's name, Mountfort, suggested a relevant image and an apt use of Theocritus. Tennyson saw his heroine as a woman whose high aspirations made her try to deny her normal female instincts. They finally 'drag' her 'down From' her 'fixt height to mob' her 'up with all The soft and milky rabble of womankind' (vi, 288-90). So she was named Ida (after the mountain in 'Oenone'), and viewed (like Emily Sellwood) as a kind of Oread. Thus the moment of her final descent (to marriage with the Prince) is marked by a 'small Sweet Idyl', beginning:

> 'Come down, O maid, from yonder mountain height:
> What pleasure lives in height (the shepherd sang) ....' (vii, 177-8)

Composed in a region dominated by another mountain-virgin, the Jungfrau, this poem is pervasively Theocritean, but most closely related to *Idyll* xi, where Polyphemus, seated on his high rock beneath the white snows of Mount Etna, tells the sea-nymph Galatea that he will learn to swim, in order to discover 'what pleasure you can find in living in the deep'. Though the Prince yearns upwards instead of downwards, he is deliberately allowed to remain, like Polyphemus, partly a figure of fun.

The story of the poem owes something to *Love's Labour's Lost*, where a one-sex academic programme is broken up by love affairs, and to the Persian tale of the Princess Tourandocte, who avoids marriage by having all suitors executed who cannot answer her riddles; an analogue of the Sphinx-myth, comparable to that in the Latin novel *Apollonius of Tyre*, the source of Shakespeare's *Pericles*.

The point of discussing a topical issue in a context of myth and romance was to take it out of time, and show it *sub specie aeternitatis*. This is implied by the references in the Prologue to *The Winter's Tale*. The story, improvised by seven young men, is compared to a 'Seven-headed monster'

> only made to kill
> Time by the fire in winter.'
>   'Kill him now,
> The tyrant! kill him in the summer too,'
> Said Lilia; 'Why not now,' the maiden Aunt.
> 'Why not summer's as a winter's tale?'   (200-4; cf. 230-1)

The narrative method, based on a game that Tennyson had often played at Cambridge, justified internal contradictions, lowered the emotional temperature, and presented the poem as a forum for all shades of opinion; but 'killing Time' meant not only passing it, but asserting the poet's right to defy Time's tyranny, as Shakespeare had done in jumping sixteen years between Acts III and IV, so as to show how things can improve between one generation and another, and justifying the licence in a speech by 'Time, the Chorus', who says, 'it is in my power To o'erthrow law, and in one self-born hour To plant and o'erwhelm custom'. Tennyson implies that he will be equally achronic, in order to show how Time will ultimately abolish the law and custom of male supremacy.

III

The Aunt wanted a story not only fitting the time, but also suiting the place (Prologue, 205-6). Tennyson had found, in the home of his friends, the Lushingtons, a wonderfully apt location for debating a contemporary question both in and out of time: in the middle of the nineteenth century, but also against a time-scheme so vast as to suggest eternity. Park House (in Sandling Park, Boxley) was built (1795) in a classical style, with a semi-circular porch, Doric columns and a triglyph Doric frieze. Less than a mile away were the ruins of Boxley Abbey (founded 1146), near the village to which the Tennysons moved in 1841. The juxtaposition of Greek and Gothic architecture, which Tennyson emphasized by a shot of the 'Grecian house' through the ruined wall of the 'Gothic' abbey (93-4, 255), was a ready-made image for 'time-killing', reinforced by the real or imagined contents of the house: a heterogeneous collection of archaeological and anthropological curios (Edmund Lushington was a Greek specialist, and his father had been a colonial administrator in Ceylon). Thus 'Ammonites, and the first bones of Time' (15) suggested geological evidence for the immense age of the earth; and 'calumets' (17), i.e. Red Indian pipes of peace from America, embodied the mingling of ancient and modern cultures.

The last significant feature of the Prologue's setting is the festival of the Maidstone Mechanics' Institute which took place in the grounds of Park House on 6 July 1842. This had a special relevance to the poem's theme, since the Institutes were among the main channels of Robert Owen's Socialist and feminist propaganda; but Tennyson, who was there, saw a wider meaning in the paradoxical introduction, into a scene so full of conservative, historic and pre-historic associations, of a working-class organization, educating itself with demonstrations of the latest scientific discoveries, while still enjoying such traditional forms of entertainment as cricket and country dances (54-89). It enabled him to show feminist reform as part of an incredibly long, incredibly slow process of human development. Thus 'Vivian-place' (9) became, as its name suggests, the place of life, just as the Lushingtons' home sounded an appropriate setting for a poem concerned with vigorous natural growth.

The association of feminism with life is confirmed by the fact that the Princess's country is 'a livelier land' (i, 109); and its association with technological progress was made explicit in an early draft (*Poems*, p. 754) which showed that country to be highly industrialized.

IV

When summarized, the story of *The Princess* seems scarcely pro-feminist: a talented and enterprising woman, who wants to devote her life to the education of her own sex, and has started a college for that purpose, is pressurized into marriage by appeals to her compassion.

Threatened by armed invasion, she wins the war but loses the peace. Confronted by large numbers of male casualties, she generously allows her college to be turned into a hospital, and after long spells of day-and night-duty, falls in love with one of the patients (the Prince), chiefly because he is so helpless (vii, 86–103). The college is disbanded, at least temporarily ('many a maiden passing home Till happier times', vi, 359–60), and the Principal is reduced to the status of wife and mother.

That the total effect of the poem is much less reactionary is due, first, to the poet's obvious sympathy with Ida, and secondly to some underlying thoughts, which were brought nearer to the surface in passages added to the text in 1850 and 1851.

As the title implies, Ida's is the leading part: the Prince plays only a supporting role, and the admirable side of her character is deliberately high-lighted by exaggerating the feebleness of his. The bitterness of her disappointment when her project collapses is vividly suggested in a draft (Cambridge University Library) where she speaks of her 'dark hour'

> when we almost die
> Wrench'd bleeding from our will & macerated
> In softness not our own & sick of all.

In the published version this feeling is expressed in a powerful passage (vii, 14–28) describing how her whole world 'blackened in secret'. Here Tennyson makes her a genuinely tragic figure; but he sees her tragedy as caused by her own nature, which will not allow her to forgo the biological satisfactions of sex and maternity.

That is the point of the recurrent child-theme. Ida wants women to 'lose the child' (i, 136): to stop being what Lord Chesterfield called them, 'only children of a larger growth', and become, and be accepted as, rational adults. Tennyson feared that this might lead, not only to losing 'the childlike in the larger mind' and to a failure in 'childward care' (vii, 267–8), but also to their loss of a form of natural fulfilment. From a male, this kind of argument is inevitably and rightly suspect; but Tennyson at least pointed to a real, though not insuperable, difficulty that faces professional women.

He tried to suggest this difficulty by the episode where Ida kidnaps Psyche's baby, called Aglaïa, 'glory', perhaps from a memory of the *Helen* of Euripides, where a daughter is called 'the glory *(aglaisma)* of her mother'. Finding that his point had not been understood, he added (1850) six songs between sections, presenting the child as a reconciler of sex-antagonism, an element in female attractiveness, a form of immortality for its parents, an inspiration for the father, a consolation for the widow, and (presumably) an invisible component of the sex drive ('at a touch I yield', *Poems*, p. 829). Of several songs about children written at this time, some were happily not incorporated (e.g. 'Bless thy full cheeks, my noble boy', 'Minnie and Winnie', and the first of the series, 'The Losing of the Child', in which a child is swept away by a flood, but found unhurt by what Tennyson called 'a chorus of jubilant women' (*Eversley*)).

In the 1851 edition the Prince was made subject to 'weird seizures' in which he was afflicted by a sense of dream-like unreality (i, 5–21). These attacks, resembling the 'abyss of idealism' into which Wordsworth sometimes fell, having to grasp 'at a wall or tree to recall' himself 'to reality', and doubtless related to Tennyson's own trance-like experiences, clearly served to decrease the Prince's stature as against the Princess's; but this was not their only function. A draft in Cambridge University Library shows that they mark the distinction between a 'real' woman like the Prince's mother, and a fantasy persona of a woman, like Ida the militant 'liberationist' (vii, 327–9; 291–315):

> I seem'd
> To walk among a world of hollow shows
> And framed a thousand monstrous fantasies,
> And felt myself the shadow of a dream.
> No shadow was my mother, clear throughout
> As genial daylight, mild as any saint.

Two other drafts in the same collection associate the 'seizures' with 'dilations and dreams', and a third compares the visual sensation to that of a man seeing objects through a 'hollow haze that makes his mound A mountain'. This notion of seeing things magnified by mist (just as Wordsworth, in the *Prelude*, saw a shepherd transformed by fog into 'a giant', and his sheep into 'Greenland bears') related to the 'mock-heroic gigantesque' which is the original style of the story (Conclusion, 11).

The 'seizures', therefore, occur when Tennyson wants us to see something absurdly exaggerated in characters, behaviour, or situations: Ida's histrionic pose with her foot on a leopard (iii, 162f); the expulsion of the Prince and his friends from the college by eight hefty females (iv, 527f); the extreme male chauvinism expressed by the Prince's father (435f); the tournament designed to settle inter-sexual differences by force (in which the Prince's dream-like state alludes satirically to those which precede the deaths of Hector in *Iliad* xxii, and Turnus in *Aeneid* xii; v, 472f); and the violent Roman feminists pictured on the Prince's sickroom wall (vii, 104f).

In this painting the women are 'Titanic shapes' threatening a 'dwarf-like' male, the reactionary Cato. The hero of *Eustace Conway* dismisses his momentary envy of women's capacity for 'frank affection' by thinking: 'It is abandoning our high prerogative, it is dwarfing our god-like stature, to covet their attribute.' Which sex are the god-like Titans, which the dwarfs? You might just as well ask, replies Tennyson, which ventricle of the heart is more important:

> The woman's cause is man's: they rise or sink
> Together, dwarfed or godlike, bond or free ....

They must combine to form

> The single pure and perfect animal,
> The two-celled heart beating, with one full stroke,
> Life.   (vii, 243–4, 288–9)

V

The 'seizures' also relate to Tennyson's favourite theme of time. In a draft (Cambridge University Library) the Prince says:

> I thought the world a shadow, what I was
> And where I was a shadow not a truth ....

This alludes to the Platonic doctrine that our world is a shadow of the real world of eternal ideas: in *The Republic* (vii) human beings are compared to prisoners in a cave, watching shadows of external objects and of themselves on a wall, and unaware that the shadows are not the only reality. Thus Shelley calls Time an 'envious shadow' in *Prometheus Unbound*, and Ida echoes the phrase when the Prince objects that the theory of evolution represents the Creator as a mere 'workman' 'That practice betters' (iii, 280–2). She replies that 'all creation is an act at once', and Time is a human illusion, but an illusion within which human beings are compelled to operate:

'Our weakness somehow shapes the shadow, Time;
But in the shadow will we work, and mould
The woman to the fuller day.'   (iii, 304–14)

So in one way the Prince's 'seizures' are visions of a metaphysical truth,
that the world of Time is an illusion. Having thus suggested that the
'woman-question' must be seen against a background of Eternity as
well as Time, Tennyson is free to pursue the temporal aspect of feminism in a context of evolution, derived from his reading of Lyell's
Principles of Geology and Chambers's *Vestiges of Creation*.

The evolutionary context is summarized by Psyche, when she traces
the history of the universe from its nebular origin (Laplace's theory),
and connects the subjection of women with the most primitive stage of
human development:

'then the monster, then the man;
Tattooed or woaded, winter-clad in skins,
Raw from the prime, and crushing down his mate . . . .' (ii, 102–6)

The theme recurs in the geological expedition, where the word 'crag',
like the other geological terms that follow it (iii, 314–5), refers to Lyell,
who was particularly interested in some 'shelly strata', 'provincially
termed "Crag" '. On the Suffolk coast their 'dip' was 'uniformly to the
south', with rare exceptions 'where the inclination was northerly'. That
is why the Princess decided 'to take The dip of certain strata to the
North' (iii, 153–4). What interested Lyell was that these Crag-strata
contained fossil remains of many different periods, including 'a great
mixture of recent species of shells' and 'many fragments of older rocks,
together with ammonites' and 'vertebrae of ichthyosauri'. These vertebrae fitted neatly into Ida's evolutionary argument;

below, stuck out
The bones of some vast bulk that lived and roared
Before man was. She gazed awhile and said,
'As these rude bones to us, are we to her
That will be.'   (iii, 276–80)

Another passage in Lyell enabled the Prince to compare the male
speciality, war, with 'an old-world mammoth' (v, 142).

Lyell (whose illustration of 'The Drongs', huge granitic rocks standing alone in the sea, probably suggested the image for Ida's body-guard, iv, 262-3) summarized but rejected Lamarck's theory of evolution. Chambers put forward a theory of 'Progressive Development' from which Tennyson took several details. Chambers expressed the impossibility of actually seeing such a long, slow process in operation, by comparing man to 'an ephemeron, hovering over a pool', and unable, in its one day of life, to see a tadpole turning into a frog. Earlier in the book, he had described the footprints of prehistoric animals that had been found in sandstone. Ida combines the two images:

> 'Would, indeed, we had been,
> In lieu of many mortal flies, a race
> Of giants living, each, a thousand years,
> That we might see our own work out, and watch
> The sandy footprint harden into stone.'   (iii, 250-4)

Chambers illustrated his thesis that 'sex' is 'a matter of development', by saying that bees can arrange for a larva to turn into 'a queen or true female' by arresting its development at that 'early' stage 'at which the · female sex is complete'. Another eight days would make it 'a perfect male'. Tennyson explicitly rejected this theory ('For woman is not undevelopt man, But diverse', vii, 259-60); but he was evidently struck by the implications for feminism of the fact that among bees the female is the superior sex, and also that sexual character can be determined by environmental factors (enlarging the larva's cell, keeping it warmer than usual, feeding it special food). Bee-images therefore abound in the poem. Ida is initially compared to a queen bee (i, 39); her college is a 'hive' (ii, 84); one of her students is called Melissa (a bee), and pairs off with Florian; the Prince returns to the college 'by beelike instinct hive-ward' (iv, 181); Ida calls him and his friends 'Wasps in our good hive' (iv, 514); and the last amenity mentioned to lure her down from her 'mountain-height' is the 'murmuring of innumerable bees' (vii, 207).

Chambers's mention of the bee 'imago' emerging from its 'pupa' probably suggested the name of Florian's sister, Psyche (which means 'butterfly' as well as 'soul'); and the implication that woman must cease to be a mere doll (pupa) and emerge in her fully developed character (imago) is emphasized when the three friends, in adopting the image of women students, become 'as rich as moths from dusk cocoons' (ii, 5).

Chambers saw 'nothing improbable' in the idea that the present human species was 'but the initial of the grand crowning type', 'a nobler

109

type of humanity' living in 'a much serener field of existence'. The Prince sees the perfecting of the sex relationship as the pre-condition of this final development:

> Then reign the world's great bridals, chaste and calm:
> Then springs the crowning race of humankind.'   (vii, 278–9)

Evolution gave hope for the future, but created nostalgia for the past. This aspect of the time-theme is expressed in the song, 'Tears, idle tears', composed, Tennyson said, 'on the yellowing autumn-tide at Tintern Abbey, full for me of its bygone memories', and expressing 'the sense of the abiding in the transient', as well as his habitual 'passion of the past' (*Eversley; The Nineteenth Century*, vol. 33, p. 170). Tintern Abbey, not far from Arthur Hallam's grave, was like Boxley Abbey a Gothic ruin, the subject of watercolours by Turner, and the title of a poem by Wordsworth, reflecting on the passage of time, and the loss of youthful 'joys' and 'raptures'. Tennyson's poem owes something to a Latin Alcaic stanza of Gray, addressed to an inner fountain of tears, and preceded in a letter by a Greek iambic line ('to shed new tears for ancient evils') adapted from a fragment of Euripides: 'One must not shed new tears for ancient things.' The 'idle tears' also derive from the tears shed by Aeneas, 'tears for things and for mortality', when in the new town of Carthage he sees pictures of the fall of Troy (*Aeneid*, i, 462), and from his 'empty tears' that roll down as he resists Dido's piteous appeals not to leave her (iv, 449).

Both Virgilian passages are relevant to the meaning of the song in its context. It is sung by a girl who wishes to do her duty by the future, but is torn with regret for the past (heterosexual happiness with her boyfriend, presumably the 'cousin' of vi, 229). Building a new city does not entirely compensate for the loss of the old one; but Ida, the empire-builder, is naturally contemptuous of a song that 'moans about the retrospect' (iv, 67) and urges her students to shut their ears to the Sirens of the past (iv, 44–8).

Gray addressed his inner fountain of tears as 'pious nymph', and the backslider's 'natural piety' (Wordsworth's phrase) is rewarded with a name suggestive of Wordsworth's 'violet by a mossy stone, Half hidden from the eye'. Melissa, on the other hand, a much more positive character, is 'lilylike' (iv, 143), which recalls the independently minded Lilia of the Prologue. In thus differentiating between female types, Tennyson was making a point originated by Mary Wollstonecraft,

110

when she complained that though men are allowed to be individuals, 'all women are to be levelled, by meekness and docility, into one character of yielding softness and gentle compliance'. That is what the Prince, speaking of Ida's militancy, means by his rebuke to his father:

> 'I hold her, king,
> True woman: but you clash them all in one,
> That have as many differences as we.
> The violet varies from the lily as far
> As oak from elm ....'
>
> (v, 171–5)

VI

The Princess was subtitled 'A Medley', partly to indicate its view of the nineteenth century as a 'Crag'-like mixture of modern elements with relics of many other different periods, and partly in irony, since the poem is remarkable for its artistic coherence. For instance, the casual remark that the Prince looks 'like a girl' (i, 3), and the farcical sequence where he dresses up as a girl, point forward to the serious concluding statement that the sexes must grow more like each other (vii, 263–4), as they have conspicuously begun to do during the last decade, especially in clothes and hair-styles. A more complex form of unification mentioned by Tennyson is the fact that 'there is scarcely anything in the story that is not prophetically glanced at in the prologue' (*Memoir,* vol. I, p. 251). Thus the following items in the Prologue reappear, more or less transmuted, in the story: science, a ball over a fountain, a telescope, electricity, an echo, clockwork, a fire-balloon, babies on the grass, water-lilies, a male dressed in a woman's scarf and shawl, a picnic, a college, proctors, academic gowns compared to the colours of a tiger-moth, a 'Puss', a loving eye in a cage, a face reddening with anger, and, in a rejected draft (Cambridge University Library), a baaing 'mother ewe'. In an interlude (added 1850) Lilia sings a song with as much passion (*Poems,* p. 801) as Violet sings hers, and 'cried' for war, just as Violet cried, in another sense, for love (iv, 41–3).

A Conclusion added in 1850 made clearer the middle course that Tennyson was trying to steer between the revolutionaries and the reactionaries, using an image (the Parallelogram of Forces) which may be taken to imply that, but for his fear of antagonizing his male readers, and so making them even more reactionary, he would have taken a more overtly feminist line:

> Then rose a little feud between the two,
> Betwixt the mockers and the realists:
> And I, betwixt them both, to please them both,
> And yet to give the story as it rose,
> I moved as in a strange diagonal,
> And maybe neither pleased myself nor them.　　　　(23-8)

He also used the French Revolution of 1848 to clarify the progressive character of his views both on politics and on the 'woman-question'. The 'Tory member's elder son' makes a conservative and xenophobic comment on the French habit of revolution. The poet-speaker politely slaps him down, implying a degree of tolerance for the feminist fantasies even of the French Socialists:

> 'Have patience,' I replied, 'ourselves are full
> Of social wrong; and maybe wildest dreams
> Are but the needful preludes of the truth:
> For me, the genial day, the happy crowd,
> The sport half-science, fill me with a faith.
> This fine old world of ours is but a child
> Yet in the go-cart.　　　　(72-8)

The last image replaced an allusion (Cambridge University Library) to Heracles strangling snakes in his cradle (Theocritus, *Idyll* xxiv). The published ending of the poem, a night scene which draws the attention upwards through the sky to the 'Heaven of Heavens', and concludes on a note of pleasure, was clearly modelled on the final simile of *Iliad* viii (which Tennyson later translated) and implied that though the sex-war would start again tomorrow, one could trust that 'the powers of the night' had everything under control.

VII

Since a modern biographer has solemnly described *The Princess* as 'entirely without humour', it perhaps needs pointing out that almost all the funny bits are quite intentional: it seems a pity to imitate the playgoers who feel it would be wrong to laugh at the gravediggers' scene in *Hamlet* because their image of Shakespeare does not allow for anything less than deadly serious.

One of the best comic scenes is where Ida, 'blind with rage', misses a

112

plank and falls into the river (iv, 159–60). The Prince 'plunges' in, grabs her and swims to the bank (in a parody of a feminist catch-phrase) 'Oaring one arm, and bearing in my left The Weight of all the hopes of half the world' (165–6). So far the humour is at the expense of the feminists; but the passage is also parodying Cassius' speech in *Julius Caesar*, describing a similar rescue of the great dictator. The allusion begins to deflate the Prince's conscious heroism, since Cassius is depicted as consumed with ignoble envy; and the deflation is completed by the substitution of 'woman-vested as I was' for Shakespeare's 'accoutred as I was' (163). We are left with the ludicrous picture of a man who thinks he is playing his traditional role of woman's *'natural* protector' (Mary Wollstonecraft's sardonic phrase), while looking, in his waterlogged lady's dress, more like a wet hen. In case the satire on the masculine image of the male failed to register, Tennyson underlined it in the magnificent account of the merriment that greeted the bedraggled Prince's appearance in his father's camp:

> I stood and seemed to hear,
> As in a poplar grove when a light wind wakes
> A lisping of the innumerous leaf and dies,
> Each hissing in his neighbour's ear; and then
> A strangled titter, out of which there brake
> On all sides, clamouring etiquette to death,
> Unmeasured mirth; while now the two old kings
> Began to wag their baldness up and down,
> The fresh young captains flashed their glittering teeth
> The huge bush-bearded Barons heaved and blew,
> And slain with laughter rolled the glided Squire. (v, 11–21)

7

In Memoriam A. H. H.

I

Tennyson's portrait of Arthur Hallam, as seen by the Apostles, ends with a curious detail:

> . . .we saw
>
> The God within him light his face
>
> And seem to lift the form, and glow
>   In azure orbits heavenly-wise;
>   And over those ethereal eyes
> The bar of Michael Angelo.   (lxxxvii)

The reference to 'the broad bar of frontal bone over the eyes' (*Eversley*) that Arthur shared with Michelangelo, implies that they resembled one another in more important ways. Vasari, who idolized Michelangelo and described his friendship with him as one of his greatest blessings, wrote that God had sent this universal genius into the world to be 'a beacon of light' in the darkness of the world, and 'a type of the true artist'. Wishing to transfer this exalted character to his friend, Tennyson indirectly associates him with Michelangelo by alluding to two pictures, the 'Creation of Adam' and the 'Creation of Eve'. In the first, as described by Vasari, God 'stretches out his right hand towards Adam'; in the second there are 'two nudes, one in a heavy sleep like death, the other quickened by the blessing of God'. The life-giving hand and the 'sleep like death' are combined in a euphemism for Arthur's cerebro-vascular accident: 'God's finger touched him, and he slept' (lxxxv, 20). Arthur, who spent several months in Rome, may have described the pictures to Alfred; but he probably also saw engravings of them such as

114

those in R. Duppa's *Michel Angelo Buonarroti* (1806), since in the notebook (Trinity College, Cambridge) containing the earliest sections of *In Memoriam* there are several drawings which look like attempts to copy the divine right hand in the 'Creation of Adam'.

Arthur's own creations in verse and prose, though not quite so impressive, also left their mark on *In Memoriam*. The phase 'tumult of acclaim' (lxxv, 20) comes from a poem in which the two friends had collaborated; the account of the baby gradually learning to distinguish himself from his environment (xlv) paraphrases a passage in Arthur's essay 'On Sympathy'; what he had described in his essay on Petrarch as 'the luxury of grief', 'to connect the memory of the dead with our thoughts and employments ... at the moment of their death', is enjoyed in section vi, 17-24; and Tennyson's complaint (xli, 5-8) that he has 'lost the links that bound' Hallam's 'changes' seems to echo, not only the opening of Crabbe's 'The Parting Hour', but also Hallam's remark ('On Cicero'): 'Of that immense chain of mental successions, which extends from the cradle to the death-bed, how few links ... are visible to any other person?'

Tennyson's 'hope' that 'answer' and 'redress' for the cruelty of the world presented by geology may be found 'behind the veil' (lvi, 28) parallels Chambers's hope that 'the Redress is in reserve' that 'there is a system of Mercy and Grace behind the screen of nature'; but the veil image appears to derive from Hallam's reference ('On Cicero') to the veiled image of Truth at Sais, just as the veiled statue of Hallam does in the allegorical section ciii. If it was also suggested by Hallam's letter to Emily Tennyson, describing a charade in which he played Pygmalion, and had to unveil a 'Statue draped in white', this might account for the somewhat charade-like nature of the allegory.

Hallam's most important influence, however, on the thought of *In Memoriam* stems from his attempt at rational theology, 'Theodicaea Novissima', which was included in Hallam's *Remains* (1834) at Tennyson's special request. The second sentence tacitly alludes to the Latin caption beneath the frontispiece of Baron's *Instauratio Magna* (1620): 'In these times, when knowledge is increased, and many go to and fro on the earth to spread it . . . .' Tennyson alludes (cxiv) to the frontispiece itself, which shows a ship sailing between two pillars into a boundless sea (i.e. the mind of man voyaging beyond the Pillars of Hercules, the boundary of the known world):

Who loves not knowledge? Who shall rail

> Against her beauty? May she mix
> With men and prosper! Who shall fix
> Her pillars? Let her work prevail. (1-4)

Tennyson supports Bacon's programme for the unlimited progress of science, but simultaneously makes a plea for the seven pillars of Wisdom (*Proverbs*, ix, 1, which he quoted in *Eversley*). Thus pillar-fixing at first means setting bounds to knowledge, but immediately suggests building the 'house' of Wisdom. The double attitude is in the spirit of Hallam's essay, which tries to put forward a scientifically logical argument for religious belief. *In Memoriam* insists, like 'Theodicaea Novissima', that 'God is love', and relies heavily on Hallam's type of reasoning, that strong subjective feeling must have an objective basis:

> I see that the Bible fits into every fold of the human heart. I am a man, and I believe it to be God's book because it is man's book. . . . My feelings and thoughts can no longer refuse their assent to *what is evidently framed to engage that assent*; and what is it to me that I cannot disprove the bare logical possibility of my whole nature being fallacious?

II

The composition of individual sections from 1833 onwards, originally a form of self-therapy ('The sad mechanic exercise, Like dull narcotics, numbing pain', v, 7-8), seems at first to have been controlled, not by any conscious plan, but only by half-conscious memories of literary precedents. The first section written (ix) belongs to the same form as Lycidas' song (Theocritus vii) wishing a safe voyage to his boy-friend. The adaptation of the *propempticon* to the ship bringing Hallam's corpse back from Vienna was facilitated by Lycidas' reference to another pastoral poet, who was shut up in a cedar chest, but kept alive by bees attracted by the poetic nectar on his lips. The word used for 'chest' was also used for the receptacle for Hector's bones (*Iliad*, xxiv, 795); and a cedar-wood coffin is mentioned in Euripides' *Alcestis* (about another miraculous return from death), immediately after the widower has said that, if only he had the poetic and musical gifts of Orpheus, he would go down to hell and bring his wife back. Equally relevant to Tennyson's situation was Horace's *Ode* (I, iii) wishing his friend Virgil a safe voyage to Greece, and begging the ship to preserve 'half of my soul', just as Hallam is called 'half my life' (lvii, 6).

Despite Tennyson's statement that, having been 'over-dosed' with Horace at an early age, 'It was not till many years after boyhood that I could like Horace' (*Materials*, vol. 1, p. 33), the *Odes*, which he had been made to learn by heart, were clearly a pervasive influence on *In Memoriam*. First, they were a precedent for a random collection of lyrics, written in short four-line stanzas over a long period, and unified by nothing but the poet's personal feelings and philosophy; for poems on how to deal with grief for the death of a beloved friend (I, xxiv, II, ix); and for poetic tributes, affectionate yet humble in tone, to a literary patron. The *Odes* begin by addressing Maecenas as 'my sweet source of protection and honour', which precisely defines Hallam's role as Tennyson's friend, supporter, literary agent and publicity manager. The *Odes* on the death of friends recommend stoical endurance, and an end of 'weak complaints', a policy which Tennyson claims to have adopted:

> And so my passion hath not swerved
> > To works of weakness, but I find
> > An image comforting my mind,
> And in my grief a strength reserved.   (lxxxv, 49-52, 1833)

At the same period he writes: 'I count it crime To mourn for any over-much' (lxxxv, 62-3), and in a rejected draft of section cxxiii paraphrases Horace's image (III, iii, 7-8) for steadfast patience amid universal disaster (*Poems*, p. 973).

Horace's lament for Virgil's dead friend Quintilius (I, xxiv) asks Melpomene, the muse of tragedy and lyric, to 'teach mournful songs'; the *Ode* that ends book III, where Horace claims to have 'completed a memorial more lasting than bronze', and thus achieved a partial immortality, is again addressed to Melpomene. Tennyson takes over Horace's muse, when expressing the hopeless aspect of his grief, but insists that she is 'but an earthly Muse', inferior to Urania, the 'Heav'nly Muse that inspired Milton's theodicy' (xxxvii). Melpomene is finally rejected ('the song of woe is after all an earthly song') and Hallam is left in his poetic 'shrine', which is Horace's 'memorial', but not 'more lasting than bronze':

> Come; let us go: your cheeks are pale;
> > But half my life I leave behind:

117

Methinks my friend is richly shrined;
But I shall pass; my work will fail.   (lvii, 2, 5-8)

The section ends with an allusion to Catullus' eternal farewell to his dead brother (ci), as the most perfect expression of the pagan attitude to bereavement; and the poem as a whole gives Urania the last word.

Horace seems to have suggested, not only many details, but two procedures which became central to the structure of *In Memoriam*: the conjunction of human feeling with seasonal change, and the use of anniversaries. He associated spring (*Odes*, I, iv) with mortality, which will end the delight of gazing at 'young Lycidas', which irrevocably separated the famous friends, Theseus and Pirithous (IV, vii), and which makes it urgently necessary that Virgil should come and drink wine with his friend Horace, 'while you still can, remembering death's black fires' (IV, xii). Spring and death are similarly linked in 'On a Mourner', written in October, immediately after hearing that Hallam had died; and *In Memoriam* marks the poet's gradual acceptance of his loss by his reactions to three successsive springs (xxxviii-ix, lxxxvi, cxv-vi). His use of anniversaries, such as Hallam's death-day (lxxii, xcix), and birthday (cxii), resembles that in Horace's *Odes* cursing a tree that fell and nearly killed him (II, xiii), celebrating the anniversary of his escape from death (III, viii) and celebrating the birthday of Maecenas (IV, xi).

The assumption by one reviewer of *In Memoriam* that 'These touching lines evidently come from the full heart of the widow of a military man' points to the continuing influence of Ovid. Tennyson sometimes plays the part of the deserted 'heroine', thinking of his 'spirit as of a wife' (xcvii, 8), wanting Hallam to 'come' to him in a landscape that includes a 'lonely grange' (xci, 12), and even when comparing himself to a 'widower', closely following the lines (*Heroides*, x, 9-12, 51-4). where Ariadne wakes up to find that Theseus has got out of bed and left her (xiii).

Tennyson once thought of calling the poem 'Fragments of an Elegy' (*Memoir*, vol. 1, p. 293), and FitzGerald assumed (letter of 29 January 1845) that it was in the pastoral form: 'Don't you think the world wants other notes than elegiac now? *Lycidas* is the utmost length an elegiac should reach.' The fiction that Arthur and Alfred were Arcadian shepherds is suggested only in section xxiii, though there is an allusion to the origin of the shepherd's pipe in the metaphor: 'I take the grasses of the grave, And make them pipes whereon to blow' (xxi, 3-4); but the poem conforms to the pattern of the pastoral elegy, which, originally a comfortless dirge (Theocritus i), became associated with the Adonis vegetation-myth (Bion i), and so developed a happy ending, with the dead man resurrected and deified (as in Virgil, *Eclogue* v). Apart from its general pattern, *In Memoriam* takes certain features from a number of pastoral elegies. It resembles the 'Lament for Bion' (attributed to Moschus) in suggesting (e.g. xi) that the natural environment shows signs of grief; *Eclogue* x in its final victory of love (cxxvi-ix); *Lycidas* in its title (the Greek words on Milton's title page mean 'in memoriam'), its concern with fame, religion and shipwreck, and its concluding 'nuptiall Song'; *Adonais* in its references to Urania, in its elaboration of Shelley's Greek epigraph (cxxi), and its identification of Hallam with natural beauty (cxxx); and the archetypal Theocritus i (which begins beneath a 'whispering' pine tree) in its invocation to a yew tree, immediately followed by 'whispers' from the 'lying lip' of Sorrow (ii-iii).

A complaint in *The Times* (28 November 1851) of *In Memoriam*'s 'amatory tenderness' rightly implied that the poem was partially modelled on the Petrarchan sonnet sequence. Hallam's four surviving essays on Italian literature include a life of Petrarch, containing a translation of Petrarch's line on the dead Laura: 'Death appeared lovely in that lovely face', the probable source of 'Death has made his darkness beautiful with thee' (lxxiv, 11-12). Petrarch's *Rime* were relevant to Tennyson's situation, since they were on 'the life and death of Laura'; and it may be significant that the Petrarchan sonnet begins with two quatrains in the *In Memoriam* rhyme-scheme. The opening pair of quatrains are to this effect: 'You that hear in scattered poems the sound of the sighs with which I fed my heart in my first youthful wanderings when I was not quite the same as I am now, I hope that those who understand love from experience will pity, not pardon me for the varied style in which I mourn and reason, between vain hopes and vain grief.' Variety of style, and rising above past grief, are the first two ideas in *In Memoriam* also:

> I held it truth, with him who sings
>> To one clear harp in divers tones,
>> That men may rise on stepping-stones,
> Of their dead selves to higher things.   (i, 1-4)

The last of the introductory stanzas written in 1849 picks up Petrarch's other two notions, youthful wanderings and pardon:

119

Forgive these wild and wandering cries,
    Confusions of a wasted youth;
    Forgive them where they fail in truth,
And in thy wisdom make me wise.   (41-4)

Other Petrarchan echoes include the image of walking wearily on alone, with many backward looks, when parted from the loved one (xxiii, xxxviii; cf, sonnet xv).

Tennyson thought Shakespeare 'greater in his sonnets than in his plays' (*Materials*, vol. 4, p. 460), which Jowett took to imply 'a sort of sympathy with Hellenism' (i.e. with Plato's glorification of male homosexual love in the *Symposium* and elsewhere); but this is not the only link between the *Sonnets* and *In Memoriam*. Sonnet i and section i use the same financial image:

But who shall so forecast the years
    And find in loss a gain to match?
    Or reach a hand through time to catch
The far-off interest of tears?   (i, 5-8)

Shakespeare urges a young man not to hoard up his beauty, but to invest it for the future by producing children. The Comparison of children to interest is as old as the Greek word *tokos*, which has both meanings, on which Aristophanes puns in a passage that Tennyson would have known. The interest-metaphor is applied to tears shed for 'dead lovers' in *Sonnet xxxi*, and in *Richard III* tears are regarded as money lent, which in time will be repaid with interest. A final hint for Tennyson's 'interest of tears' may have come from the *Confessions* of St Augustine, where his mother, deeply distressed at his youthful heresies, is told by a bishop: 'The son of those tears cannot possibly be lost.' With memories of *tokos*, the poet (who had similarly worried his own mother) could have taken the 'son' in a financial as well as literal sense, and created an image that concisely expressed one of the central ideas of *In Memoriam*, the progress from youthful 'confusions' to at least maturer wisdom.

There were precedents in the *Sonnets* for the night vision of Hallam (lxx); for his resemblance to 'the great of old' (lxxiv); for regarding the poems as a rich tomb (lvii); and for the question whether the poet's love could increase with time (lxxxi), but the two works resemble each other most in their emphasis on the destructive effects of time, especially on the spectacle of geological change, which makes Shakespeare fear

(*Sonnet* lxiv) 'That time will come, and take my love away'. Tennyson has the same fear:

> The hills are shadows, and they flow
>> From form to form, and nothing stands;
>> They melt like mist, the solid lands,
> Like clouds they shape themselves and go.
>
> But in my spirit will I dwell,
>> And dream my dream, and hold it true;
>> For though my lips may breathe adieu,
> I cannot think the thing farewell.
>
> (cxxiii, 5-12)

III

The philosophy of *In Memoriam* might be summarized as an attempt to harmonize two slightly discordant concepts, spiritual evolution and physical evolution, first formulated by Plato and Lucretius respectively. In the *Symposium* Plato listed the 'steps' (*epanabathmoi*) by which a soul might rise from love of a beautiful person to love of Divine Beauty, Truth and Goodness. In two sermons on the Ascension St Augustine wrote: 'We make a stairway (*scala*) of our vices, if we tread them under foot', and 'Our ascensions are not literal steps by which we climb, but conduct by which we improve ourselves.' In Keats's 'The Fall of Hyperion' (89-153), the unpublished manuscript of which Tennyson's friend Milnes must have let him see, progress towards poetic immortality is imaged as a laborious ascent up marble altar-steps. In a section expressing the extreme difficulty of reconciling the scientific with the religious view of the universe, Tennyson speaks of 'the great world's altar-stairs That slope through darkness up to God' (lv, 15-16); but already in the first stanza of the poem he asserts the possibility of spiritual evolution through the stair-image:

> That men may rise on stepping-stones
> Of their dead selves to higher things.
>
> (i, 3-4)

Keats had been allowed to climb the altar-steps, because he intensely felt 'the miseries of the world': Tennyson hopes that his own misery at Hallam's death will somehow prove a means of 'ascension'.

Lucretius (*De Rerum Natura*, v, 416-1457) outlined a purely mate-

121

rialist theory of evolution, from the chance collision of atoms to the 'peak' of human development. His picture of the bestial life, diet and mating habits of primitive man is alluded to in the argument that, but for a belief in an after-life, 'Love' would never have developed beyond lust, but 'in his coarsest Satyr-shape Had bruised the herb and crushed the grape, And basked and battened in the woods' (xxxv, 22-4). In book iv Lucretius depreciated love as an illusion and a perpetual source of bitterness, while recommending the simple gratification of the sexual instinct; in book iii he argued against the possibility of survival after death; in book i he denounced religion as a cause of unnecessary human suffering, and in several passages denied that the gods took any interset in human affairs.

After reading books iii and v with Palgrave one night Tennyson 'laughingly agreed that Lucretius had left' him 'all but' a convert to 'his heart-crushing atheism' (*Materials*, vol. 4, p. 311); but the laughter concealed a real disquiet, and much of *In Memoriam* was written in reply to the Lucretian philosophy.

The imagery of the poem shows a more positive debt to Lucretius, who supplied precedents for 'nature red in tooth and claw' (lvi, 15: book v, 1036-8); for the stress on Hallam's inability to 'strike a sudden hand in mine' (xiv, 11, vii, 5: book v, 148-51); for Tennyson's picture of himself as 'An infant crying in the night: An infant crying for the light' (liv, 18-19: book ii, 54-61, iii, 87-92); and for the idea of a soul standing by to adopt a body at the moment of conception (Concluding Stanzas, 121-4), which inspires one of Lucretius' rare jokes (book iii, 776-83).

The opening lines of section i attribute the doctrine of spiritual evolution to 'him who sings To one clear harp in divers tones', identified by Tennyson as Goethe (*Eversley*). The harp image clearly alludes to *Wilhelm Meister*, which contains a deeply depressed harper (eventually cured of his gloom) with a varied reportoire of songs. In one of these he says (Carlyle's translation, 1824-7): 'I sing but as the linnet sings', just as Tennyson says: 'I do but sing because I must, And pipe but as the linnets sing' (xxi, 23-4). Though he evidently knew Carlyle's version, he had also read the German text, which he acquired in 1838, and supplied with a MS glossary. Goethe's novel contains prototypes of section vii, when Wilhelm visits the front door of his beloved Mariana in the early morning, leaving only when the business of the town begins to come 'alive' again (*lebendig*); and of section xcv, when the dead Mariana 'speaks to' her lover through her letters.

The theme of *Wilhelm Meister*, Goethe told Eckermann, was that 'a man, despite his follies and errors, being led by a higher hand, reaches some happy goal at last'; or, as Carlyle put it ('Goethe', 1828), 'Anarchy has now become Peace; the once gloomy and perturbed spirit is now serene, cheerfully vigorous, and rich in good fruits.' In the same essay Carlyle made clear, with extracts from Goethe's autobiography, *Dichtung und Wahrheit*, that this kihd of spiritual evolution from despair to fruitful serenity had taken place in Goethe's own life. He cured himself of his suicidal depression, first by testing his capacity for actual suicide (he experimented every night with a sharp dagger, to see if he could bear to insert the point an inch or two into his chest, and found he could not), and secondly by writing his gloomy feelings out in *The Sorrows of Young Werter*. The 'fable' of this novel, a 'poetical task' intended to prove he had got over his 'hypochondriacal crotchets', came to Goethe quite suddenly when he heard of the suicide of a young man called Jerusalem: 'in this instant the plan of *Werter* was invented: the whole shot together from all sides, and became a solid mass; as the water in the vessel, which already stood on the point of freezing, is by the slightest motion changed at once into firm ice.' Tennyson ingeniously adapted the image to express the sense of grief that haunted his sleep even when he had ceased to be conscious of the reason for it:

> Something it is which thou hast lost,
> > Some pleasure from thine early years.
> > Break, thou deep vase of chilling tears,
> That grief hath shaken into frost! (iv, 9-12)

The use of 'vase' rather than 'vessel' suggests that he had read the image not only in Carlyle's 'Goethe', of which he owned a copy (1840 edition), but also in the 1824 translation of *Dichtung und Wahrheit*.

The special importance of Goethe in the thought of *In Memoriam* is that he was an authority for linking spiritual with physical, or scientific evolution. Darwin mentioned Goethe (1859) as a pioneer of evolutionary thought, who had 'pointedly remarked . . . that the future question for naturalists will be how, for instance, cattle got their horns, and not for what they are used'. Nor was he merely a theorist: in 1784 he had discovered a bone in the human species (the pre-maxillar) which was supposed to be found only in animals.

The chief sources, however, for Tennyson's ideas about physical evolution were Lyell's *Principles of Geology*, which he studied closely in 1837, and Chambers's *Vestiges of Creation*, which he read with anxious curiosity in 1844, having heard 'that it came nearer to an explanation than anything before it'. 'I trembled as I cut the leaves', he told Allingham (*Diary*, p. 148).

Though Lyell rejected Lamarck's evolutionary theory, he carefully summarized it. He also mentioned Tiedemann's discovery that the embryonic human brain went through stages in which it successively resembled the brains of fish, reptiles, birds, and lower mammals. Tennyson, who had probably known of this discovery from articles in the *Westminster Review* (1828), had alluded to it in 'The Palace of Art' (*Poems*, p. 409), and did so again in the concluding stanzas of *In Memoriam* (123-6), when the soul embodied on the wedding-night is 'moved through life of lower phase'. Finally, Lyell made a point that would figure largely in Darwin's theory of Natural Selection: 'In the universal struggle for existence, the right of the strongest eventually prevails; and the strength and durability of a race depends mainly on its prolificness.' This 'prolificness' was one of Tennyson's nightmares: 'The lavish profusion ... in the natural world appals me, from the growths of the tropical forest to the capacity of man to multiply, the torrent of babies' (*Eversley*).

Lyell's whole picture of the world was profoundly depressing. His main emphasis was on perpetual change and destruction: the title-page of vol. 2 carried the motto: 'The inhabitants of the globe, like all the other parts of it, are subject to change. It is not only the individual that perishes, but whole species.' In a cool, objective style which often sounds cruelly satirical , Lyell dwells on the 'vicissitudes' (floods, earthquakes, volcanic eruptions) 'essential to the stability of the system', but are 'so often the source of death and terror to the human race'. On a town built near a quiescent volcano he comments briskly: 'the volcano burst forth again with renewed energy, annihilating one half of the inhabitants'. He seems, like Hamlet, fond of showing 'To what base uses we may return'. He mentions, 'a side of a human skeleton' found, along with the bones of birds, moles, water-rats, mice and fish, in a cave forty feet up a limestone cliff, under 'six inches of earth', 'apparently derived from dust driven in continually by the wind'; human bones 'encrusted with stalactite' and a human skull filled with it, in another 'cave of mountain-limestone; human bones', with the remains of 'rhinoceros, bear, hyena, and many other terrestrial mammifers', 'embedded in alluvial mud', also in limestone; and he has a whole section entitled 'Imbedding of Organic Bodies and Human Remains in Blown Sand'. All this is what Tennyson had in mind when he refused to 'dream of human love and truth, As dying Nature's earth and lime' (cxviii, 3-4), or asks in horror: 'And he, shall he, Man, her last work, who seemed so fair,'

> Who loved, who suffered countless ills,
>> Who battled for the True, the Just,
>> Be blown about the desert dust,
> Or sealed within the iron hills? (lvi, 8-20)

While resisting, however, the implications of Lyell's evidence, Tennyson often adapted it to his own purposes. Lyell's 'Uniformitarianism' (i.e. his attempt 'to explain the former changes of the earth's surface by reference to causes now in operation') is trasmuted to form the poem's peroration: 'One God, one law, one element, And one far-off divine event, To which the whole creation moves' (where 'event' means not 'incident' but 'outcome'); and as late as 1868 Tennyson wrote section xxxix, giving a serious significance to Lyell's jocular comparison of yew trees in spring to the mares mentioned by Virgil (*Georgics*, iii, 271-5) that are impregnated by the wind, when 'the warmth returns to their bones'. The warmed bones of the mares, with their promise of new life, become the 'buried bones' watched over by the yew tree; thus Lyell's flippant allusion is made to hint delicately at the question put to Ezekiel, the central question of the poem: 'Can these bones live?'

Lyell ends with a perfunctory gesture towards Paley's argument for the existence of God, which Tennyson found unconvincing (cxxiv, 5-6): 'in whatever direction we pursue our researches . . . we discover everywhere the clear proofs of a Creative Intelligence, of His foresight, wisdom and power.' Chambers subscribes much more heartily to natural theology, and is at pains to show the Creator's benevolence, while admitting that it is sometimes heavily disguised; but what Tennyson probably liked best about his religious thought was his use of Arthur Hallam's type of argument in 'Theodicaea Novissima': that human 'conscientiousness and benevolence', and the human instinct 'prompting us to the worship of the Deity', imply that there is a Deity. 'The existence of faculties having a regard to such things is a good evidence that such things exist. The face of God is reflected in the organization of man, as a little pool reflects the glorious sun.'

Chambers's version of evolution was a 'Great Progress' organized by God, and he concluded his book with the words 'Let us wait the end with patience and be of good cheer', just as Tennyson ended his poem with 'the whole creation' moving towards a 'divine event'. Above all, in Chambers, physical and spiritual evolution were parts of a single process: as far as human beings were concerned, it was a long development towards a higher type of humanity, 'the grand crowning type . . . superior to us in organization, purer in feeling, more powerful in device and act'. This is the 'crowning race' that Tennyson describes in the concluding stanzas (128-36).

Chambers had even suggested a way of bringing Arthur Hallam into the system, when he explained that Providence arranges for the development of the human race by 'the production of original, inventive, and aspiring minds' who help to bring 'mankind from the darkness of barbarism to the day of knowledge and mechanical and social improvement'. Hallam therefore became one such Providential 'arrangement', 'a noble type' of the 'crowning race', born before his time (138-9).

Of the many other ways in which *Vestiges* seems to have affected *In Memoriam*, two may be mentioned. The image of Arthur Hallam as 'a central warmth' (lxxxiv, 6), reinforced by the 'solid core of heat' in the fire (modelled on one in a Horace *Ode*) to celebrate his birthday, was probably inspired by Chambers's discussion of a 'central heat' in the earth; and the concluding epithalamion, though partly a response to Tennyson's sister Cecilia's marriage to his friend, Edmund Lushington (10 October 1842), was given a special significance by the theory of Progressive Development. Chambers had suggested that this operated 'through the medium of the ordinary process of generation': 'the simplest and most primitive type, under a law to which that of likeproduction is subordinate, gave birth to the type next above it, . . . this again produced the next higher, and so on to the very highest'. The conception of another Lushington was thus an essential step in the 'Great Progress'.

The thought of *In Memoriam* combines respect for science with a rejection of its claim to be the final source of truth. This attitude, which is made explicit in section cxiv, must have been partly, at least, derived from a University Sermon preached by a member of Tennyson's college, Julius Hare, on Advent Sunday 1828. The poet probably heard it, but he could also have read it later, when published in *The Victory of Faith* (1840). Hare tries to define the proper attitude to Reason, with reference to 'philosophy and science'. He anticipates many features of section cxiv (the first stanza of which was written 1831-3): the allusion to the only published instalment of Bacon's *Instauratio Magna*; the idea of science 'submitting all things to desire' ('if Reason of late has been somewhat overbearing, the Will has pusht her on'); the use of the Pallas myth; the image of racing ahead too fast; the need for 'love' ('the vital warmth of the Affections'); the notion of 'moving side by side' (Reason should 'act in consort and co-ordination with our other faculties'); and the reference to the house of Wisdom. Tennyson also assimilates one of Hare's images to the 'go-cart' image of *The Princess* (Conclusion, 78): where Hare had recommended holding 'a tight rein over' Reason (a metaphor from horse-riding), Tennyson thought of the reins used to control the movements of a toddler: 'A higher hand must . . . guide Her footsteps, moving side by side With Wisdom, like the younger child' (17-20). Few University Sermons can have had such a far-reaching effect.

IV

Under all these influences the individual sections were composed, at first quite spontaneously, 'as the phases of our intercourse came to my memory and suggested them' (Tennyson, *Eversley*); but there was only one important influence on their organization into a unified structure. 'It was meant,' said Tennyson, 'to be a kind of *Divina Commedia*, ending with happiness' (*Eversley*); or, as he told Knowles, 'It . . . begins with death and ends in promise of a new life – a sort of Divine Comedy, cheerful at the close' (*Reminiscence*, p. 182). FitzGerald once asked him (1833-5), when they were looking at busts of Dante and Goethe in a shop window, 'What is there wanting in Goethe which the other has?' 'The Divine!' he answered (*Memoir*, vol. 1, p. 121). If Goethe the evolutionist presides over the start of the poem, Dante the religious visionary determines its final form.

This use of Dante would have pleased Arthur Hallam, who had planned to edit the *Vita Nuova* (a title which doubtless suggested Tennyson's 'promise of a new life'), had translated in verse twenty-five sonnets from it, and had praised the *Divina Commedia* as the perfect expression of 'the magnificent idea' that love was 'at once the base and pyramidal point of the entire universe', and that 'the union of souls' was 'the best and appointed symbol of our relations with God'.

The *Vita Nuova* itself has analogies with *In Memoriam*. Part allegory, part autobiography, it relates how Dante fell in love with Beatrice, how she died , and how, when he was tempted to be unfaithful to her, his constancy was restored by a vision of her, as he had first seen her, which revived memories of her in 'past time'. Similarly, Tennyson's religious faith is restored (xcv) by a mystical experience: while reading Hallam's letters about 'that glad year which once had been', the poet felt that 'The dead man touched me from the past, And all at once it seemed at last His living soul was flashed on mine' (*Poems*, p. 946). The *Vita Nuova* also resembles *In Memoriam* in presenting autobiographical material through short poems expressing different moods, and in commenting on these poems (in prose) rather as Tennyson comments on his in verse (e. g. v, xxi, xxxvii, xlviii). Dante was composing a poem in Beatrice's honour at the moment of her death, just as Tennyson 'wrought At that last hour to please him well' (vi, 17-18); and he may have been struck by Dante's remark that Beatrice died in 'the ninth month' of the Syrian calendar (Hallam died in September), and by his curious insistence that the number nine 'was herself'. Between a prophetic dream that she was dead, and her actual death, Dante had a vision of Love, who 'seemed to tell me joyfully in my heart: "Be sure that you bless the day that I seized upon you, for that is what you should do" '. This thought (elaborated in a sonnet of Petrarch) reappears in Tennyson's article of faith: "Tis better to have loved and lost Than never to have loved at all' (xxvii, 15-16, lxxxv, 3-4).

In the *Divina Commedia* Dante passes from Hell, through Purgatory, to the Earthly Paradise, where he meets Beatrice. She then takes him up to the Empyrean, where he has a vision of God, and of all 'the scattered leaves of the universe bound together by love in one volume'. *In Memoriam* shows Tennyson passing from a hell of total despair, through a purgatory of 'Doubt and Death' (lxxxvi, 11) to a mystical reunion with Hallam, as he reads 'Those fallen leaves which kept their green, The noble letters of the dead', after which he is 'whirled About empyreal heights of thought', and comes on 'that which is', and catches 'The deep pulsations of the world' (xcv, 23-40).

There are detailed as well as general parallels. Tennyson's hell is most powerfully expressed in the setting of Wimpole Street ('And ghastly through the drizzling rain On the bald street breaks the blank day', vii, 11-12): Dante's *Inferno* is 'a city of sorrow' (*città dolente*). The first hint of Tennyson's release from purgatory is marked by the 'sweet. . . air' of spring, with its 'new life', fanning his 'brows' (lxxxvi), just as Dante's arrival at the Earthly Paradise is marked by a 'sweet air' (*aura dolce*) striking his 'brow' (*Purgatorio*, xxviii, 7). Tennyson's beatific 'trance' is 'cancelled , stricken through with doubt'; he complains of the inadequacy of language to convey his experience, but finally suggests the unity of all things by making the sunlight and the starlight mix 'like life and death' (xcv, 43-64). Dante's vision was interrupted, when 'the lofty imagination lost its power'; he made the same complaint against language, and concluded with his 'desire and will, like an evenly spinning wheel', being 'revolved by the love that moves the sun and the other stars' (*Paradiso*, xxxiii, 120-45).

This image of rotation is, after the general pattern of progress from hell to heaven, the most important element in the structure of *In Memoriam* that derives from Dante. The Inferno is first experienced as a tumult of lamentation 'revolving' like a whirlwind in the darkness. Dante's first sight in it is a 'circling' ensign pursued by multitudes of the damned. Hell is a funnel that goes down in narrowing concentric circles; purgatory is a hill which must be climbed spirally, by 'circling' its terraces; heaven is reached by passing through Ptolemy's revolving planetary spheres; the angels are neatly arranged in circles; and the whole universe is controlled by the 'great wheels' (*magne rote*), which 'direct each seed to some end' (*Purgatorio*, xxx, 109-10). That is what Tennyson has in mind when he 'trusts' 'That nothing walks with aimless feet; That not one life will be destroyed'; a faith apparently contradicted by 'Nature', when 'of fifty seeds She often brings but one to bear' (liv, 5-6, lv, 11-12).

For Tennyson the wheel image had developed new associations. It suggested the works of a clock or watch (Paley's famous simile for a divinely created universe), and so time passing 'with every kiss of toothèd wheels' (cxvii, 11); the origin of the solar system and all other stellar systems (Laplace's cosmogony, as summarized by Chambers, pictured the universe developing from 'rotary motion' round 'aggregations' of nebulous, 'luminous matter'); and also, of course, the railway, the grand symbol of progress by rotation. In the psychological sphere, the wheel image suggested obsessive circling round a single idea, a single object of love or grief ('I . . . circle moaning in the air: "Is this the end? Is this the end?" '; 'My centred passion cannot move, Nor will it lessen from today', xii, 5-16, lix, 9-10). This suggestion was in line with Love's statement in the *Vita Nuova*: 'I am like the centre of a circle, to which all parts of the circumference are similarly related'; but by the end of the poem Hallam is more like the circumference than the centre ('I prosper, circled with thy voice', cxxx, 15), since he has become a presence diffused through the whole universe, and approximating to the definition of God (attributed to Empedocles): 'a circle whose centre is everywhere and whose circumference is nowhere.' Rotation was thus the ideal image on which to base the structure of a poem about love, religion, biological evolution operating through the reproductive cycle, and spiritual evolution operating through the passage of time, as marked by the revolving hands of the 'clock' that 'Beats out the little lives of men' (ii, 7-8), and hinted at even by the champagne that 'circles round' to celebrate the prospect of a new little life (Concluding stanzas, 81).

A sense of rotation is conveyed by the *In Memoriam* rhyme-scheme (as it is, to a lesser degree, by that of Dante's *terza rima*). FitzGerald wrote (31 December 1850) that *In Memoriam* was 'monotonous', and had 'that air of being evolved by a Poetical Machine of the highest order'. Certainly one has an impression of turning wheels, but the effect was deliberate, and subtly expressive of the poem's philosophy, as one passage in the introductory stanzas (1849) makes clear:

> Let knowledge grow from more to more,
>> But more of reverence in us dwell;
>> That mind and soul, according well,
> May make one music as before . . . .   (25-8)

The final rhyme takes us back, both in sense and in sound, to where we started. The turning wheel, however, has carried us a stage forward: the next revolution begins 'But vaster'. Keats described his own miniature account of spiritual evolution (*Endymion*, 777-811) as 'a regular stepping of the Imagination towards a Truth', a process for which the rhyming couplet was eminently suitable; but for Tennyson's idea of progress, not 'pedestrian', but by a kind of wheeled transport, the ABBA rhyme-scheme was perfectly adapted.

The rotatory character of the total structure is implied by Tennyson's note: 'After the death of A. H. H., the divisions of the poem are made by First Xmas Eve (Section xxviii), Second Xmas (lxxviii), Third Xmas Eve (civ, cv, etc.)' (*Eversley*). Christmases, however, are only one example of a general system of recurring occasions, which include seasons, anniversaries, and returns to the same place or subject of thought (e. g. the yew tree in the churchyard, ii, xxxix; or Hallam's front door, vii, cxix). The function of this system is to convey the passage of time, and the gradual changes in feelings, thought and attitudes that take place between one such occasion and its repetition: the spiritual progress made by one revolution of 'the great wheels', or of the smaller wheels with which they engage.

130

V

In adapting a wide variety of literary and philosophical materials to the expression of an intense personal experience, Tennyson produced a work of enormous originality, which had a profound significance for his age, and has an equal, though different, significance today. The build-up of a potential MP (cxiii, 11) into a figure of cosmic, and even divine, stature may seem implausible; and 'I have felt' (cxxiv, 16) may seem inadequate evidence for God's existence; but *In Memoriam* remains an accurate and moving statement of the human predicament, and an honest, if idiosyncratic, attempt to cope with two of its most unacceptable features: the fact of death, and the fact of living in a world of which increasing knowledge makes it increasingly hard to believe that 'Whatever is, is right'.

8

Maud

'Allingham, would it disgust you if I read "Maud"?' asked Tennyson in 1865. 'Would you expire?' (*Diary*, p. 117). It was his favourite poem, and the one he most enjoyed reading aloud. It developed from 'Oh! that 'twere possible' (*Poems*, pp. 598–602), a lyrical monologue begun (1833) as a dramatization of his feelings about Arthur Hallam's death, and completed and published in *The Tribute* (1837). The speaker of this poem is haunted by the ghost of a dead girl that he has loved, who lived in an 'old Manorial Hall' with 'laurels' in its 'garden', and used to meet him in 'woody places' (51–4,6). The piece ends with the thought that her 'Spirit waits To embrace' him 'in the sky' (109–10). *Maud* was designed to provide a complete narrative context for 'this somewhat mysterious contribution', as a reviewer had called it. The ghost was to be explained as a hallucination experienced by a mentally unstable lover, who was about to go mad with grief and guilt, because he had caused the girl's death by killing her brother in a duel.

According to the *Memoir* (vol. 1, p. 379), Tennyson 'accidentally lighted upon' his early poem, and attempted to make it more 'intelligible' by writing one to precede it: 'the second poem too required a predecessor; and thus the whole work was written, as it were, *backwards.*' What Tennyson 'lighted upon' was evidently not the complete poem, but some fragmentary draft of it, since a letter of 12 October 1853 (now at Harvard) from Emily's father shows that she had asked him to get a copy made of the poem from *The Tribute*. Mr Sellwood replied: 'Not knowing anyone who would work cheaper than myself I have copied & now send you Alfred's poem . . . .'

Besides reading this transcript, Tennyson seems shortly afterwards to have glanced through some copy (perhaps belonging to Sir John

Simeon) of the book itself; if not, some striking parallels between *Maud* and other poems in *The Tribute* must be attributed to memories up to sixteen years old. The anonymous ballad 'The Wicked Nephew' relates how the lover of 'Lady Maud' is haunted by the ghost of his uncle, whom he has murdered. Sir Aubrey de Vere's 'The Passion Flower' ('Art thou a type of beauty or of power, Of sweet enjoyment, or disastrous sin?') suggests the symbolic passion flower at Maud's garden gate (I, xiv, 496); A. Bradstreet's 'Julia in her Garden' resembles Maud in hers, with flowers capable of 'preaching', and raindrops in them, emblematic of 'tears' (I, xxii, 908-9); and the Italian sonnet immediately before Tennyson's contribution, telling an operatic singer that if Dido could have produced 'that sweet song', Aeneas would have forgotten everything else, and stayed with her, seems close in thought to the passage where Maud's lover is ready to fall down and worship 'Not her, not her, but a voice' (I, v, 189). Finally Lady Northampton's 'The Idiot Boy' shares with *Maud* its general theme (a contrast between the elevating effect of love and 'the thirst of gold'), the main features of its plot (a mentally deranged boy falls in love with 'a damsel brighter than the rose', with 'rosy cheeks', and a 'rightful heir' has been robbed of his 'manor' by 'treacherous wiles'), its seaside setting, and two notable images: the waves beat against the rocks 'in madd'ning fury' ('the scream of the maddened beach dragged down by the wave', I, iii, 98), and the dead hero, like Maud's dying brother (II, ii, 117), is called a 'poor worm'.

The precise sense in which *Maud* was composed *'backwards'* can be seen in a manuscript at Trinity College, Cambridge. The first section (designed to make the hero's hallucination 'intelligible') describes the killing of Maud's brother in a duel (II, i). This incident may have been suggested by Browning's 'Before' and 'After', a pair of poems concluding with the horror and remorse of an injured party who has killed his wronger in a duel. These poems, probably written soon after 1846, could have been shown or mentioned to Tennyson by Browning, along with other poems that he was collecting for *Men and Women* (1855), when he visited the Tennysons for Hallam Tennyson's christening (5 October 1852).

The next section (I, xiv) begins to account for the duel by introducing Maud, and subtly preparing for the hero's hallucination, and also for his final dream of her speaking to him from among 'a band of the blest' (III, vi, 9-13), by suggesting that, as he stands outside her window, it would be easy for her 'like a glorious ghost, to glide, Like a beam of the seventh Heaven, down to my side' (508-9). The poet then goes back again in time to present the hero's depressive temperament and depressing situation, and the process by which he gradually falls in love with Maud (I, iv-vi) in spite of his gloomy suspicions. After this the story is worked out in roughly chronological order up to and including the scene in the madhouse (II, v), which is then followed by the chronologically earlier shell lyric (II, ii), indicating that the delicate balance of the speaker's mind is about to be upset. This lyric had been written in the 1830s, doubtless in response to Lyell's remark (vol. 2, p. 281): 'It sometimes appears extraordinary when we observe the violence of the breakers on our coast . . . that many tender and fragile shells should inhabit the sea in the immediate vicinity of this turmoil' ('Frail, but of force to withstand, Year upon year, the shock Of cataract seas . . .'). 'The shell undestroyed amid the storm', Tennyson explained (*Eversley*) 'perhaps symbolizes to him his own first and highest nature preserved amid the storms of passion.'

The rest of the manuscript contains only rewritings of, or additions to, earlier sections. There is no sign of the introductory section (I, i) relating the speaker's family history and expressing his horror at contemporary social conditions; nor of the conclusion (III) in which he sees 'a hope for the world in the coming wars' (vi, 11). The introduction seems unlikely to have been written before April 1854, when the adulteration of food and drugs to which it refers (I, i, 39-44) was first highlighted by John Postgate's revelations at a special conference held at Birmingham to discuss the subject (20 April); and the date of composition was probably after the second Birmingham meeting (28 November 1854), which was brought to the attention of readers, not only of the *Lancet*, but also of *The Times*, the *Morning Post* and *Punch*. The conclusion was stated by Tennyson (*Eversley*) to have been 'written when the cannon was heard booming from the battleships in the Solent before the Crimean War' (declared 28 March 1854). The last four lines of the poem (54-9) were added in the 1856 edition, to explain the moral significance of the apparently bloodthirsty 1855 peroration ('The blood-red blossom of war with a heart of fire), and to hint that the speaker might not be wholly recovered. 'Take this with the first', said Tennyson, 'where he railed at everything. He is not quite sane – a little shattered' (G. Ray, *Tennyson reads 'Maud'*, Vancouver, 1968, p. 23):

And myself have awaked, as it seems, to the better mind;

It is better to fight for the good than to rail at the ill
I have felt with my native land, I am one with my kind,
I embrace the purpose of God, and the doom assigned.

II

The raw materials from which Tennyson created *Maud* included a lot
of personal experience. The speaker's unfairly treated and pathologic-
ally resentful father sounds very like Dr Tennyson; and the 'vast spec-
ulation' that 'failed' (I, i, 9) recalls the poet's own involvement in the
collapse of the 'pyroglyph' project. Maud, 'Queen rose of the rosebud
garden of girls' (I, xxii, 902), has obvious links with Rosa Baring,
whom Tennyson heard (June 1854) to be staying with her husband at
Ryde, only eighteen miles from Farringford. Maud's 'little oak-room'
(I, xiv, 497) and her 'high Hall-garden' (I, xii, 412) were features of
Rosa's home, Harrington Hall; and the theme of young love thwarted
by the financial requirements of a girl's family had been 'proved upon'
Tennyson's 'pulses' a second time, when his engagement to Emily was
broken off. That 'gray old wolf' (I, xiii, 471), Maud's unscrupulous
father, carries much of the odium attached to the poet's grandfather;
and her favoured suitor, the 'new-made lord' whose 'old grandfather
has lately died', leaving his wealth to 'a grandson, first of his noble line',
to be spent on building a 'gewgaw castle' (I, x, 332-51), was clearly
modelled on Tennyson's uncle Charles, and his conversion of Bayons
Manor into a Gothic castle.

All this belonged to the past; but Tennyson's present made an equally
important contribution. The ecstatic love lyric beginning 'I have led her
home, my love, my only friend' (I, xviii) reflects the long-delayed
satisfaction of establishing a permanent home with Emily, and the start
of what his grandson has called 'probably the happiest period of Tennyson's life' (*Alfred Tennyson*, pp. 277-8). *Maud,* the first major poem
written at Farringford, is full of touches suggested by his delightful new
environment.

The 'shipwrecking roar' of the sea that the speaker hears in his 'own
dark garden ground' (I, iii, 97-8) could be heard by Tennyson in his.
Because of frequent fogs, variable currents, and a broad submerged shelf
fringing the shore, the adjacent coast was particularly dangerous to
shipping. At Chale Bay, about twelve miles away, fourteen ships had
once been wrecked on a single night. The 'shining daffodil' and the
'emeralds' breaking 'from the ruby-budded lime' were features of the

Farringford garden in April 1854 (*Memoir*, vol. 1, p. 374); and from the top of High Down (now Tennyson Down) where the poet often walked, one really does have the impression of being 'ringed' by sea (I, iii, 101–7).

When the speaker admits that his resistance to contemporary social ethics may finally be worn down, that he may 'passively take the print Of the golden age', and set his 'face as a flint' (I, i, 29–31), the image was probably suggested by the abundance of flints on the foreshore at Freshwater, on which a modern guide-book comments: 'It is curious to notice how these are continually rolled eastward by the drift of the tide, and how rapidly they grow rounder and smaller in the process.' High Down is littered with small pieces of chalk that look like bread thrown out for birds; and Alum Bay, to which the Down leads, was so named because alum had been found there around 1561. The visual effect and the name must have helped to impress on Tennyson's mind Postgate's statement that 'BREAD is made of flour which . . . contains alum in variable but injurious quantity. It is white, dry, and readily crumbles; produces acidity and flatulency, and often leads to permanent dyspepsia and ill health'. He had also analysed some 'cream' which 'consisted of very finely prepared chalk and a modicum of cow cream'. Hence the speaker's charge that 'chalk and alum and plaster are sold to the poor for bread' (I, i, 39). This contradiction of the Gospel ('What man is there of you, whom if his son ask bread, will he give him a stone?') looks forward ironically to the 'Christless' failure of the social critic himself to 'forgive' the brother (II, i, 26, 44).

The Isle of Wight is a geologist's paradise (Alum Bay is remarkable for its vertical strata) which may once have been the estuary of a great river flowing eastwards, and in which remains of prehistoric reptiles had been found. On 22 May 1854 Tennyson was 'much pleased with the Iguanodons and Ichthyosaurs' at the Crystal Palace (*Memoir*, vol. 1, p. 376). *Vestiges of Creation* (1853 edition) painted a vivid picture of a world dominated by 'tyrant sauria' and 'huge megalosaurs', 'whole millenniums before' human beings appeared: 'the stream flowing and glittering in the sun, but not to cheer the eye of man. . . . And yet the certainty that in good time . . . the higher animals were to come, and among the last the Creature of Creatures . . . the historical being of the world!' In his initial disillusionment, the speaker of *Maud* paraphrases this passage, but rejects its anthropocentric optimism:

A monstrous eft was of old the Lord and Master of Earth,

For him did his high sun flame, and his river billowing ran,
And he felt himself in his force to be Nature's crowning race . . . .
So many a million of ages have gone to the making of man:
He now is first, but is he the last? Is he not too base?   (I, i, 131-7)

The laurels around Maud's home are a legacy from the poem of 1837; but the sound they make ('the dry-tongued laurels' pattering talk', I, xviii, 606) was first heard at Farringford (screened by laurels to north and south), just as the stars addressed by Maud's lover (I, xviii, 628-80) are those that Tennyson watched from open fishing boats, from his garden, and from his roof-top observatory.

A few feet away from this was the small room in which he wrote *Maud*. Close to his window were the upper branches of a magnificent cedar of Lebanon, which, though now symmetrically lopped, probably shared the general tendency of trees in that area (where the prevalent winds are westerly) to imitate the movement of the flints on the fore-shore, and of the prehistoric river, by 'bending toward the East' (T. Varley, *Isle of Wight*, Cambridge, 1924, p. 13). That is perhaps why the happy lover suddenly asks the cedar: 'O, art thou sighing for Lebanon In the long breeze that streams to thy delicious East', and streams back with it, in one of the poem's loveliest passages, to the dawn of the human race in the Garden of Eden, and 'the snowlimbed Eve from whom she came' (I, xviii, 613-26).

Living, as he virtually does, in the Isle of Wight, the speaker of *Maud* has good geographical grounds for retiring after the duel to the 'Breton, not Briton' coast (II, ii, 78). Proximity to that land 'of ancient fable and fear' (80) had made Tennyson study E. Souvestre's *Les Derniers Bretons* (*Memoir*, vol. 1, p. 381), where he would have come across a 'fable' that the Druid stones of Carnac were soldiers who had been turned into stone by a Christian saint. This may have suggested an important pattern of images in *Maud*. The speaker begins with 'a heart half-turned to stone' by hatred. It is turned to flesh by love for Maud (I, vi, 267-9), turned back to stone by the brother's contempt ('Gorgonised me from head to foot With a stoney British stare', I, xiii, 457-65), which climaxes in the duel; it remains a 'poor heart of stone' on the 'Breton strand' (II, iii, 132), and is finally reconverted into flesh ('The blood-red blossom of war with a heart of fire . . . we have hearts in a cause', III, iv-v). The saint turned soldiers into stones: 'the purpose of God' turns a stone into a soldier.

III

The literary materials of *Maud* are as important as the autobiographical ones. When the speaker says of Maud's brother, 'This lump of earth has left his estate The lighter by the loss of his weight' (I, xvi, 537-8), Tennyson is adapting a Homeric phrase, 'a useless weight on the earth', applied to himself by Achilles, in remorse at having kept out of the fighting, and so failed to protect his friend Patroclus. The brother, constantly denigrated by the speaker, turns out at the end to be the more magnanimous (' "The fault was mine," he whispered, "fly!" '), and the Homeric allusion already hints at this truth. It is the speaker himself who is the 'useless weight', the caricature of Achilles, raging about a private grievance in his tent, and letting other people do the fighting. The recurrent weight image is used to mark his gradual movement from the negative to the positive aspect of Achilles. He begins weighed down by the 'dead weight' of hatred (I, xix, 782) associated with the 'dead weight' of his suicide father's body (I, i, 14): he finally throws it off and can 'rise from a life half-lost with a better mind' (draft, *Poems*, p. 1092).

The corresponding movement in his society is from 'Peace' 'on her pastoral hillock' to epic warfare (III, vi, 23-8). The model here is Theocritus, *Idyll* xvi, which complains of the age's commercial greed, celebrates the approach of war against the Phoenicians (traditionally as dishonest as the Russian Czar), and contains a prototype for Tennyson's image of cobwebs 'woven across the cannon's throat' (as well as for his earlier phrase 'the mattock-hardened hand', I, xviii, 632).

The last major contribution of classical literature is the somewhat ambiguous technique of voicing sound social criticism through a character of unsound mind (I, i). Horace's *Satire* II, iii uses as its persona a bankrupt business man called Damasippus, who is generally thought to have gone mad, but goes round preaching the Stoic doctrine that the rest of the world is madder than he is. He resembles the *Maud*-speaker's father in having decided to commit suicide when his speculations failed, and the speaker himself in concerning himself with other people's business, because he has none of his own (19-20).

This satire contains the source of Shakespeare's phrase, 'Though this be madness, yet there is method in't'; and having noticed a trace of Dante (the speaker begins in a 'dark wood' and ends seeing his beloved among 'the blest') we may turn to an influence that Tennyson himself pointed out: 'This poem is a little *Hamlet,* the history of a morbid poetic soul, under the blighting influence of a recklessly speculative age'

(*Memoir*, vol. 1, p. 396). The comment recalls Hamlet's statement: 'The time is out of joint; – O cursed spite, That ever I was born to set it right!' In his preface to *Points of War* (1855), denouncing the peace party, Tennyson's friend Franklin Lushington quoted this passage, and drew the moral that one must not, like Hamlet, try to shirk the unpleasant duty of setting the time right: 'Let Hamlet stand aside . . . : we want Fortinbras just now.' Hamlet finally emerges from his intellectual isolation, takes decisive action, and is carried off 'like a soldier'. Thus, too, the hero of *Maud* begins like Hamlet the ineffectual recluse, and ends like Hamlet the potential Fortinbras.

Besides this basic parallel, there are numerous connections between *Maud* and *Hamlet*. The speaker virtually alludes to Hamlet's 'We are arrant knaves all', when he remarks: 'One says, we are villains all' (I, i, 17). Like Hamlet he is obsessed by a wish to avenge his father's death, and tries to silence his own vindictiveness in words resembling Hamlet's to his father's ghost: 'Peace, angry spirit . . . ' ('Rest, rest, perturbed spirit'). Like Hamlet he is profoundly disgusted by himself and the whole human race, is haunted by a ghost, and kills the brother of the girl he loves in a duel. This is foreshadowed by his prayer, 'Let all be well, be well' (I, xviii, 683), which ominously echoes Claudius's 'All may be well' before praying to be forgiven for 'a brother's murder'.

Other Shakespearian features include the setting of a love affair in the context of a family feud (*Romeo and Juliet*), and the characterization of a satirist who does 'Most mischievous foul sin, in chiding sin', by projecting his own vices on the world (Jaques in *As You Like It*, whose phrase the speaker borrows when he says: 'I to cry out on pride . . . ; I, xi, 428). The notion that a marriage between Maud and the speaker was arranged long ago by their parents (I, vii) comes from the story of Noureddin Ali and Bedreddin Hassan in the *Arabian Nights*, which begins with a farcical quarrel between two unmarried brothers about a marriage-settlement for their purely hypothetical offspring. Scott's novel, *The Bride of Lammermoor*, has a plot very like *Maud*'s: Edgar, the master of Ravenswood (cf. the speaker's 'dark wood' and 'a raven ever croaks at my side', I, vi, 246), is a gloomy young recluse consumed by hatred of the man who dispossessed his father of his 'ancient family seat'. Nevertheless, he falls in love with the dispossessor's daughter (first introduced as a voice singing). He sees a 'spectre', which he first assumes to be hers; and is finally buried alive in a quicksand (cf. the speaker's sense of being buried alive in the madhouse) while riding to fight a duel with her brother.

Carlyle's *Past and Present* (1843) supplied a precedent for the speaker's contention that peace in his day is worse than war, with the example of parents poisoning their children to get money out of a 'burial society' (I, i, 44); and his *On Heroes* (1841) prompted the speaker's wish for a dictator ('One still strong man in a blatant land', I, x, 392). *Alton Locke* (1850), a novel by another of Tennyson's friends, Charles Kinglsey, has a narrator whose father died 'of bad debts and a broken heart', while his 'more prudent' brother became rich; who goes in for 'wholesale denunciations' of the ruling classes, but falls in love with one of them (especially when he hears her singing); who feels as though buried alive in prison, and whose long delirious dream (introduced by a visionary female figure standing at the foot of his bed) corresponds with the *Maud*-speaker's delirium (II, v). In this dream he is at one point 'buried' (like Scott's Edgar) in 'a cloud of yellow dust'; at another, the girl he loves looks down at him, as he lies dying, with 'beautiful, pitiless eyes', rather like the 'pitiless, passionless eyes' of the stars that Maud's lover sees above him, as he lies under the cedar (I, xviii, 636). The novel also contains a 'man of science' (I, iv, 138-9), both 'vain' and 'bounded' in spirit (he has spent thirteen years writing a pamphlet on a small reptile, and complains that a fellow-scientist has plagiarized his discoveries). In Kingsley's horrific descriptions of slum life (cf. I, i, 34-46) 'the British vermin, the rat' (II, v, 296-9) figures memorably, when it is shown 'busy already with' the naked corpses of a mother and her two 'shrivelled' children; and the basic image of the madhouse section appears in Sandy Mackaye's comment on the alleged death of the devil: 'I'd no bury him till he began smell a wee strong like. It's a grewsome thing, is premature interment.'

Tennyson had also read two recent commercial successes by the so-called 'Spasmodics', Alexander Smith's *A Life-Drama* (1853) and Sydney Dobell's *Balder* (1854). The effect of these preposterous works was to suggest that the public might accept an oblique and potentially obscure narrative technique (the plots of both, which abound in short lyrics, are extremely hard to follow); and to suggest the poetic possibilities of madness (as exploited by Shakespeare in *Hamlet*). *A Life-Drama* is a verse-play (full of borrowings from Tennyson's earlier works) about a poet who, after the girl he loves is married off to a rich, elderly man, becomes deeply depressed, and urges a passing 'Peasant': 'O die, man, die! Get underneath the earth for very shame!' but finally marries another girl and goes 'forth 'mong men . . . in the armour of a pure intent' to do 'God's work'. The features of *Maud* which it anticipates include a fawn (called Flora); falling in love with the voice of 'a maiden singing in the woods alone'; 'evenings cawed by clouds of rooks'; the extinction of the whole human race 'with a master-stroke'; a contrast between love and the 'cold' stars; haunting by the reproachful face of a girl; a call for 'mad War!'; and a tiny dash of humour (an ode to Scotch whisky).

Balder, Part I (mercifully no more was published), is a verse drama in forty-two scenes about a poet and his wife Amy. For the first twenty-two scenes she is merely a voice singing songs off stage. She gets more and more depressed, and goes mad. Her husband, who has hitherto done nothing but write or recite poetry, decides that the kindest thing to do is to undress her, put a handkerchief over her face, and kill her; which he does.

Apart from love and madness the most important ingredients of *Maud* that are found in *Balder* are the stars as 'pitiless signs'; a 'phantom' (of Amy's past beauty and singing); her repeated use in her madness of the buried-alive image ('I hear the sound of life above my head . . . the very rock Shakes with the overgoing . . . my cry Can never struggle to the day'; cf. II, v, 242-51, 339); talking flowers, including an 'imperial Lily' by 'Eden-gate'; and above all the Crimean War. Besides a nautical chorus, recalling *The Bab Ballads*, about a sea-battle with the Russians, Tyranny (i.e. the Czar) is allegorized as an insatiable limbless trunk riding on a perpetually excreting, headless, black monster with innumerable hands and feet. Balder also compares himself to 'one who crossed in hapless love, Betakes him to the wars, and tells in blows His bitter need of kisses'.

The war had also been used for poetry by Tennyson's close friends, Henry and Franklin Lushington in *La Nation Boutiquière* (1855), which Tennyson may have seen in manuscript, although Henry was living in Malta. The poem by Henry, which gave its title to the volume, denounced 'the peace of baseness' and 'the years of gains', and lamented that 'so great a land' might die of 'so vile a canker'. A leader in *The Times* asked (14 February 1855): 'What if . . . "the cankers of a long peace" should be found almost as destructive as the more confessed plagues of war?' The phrase quoted from Falstaff was adapted by Tennyson in his first edition: 'the long, long canker of peace', (III, 49; *Poems*, p. 1092), but he withdrew the image, however, in response to a protest by a reviewer.

In Henry's 'The Morn of Inkerman' a soldier dreams that his dead wife kisses him on the brow, and tells him that he will survive the battle

and see his children again (cf. III, 9–13) ; and Franklin's 'Points of War'
makes the conclusion of *Maud* seem pacifist by comparison:

> Peace, peace, peace, with the vain and silly song
> That we do no sin ourselves, if we wink at other's wrong;
> That to turn the second cheek is *the* lesson of the Cross,
> To be proved by calculation of the profit and the loss:
> Go home, you idle teachers! you miserable creatures!
> The cannons are God's preachers, when the time is ripe for war.

IV

A third kind of material that went into *Maud* was drawn from contemporary life. The horrors of peace described by the speaker (I, i,
37–44) are all based on fact. The 'yell of the trampled wife' may be
documented in *The Times* by two cases of savage assault (24 August
1854), and by a third (4 September 1854), in which a wife, when
'compelled to scream for assistance' against her husband's brutality, was
given 'a terrific kick on the lower part of the abdomen'. The 'vitriol
madness' that causes the 'ruffian's' attack comes partly from *Alton
Locke*, where gin is called 'vitriol', and partly, perhaps, from a *Times*
report (8 December 1854) of a 'Vitriol Man' with 'a monomania' for
squirting vitriol on ladies' dresses.

The paradox that 'the spirit of murder works in the very means of
life' may derive from 'The Poisoners of the Present Century', an article
on the adulteration scandal in *Punch* (9 December 1854), which refers
to 'the staff of life' ('for staff, read stuff, and omit life – or substitute the
reverse') and points out that bread is now full of 'azote . . . that which
does not support life'. The charge that the chemist pestles 'a poisoned
poison' plays with Juvenal's charge that doctors poison their patients, by
referring to Postgate's statement that prescriptions are seldom honestly
dispensed. There is also the implication that chemicals used for adult-
erating food and drink are themselves adulterated. Thus *Punch* remarks
'The brewer who cheats his customers' with 'Grains of Paradise' (a
practice mentioned in *Alton Locke*) has 'himself been cheated by his
druggist'.

The speaker's attitude to the Crimean War is roughly that of *Punch*
and *The Times*. Tennyson denied (*Eversley*) that the 'broad'brimmed'
pacifist 'Whose ear is crammed with his cotton' (I, x, 370–1) represented John Bright; but in the cartoon 'Pet of the Manchester School'

(15 April 1854), which showed Cobden and Bright trying to appease a small boy in a tantrum (the Czar), the broad-brimmed hat was conspicuous; and in 'Mrs Grundy to Mr Bright' (18 November 1854) he is called 'a calico feller . . . all made of cotton, like my umbereller'. *Punch* had previously made fun of the Quaker deputation which had visited the Czar in St Petersburg (January 1854), in an effort to prevent the war ('the broad-brim would, undoffed, approach the casque').

The speaker's hope that 'God's just wrath shall be wreaked on a giant liar' (III, 45) echoes statements in *The Times* that the Czar had 'set truth at nought' (12 November 1853); that England 'will not flinch from a quarrel in which she believes HEAVEN will still be her friend '(23 February 1854); that the war will end in 'the signal punishment of the gigantic offender' (29 March 1854). *Punch* was full of references to the Czar's dishonesty ('I've no Allies, and must depend On Lies without the Al'), and the view of the war as essentially just was expressed in a famous cartoon, 'Right against Wrong', showing an indignant Britannia standing with drawn sword beside a Lion whose massive countenance imitates her frown of stern disapproval. The belief that the heart of the English people beats 'with one desire' (III, 48) comes from the assertion (*Times*, 20 February 1854): 'it is a war to which every party in the State, and almost every man in the country, gives assent'; and not only the suggestion that war may be better than the 'canker' of peace, but even the image: 'many a darkness into the light shall leap' (III, 46) appears in a *Times* leader (14 February 1855): 'war has some positive advantages . . . it . . . raises to the surface of affairs many an ardent spirit that would otherwise have smouldered in obscurity.'

Such is the speaker's attitude towards the war; but in two important ways the poem as a whole implies a quite different attitude. First, the speaker's own private war is against a man nicknamed 'the Sultan' (I, xx, 790), which subtly suggests that the speaker himself is a kind of Czar, untrustworthy and aggressive. Second, just as the Czar was pictured by *The Times* (23 December 1854) as 'a madman, armed with the torch and the sword', and in a *Punch* cartoon (11 March 1854) as a 'mad dog', so the speaker is presented as partially insane. His view of the war is therefore profoundly suspect. This point was completely missed by Cobden when he attacked the writer of *Maud* (*Times*, 5 November 1855) as a war-monger 'who would be ready to mop and mow with madmen tomorrow if Bedlam could be but one day in the ascendant'.

Tennyson emphasized the fundamental ambiguity of the poem's statement about the war in an unpublished letter (6 December 1855) to the clergyman-poet Archer Gurney (whom he had wrongly suspected of writing the anonymous abusive letter that was quoted earlier on p. 29):

> now I wish to say one word about *Maud* which you and others so strangely misinterpret. I have had Peace party papers sent to me claiming me as being on their side because I had put the cry for war into the mouth of a madman. Surely that is not half so wrong a criticism as some I have seen. Strictly speaking I do not see how from the poem I could be pronounced with certainty either peace man or war man. I wonder that you and others did not find out that all along the man was intended to have an hereditary vein of insanity, and that he falls foul on the swindling, on the time, because he feels that his father has been killed by the work of the lie, and that all through he fears the coming of madness. How could you or anyone suppose that if I had to speak in my own person my own opinion of this war or war generally I should have spoken with so little moderation. The whole was intended to be a new form of dramatic composition . . . I do not mean to say that my madman does not speak truth too . . .

So far, then, as *Maud* comments on the Crimean War, it is a dramatic dialogue between a madman arguing without moderation, but not without a modicum of truth, that war is preferable to peace, and an implicit sane assumption that war is the ultimate horror. The hint for such a dialogue probably came from a piece in *Blackwood's* (November 1854, vol. 76, pp. 589-98) called 'Peace and War: A Dialogue'. Apart from its subject-matter (and the fact that its conclusion contained a misquotation from *The Princess*) its classical allusions would have caught Tennyson's eye. It began with a quotation from Horace, with the word *alma* italicized to make a topical pun. The Platonic-type dialogue was between Tlepolemos (a Homeric hero whose name means 'enduring of war') and a Quaker called Irenaeus (from the Greek word for 'peace'). It quoted in Greek three lines from the *Eumenides* of Aeschylus, which epitomize the speaker's distinction between 'lawful and lawless war' (II, v, 327-33): 'Let it be foreign war, and plenty of it, with a terrible love of glory. I do not mean domestic cock-fights.' The words are spoken by Athena, when trying to persuade the Furies to stop tormenting Orestes for the murder of his mother; hence the two passages assimilating *Maud* to the *Oresteia* ('The household Fury sprinkled with blood By which our houses are torn', I, xix, 715–6; 'Wrought for his house an irredeemable woe', II, i, 22).

The *Blackwood's* dialogue anticipates many other points in *Maud*: a contrast between 'love-making' and 'polemics'; the idea of war as an appeal to a higher judge ('I embrace the purpose of God, and the doom assigned'); a comparison between wars and duels; war as preferable to 'the everyday life of a peaceful commercial society'; adulteration included among 'the horrors of peace'; madness ('railway-mania' versus the 'madness' of war); and finally an inconclusive argument. Tlepolemos does most of the talking, but Irenaeus complains at the end that he has not been 'given a chance' to produce all his counter-arguments. *Maud* similarly ends with the pacifist case suggested, but not fully stated.

In one other way, not unconnected with the war, contemporary life contributed to *Maud*. In September 1850 the great winged Assyrian bull discovered by A. H. Layard arrived at the British Museum. Tennyson probably saw it soon afterwards, and certainly saw it (or a reproduction of it) in the Nineveh Court of the Crystal Palace, which he visited 21 May 1854. In 1852 he had read Layard's *Nineveh and its Remains* (1849), which illustrated (frontispiece) and minutely described the difficult process of lowering this enormously heavy, sculptured stone from its original position into a trench containing rollers. The ropes broke when the bull was four or five feet above the rollers. Layard rushed down, expecting to find it 'in many pieces', but it was miraculously undamaged.

The fall of this human-headed stone into the trench seems to have suggested the fall of the speaker's father into the pit: 'Mangled, and flattened, and crushed, and dinted into the ground: There yet lies the rock that fell with him when he fell' (I, i, 7–8). This initiated the related patterns of weight imagery and petrifaction imagery already mentioned; and the bull also supplied an appropriately ambiguous image for the brother : 'That oiled and curled Assyrian Bull' (I, v, 233). The speaker means merely to sneer at the brother's combination of powerful physique (which he clearly envies) with his dandy-like coiffure ('With hair curled like that of the bulls on Assyrian sculpture', Tennyson, *Eversley*); but he inadvertently implies also that the brother is a kind of winged god; and in the context of the Crimean War, the image has even more admirable associations, since *Punch* cartoonists used the Assyrian Bull to represent Layard himself (5 March 1855), and also 'the British Bull' dug out by Layard, when buried beneath the weight of official incompetence (26 March 1855). For Layard was an energetic MP, who had gone

145

to the Black Sea the moment war was declared, witnessed the Battle of Alma from a battleship, returned to England with evidence of the appalling conditions faced by the army before Sebastopol, and then worked hard to improve them. The brother thus acquires, in contrast with the speaker, an aura of a man who goes out and does something for the heroes at the front; and his 'British stare' (I, xiii, 465) suggests that he is really at heart that estimable, if limited, character, John Bull.

V

The original title of the poem, to which Tennyson intended to revert (*Poems*, p. 1038), was *Maud or the Madness;* and madness is the central theme. It was relevant not only to Tennyson's own temperament and family history, but also to the war, since, while the madness of the Czar was a commonplace, the war in defence of the Sultan seemed to some people equally mad. Carlyle wrote in his diary: 'Russian war: soldiers marching off, etc. Never such enthusiasm among the population. Cold, I, as a very stone to all that: it seems to me privately I have hardly seen a madder business . . . .'

Tennyson's treatment of madness is both psychological (an attempt to portray it accurately) and philosophical (an attempt to define the function of madness, i.e. of the irrational element, in human life). For the first, he relies heavily on technical information from his psychologist friend, Dr Matthew Allen; for the second, on an assessment of Stoic and Epicurean ethics in the light of his own experience.

Tennyson referred to the madhouse in II, v as 'Bedlam' (G. Ray, *Tennyson reads 'Maud'*) and the influence of Hogarth's *A Rake's Progress* (Plate 8) is confirmed by a manuscript (Trinity College, Cambridge), which includes an equivalent of Hogarth's mad musician; but the real-life source was Allen's private asylum at High Beech, which Tennyson spent a fortnight visiting (soon after 1837). According to Spedding (Hallam Tennyson, *Tennyson and his Friends*, 1911, p. 408) he was 'delighted with the mad people, whom he reports the most agreeable and the most reasonable persons he has met with'. His knowledge of madness and its treatment was otherwise based on Allen's conversation, and on his *Essay on the Classification of the Insane* (1837).

Allen's asylum consisted of several houses, including 'Springfield', 'Fair Mead House'(for convalescents), and 'Leopard's Hill Lodge'; its address he habitually spelt 'High Beach'. It cannot be merely coincidence that the *Maud*-speaker's mental state is at first reflected by 'a maddened beach' (I, iii); that he begins to recover in spring (I, iv); that his convalescence is accelerated by hearing Maud singing in 'the meadow' (I, v); and that he finally returns to near-normality under the auspices, not of a leopard, admittedly, but of a 'Lion' (III, 14), which has earlier appeared over Maud's garden-gate, as what Tennyson called 'a token – I hardly write anything without some meaning of that kind' (G. Ray, *Tennyson reads 'Maud'*).

Allen's theory of treatment was to encourage, by kindness, the patient's positive moods ('light, cheerful, and full of kindness') rather than, by harshness, to encourage the negative ones ('dark, gloomy, and vindictive'). Maud begins this type of treatment when she touches the speaker's hand with a smile (I, vi, 201); her brother counteracts it by snubbing him (i, xiii), and this is particularly disastrous because the patient is at this moment longing to be friendly (457–9). As Allen wrote, 'the disagreeable excitement' caused by frustrating 'ardent desires for the joys of moral and intellectual friendship . . . may amount to pain, aversion, hatred, contempt, and fury'.

The speaker's history precisely follows Allen's 'most obvious history of most cases': an obsessional concentration on 'certain thoughts and feelings . . . to the detriment or suppression of others' (triggered off by the traumatic experience of his father's death) leads ultimately to insanity. The 'shriek' in the 'shuddering' night which marks the initial trauma (I, i, 16) seems to echo Allen's account (Case 24) of a girl who 'received a severe shock', the news of her father's suicide, and then went totally mad when she read in a newspaper that her lover was engaged to someone else: 'she shuddered and shrieked'.

Tennyson had authority in Allen's *Essay* for most of the speaker's symptoms, including his violent oscillations of mood, sometimes associated with changes in the weather (e.g. I, vi, 204–11); his sudden concentration on the shell (II, ii: 'excessive importance is attached to the merest trifles'); and his 'fantastic merriment', the silliness (deliberately ascribed to him by Tennyson) of the 'Rosy' sequence (I, xvii, 575f: 'When their spirits are buoyant, they strangely exhibit their inherent defects of mind').

Among Allen's other contributions to *Maud* may be mentioned: 'that hole in his side' (II, v, 320), suggested by the patient who 'thought he was Jesus Christ', but was cured of the delusion when told that the 'hole in the side' that he was always pointing at was on the wrong side; the idea that the 'spirits' of asylum patients are 'prematurely entombed within them'; and the unifying thought of the poem, that 'One part of

147

society, as well as one part of the mind, is at war with another'.

The philosophical treatment of the madness theme starts from the Stoic and Epicurean doctrine that love and anger are forms of madness (Horace's Stoic madman, Damasippus, links them together when he says: 'In love are these evils, war alternating with peace'). The state of mind recommended by these philosophers was 'a passionless peace'. (I, iv, 150–1), the Stoic *apatheia* (freedom from passion), the Epicurean *ataraxia* (freedom from disturbance), or the Pythagorean *athaumastia* (freedom from admiration).

Tennyson's speaker tries to sescape madness, especially 'the cruel madness of love' (I, iv, 156) by leading 'a philosopher's life', modelled on that of 'the stoic' or 'wiser epicurean', or Pythagorean ('not to desire or admire': I, iv, 121–2, 149–56). On this principle he refuses to be angered or 'disturbed' by the Czar's crimes: 'Shall I weep if a Poland fall? shall I shriek if a Hungary fail? Or an infant civilisation be ruled with rod or with knout?' (I, iv, 147–8).

The immorality, however, of *apatheia* in the face of foreign or domestic crime had been pointed out by *The Times*. Reporting the case of a six-year-old boy battered to death by his stepmother, it commented on the 'strange apathy and indifference of the neighbours' who did nothing to interfere (6 May 1854); and the previous month it had condemned Bright's peace policy as inviting England to 'look on passively at the imminent disruption of' the European 'confederacy' and 'to await with indolent and reckless apathy the time when' she herself would become the Czar's victim (3 April 1854).

Abandoning his 'philosophy', the speaker comes to 'accept' the 'madness' of love (I, xviii, 642), and finally accepts the madness of 'wrath' against the Czar, feeling that he shares it with God (III, 45). Tennyson means that the 'madness' of passion, though potentially destructive, is a valuable part of human nature, which must not be denied. He is saying what Chambers had said of the 'sex passion' (*Vestiges*, 1853 edition): it 'leads to great evils' but it creates such a 'vast amount of happiness' that 'every ill that can be traced to it is but as dust in the balance'. Love is the great elevating force, and anger is sometimes necessary to preserve civilization. That is why the lion, finally associated with Mars, first appears 'claspt by a passion-flower', traditionally a symbol of divine suffering, but now also of sexual passion (III, 13–14, I, xiv, 495–6); and why the roses of love, which after the duel come to seem 'not roses, but blood' (II, v, 316), conclude by symbolizing 'God's just wrath': 'The blood-red blossom of war with a heart of fire.'

9

Idylls of the King

Tennyson's plans for a large-scale work on what he called 'the greatest of all poetical subjects' (*Memoir*, vol. 2, p. 125) developed from his boyish hero-worship of King Arthur, when he first read about him in Malory, combined with his knowledge that Milton had once meant to write an Arthurian epic. The earliest hint of a method by which this legendary material could be given contemporary and universal significance probably came from Lyell's *Principles of Geology*, vol. 1 (1830). After describing the gradual erosion of 'a projecting tongue of land, called the "Green"', near Penzance, and the transformation of St Michael's Mount from 'the Hoare Rock in the Wood', several miles from the sea, into 'an insular rock', Lyell mentioned, as a 'romantic tale' based on some historical 'inroad' of the Atlantic, 'the celebrated tradition in Cornwall of the submersion of the Lionnesse, a country which formerly stretched from Land's End to the Scilly Islands'. Such disappearances of land beneath the sea were linked by Lyell with the rise of islands out of it, comparable to the islands 'many times larger than the whole of Portland' that 'slight obstructions in the course of the Ganges' could create 'in the course of a man's life'.

In a prose sketch entitled 'King Arthur' (about 1833) Tennyson adapted Lyell's emerging and submerging islands into a splendid image for the rise and fall of an ideal civilization in the course of one man's life:

> On the latest limit of the West in the land of Lyonnesse, where, save the rocky Isles of Scilly, all is now wild sea, rose the sacred Mount of Camelot. It rose from the deeps with garden and bowers and

palaces, and at the top of the Mount was King Arthur's hall, and the holy Minster with the Cross of gold . . . The Mount was the most beautiful in the world, sometimes green and fresh in the beam of morning, sometimes all one splendour, folded in the golden mists of the West. But all underneath it was hollow, and . . . there ran a prophecy that the mountain and the city on some wild morning would topple into the abyss and be no more (*Memoir*, vol. 2, pp. 122-3).

Arthurian civilization was to be precariously poised over a sea of barbarism, and doomed to collapse because its foundations were hollow. The idea (not found in Malory) that this 'hollowness' was the hypocrisy originating in Guinevere's secret adultery with Lancelot is suggested by some notes (also of about 1833) which include 'King Arthur's three Guineveres' and 'Two Guineveres, ye first prim. Christianity. 2ª Roman Catholicism' (*Memoir*, vol. 2, p. 123). In the Welsh *Triads* there are three Guineveres; and in the prose romance of *Merlin* (from which Southey quoted in his edition of Malory) there are two Guineveres, very hard to tell apart: a legitimate and an illegitimate daughter of King Leodegan. Arthur married the 'true' one, but a plot was laid to kidnap her, when she went into the garden at night (for a purpose, Southey wrote, which indicated that chamber-pots had not yet been invented), and convey the 'false' one into Arthur's bed. The religious allegory of the 'two Guineveres' (modelled on that of Una and Duessa, who represent 'true religion' and Roman Catholicism in *The Faerie Queene*) was fortunately dropped; but the story of Leodegan's two daughters seems to have influenced Tennyson's choice of subject for the first two *Idylls* that he wrote, which were printed (1857) under the title: *Enid and Nimuë: The True and the False*, and for the first four *Idylls* that he published (1859), which presented the same contrast of character (Enid, Elaine: Vivien, Guinevere). The antithesis became central to the whole ethical scheme of *Idylls of the King*.

Although the rigid allegorical framework implied by these early notes was jettisoned, some of the symbolic equations mentioned in 1833 continued to operate in the development of the poem, and are part of its total meaning, e.g. 'K.A. Religious Faith'; 'Modred, the sceptical understanding'; 'Merlin . . . Science'; and 'The Round Table: liberal institutions'. Tennyson tried, however, to discourage interpretations of the *Idylls* which laid too much stress on the allegory (*Memoir*, vol. 2, pp. 126-7):

They have taken my hobby, and ridden it too hard, and have explained some things too allegorically, although there is an allegorical or perhaps rather a parabolic drift in the poem ... Of course Camelot for instance, a city of shadowy palaces, is everywhere symbolic of the gradual growth of human beliefs and institutions, and of the spiritual development of man. Yet there is no single fact or incident in the 'Idylls', however seemingly mystical, which cannot be explained as without any mystery or allegory whatever.... I hate to be tied down to say, *'This* means *that,'* because the thought within the image is much more than any one interpretation.... Poetry is like shot-silk with many glancing colours. Every reader must find his own interpretation according to his ability, and according to his sympathy with the poet.
The whole is the dream of man coming into practical life and ruined by one sin. Birth is a mystery and death is a mystery, and in the midst lies the tableland of life, and its struggles and performances. It is not the history of one man or of one generation, but of a whole cycle of generations.

The poem, then, is primarily not an allegory, which means something quite different (*allos*) from what it says, but a parable, which implies, alongside (*para*) a realistic narrative, a generalizing comment on human life. Thus Arthur's life-cycle (corresponding to one revolution of the mediaeval Wheel of Fortune) is made to typify a 'cycle of generations', the historical process by which the human race advances, through alternating periods of progress and regress, rise and fall. The first four *Idylls* ('The Coming of Arthur', 'Gareth and Lynette', 'The Marriage of Geraint', 'Geraint and Enid') depict the rise of Arthur's island of spiritual culture, 'green and fresh in the beam of morning'. The next four ('Balin and Balan', 'Merlin and Vivien', 'Lancelot and Elaine', 'The Holy Grail') show it being gradually eroded from beneath by hypocrisy, disillusionment, depression leading to the abdication of reason, refusal to believe in anything better than oneself, misdirected love, and misdirected religious instincts. The last four ('Pelleas and Ettarre', 'The Last Tournament', 'Guinevere', 'The Passing of Arthur') show the island finally toppling 'into the abyss' as t e undermining forces culminate in open treachery, sexual promiscuity, and the reasoned rejection of all moral codes that frustrate the desires of the individual. Only the rising of the 'new sun' in the last line of the poem hints that 'the great wheels' may soon bring in another phase of progress.

II

The phase of human life on which the *Idylls* comment is the history of England during Tennyson's lifetime, which he saw as a period of political and scientific progress followed by one of spiritual decline. This decline might be summarized as the ousting of religion by science, of traditional morality by rationalistic, materialistic, and individualistic ethics, and of common decency by a new, permissive attitude to sex. Thus Darwin's *The Origin of Species,* which led to Thomas Huxley's Agnosticism, synchronized with J. S. Mill's *On Liberty* (1859), which argued that 'whatever crushes individuality is despotism', and denied the right of society to interfere 'with the liberty of action of any of' its members, except in 'self-protection'; and Herbert Spencer's evolutionary philosophy, while denying that either science or religion had a monopoly of truth, asserted in *First Principles* (1863) that every individual should consider himself an 'agency' of 'the Unknown Cause; and when the Unknown Cause produces in him a certain belief, he is thereby authorized to profess and act out that belief'. Of 'the sexual insurrection' (as the *Daily Telegraph* called it in 1868) the great symptoms were the establishment of the Divorce Courts (1857), in spite of Gladstone's hundred speeches against the bill; the attempts, from 1866 onwards, to legalize marriage with a deceased wife's sister; the success of Swinburne's sex-centred *Poems and Ballads* (1866); and the popularity of what was known as 'the literature of prostitution': in Tennyson's phrase, 'the troughs of Zolaism' ('Locksley Hall Sixty Years After', 145).

This apparently backward movement contradicted Chambers's theory of evolution, but not Darwin's. The first edition of the *Origin* contained the cheering statement: 'as natural selection works solely by and for the good of each being, all corporeal and mental endowments will tend to progress towards perfection'; but in 1866 a sentence was added, allowing for the possibility of 'some forms having retrograded in organization, though becoming under each grade of descent better fitted for their changed and degraded habits of life'. In 1869 the concessive 'though' became the causative 'by'.

The thought that evolution has gone into reverse is expressed by an important image-pattern in the *Idylls,* based on the antithesis between 'man' and 'beast'. Arthur comes into a world 'Wherein the beast was ever more and more, But man was less and less' ('The Coming of Arthur', 11-12). His life-work is an attempt, at first successful, to make 'men from beasts' ('The Last Tournament', 358), but as he dies he realizes that his whole realm 'Reels back into the beast' ('The Passing of Arthur', 26). The pattern is emphasized by the constant attachment of beast images to characters representing threats to his humanizing programme. Edyrn begins by leading the life of a 'wolf'; Balin at first has a 'rough beast' on his shield; Vivien is associated with a snake, a rat, a worm, and a kitten; Pelleas and Gawain are both compared to dogs; Modred is 'like a subtle beast' (i.e. the snake in the Garden of Eden) and also like a 'green caterpillar'; and Tristram, 'from ever harrying wild beasts', is 'grown wild beast' himself.

A method of reconciling retrogression with a hope of long-term progress was suggested by Julius Hare in the 1866 edition (which Tennyson possessed) of *Guesses at Truth* (pp. 302-9). After describing as 'baseless and delusive' the 'vulgar notion of the march of mind, as necessarily exhibiting a steady, regular advance, within the same nation, in all things', he concluded that 'it is only when applied on the widest scale to the whole human race, that there is the slightest truth in the doctrine of the perfectibility, or rather of the progressiveness of man'. All experience of history showed rather his 'corruptibility', and the inevitable decline and fall of every human civilization: 'The natural life of nations, as well as of individuals, has its fixed course and term. It springs forth, grows up, reaches its maturity, decays, perishes. Only through Christianity has a nation ever risen again.'

The hope of such an ultimate resurrection is expressed by Bedivere's doubtful faith that Arthur 'comes again' ('The Passing of Arthur', 451); for the rest, the *Idylls* conform to Hare's prescription for poetry: 'epic poetry delights chiefly to dwell on the glories and fall of a nobler bygone generation.'

Apart from its general statement that everything is getting worse, the poem also comments on some individual features of the age. The Oxford Movement which began in 1833; Newman's conversion to Roman Catholicism (1845); the so-called 'Papal Aggression' of 1850, when a Roman Catholic hierarchy was established in England under Cardinal Wiseman; and the anti-liberal pronouncements of Pope Pius IX from 1864 onwards are all obliquely criticized in the character of King Pellam ('Balin and Balan', 1-116), a 'Christless foe' of King Arthur, who becomes a religious fanatic and collects large numbers of holy relics, but is totally untrustworthy, and closely associated with the murderous Garlon and the slanderous harlot, Vivien. A similar condemnation of Roman Catholicism and Anglo-Catholicism is implied by Arthur's comment on the effects of the quest for the Holy Grail. In his view, concentration on private religious experience, 'leaving human wrongs to right themselves', is a dereliction of duty ('The Holy Grail', 884-905). Here King Arthur is a good Evangelical, if not, like Newman's critic, Charles Kingsley, a Christian Socialist; but he also shares with Tennyson himself the trance-like states in which

> this earth he walks on seems not earth,
> This light that strikes his eyeball is not light,
> This air that strikes his forehead is not air
> But vision – yea, his very hand and foot –
> In moments when he feels he cannot die,
> And knows himself no vision to himself,
> Nor the high God a vision, nor the One
> Who rose again . . . . (908-15)

The first two lines that Tennyson wrote of 'Guinevere' date from the year in which the Divorce Courts were established (1857), and epitomize the sadness of divorce: 'But hither I shall never come again, Never lie by thy side; see thee no more – Farewell!' (575-7). The *Idyll* itself, where Arthur reproaches his wife for her adultery in terms that now seem intolerably self-pitying and self-righteous, was thought by Tennyson to be one of 'the finest things' he had written (*Reminiscence*, p. 187), and was much admired by his contemporaries. Modern readers may find it easier to enjoy the poem, if they see it as a first reaction to a momentous change in the nature of English society, and also as expressing a happily married man's revulsion from the idea of separation from his wife.

In 1856 Florence Nightingale returned from Scutari a national heroine, and Lewis Carroll wrote a poem in her honour, 'The Path of Roses', which contained a brilliant pastiche of 'The Two Voices'. In August 1857 Florence became an invalid, and in September Carroll met Tennyson, whom he described as 'a strange shaggy looking man', and had several conversations with him, on subjects ranging from *Maud* to 'the similarity of the monkey's skull to the human'. By November Florence was thought to be dying: she had a long conversation with Clough, arranging the details of her funeral, and wrote many letters 'to be sent when I am dead'. Tennyson doubtless heard of this from Clough, who since 1856 had been taking holidays at Freshwater, near Farringford. In July 1858 Tennyson started writing 'Elaine' (later 'Lancelot and Elaine'), a subject which his friend Thomas Woolner had urged him to tackle; but having recently conversed with the author of a poem in quasi-Tennysonian verse on Florence Nightingale, he must already have been struck by the curious coincidence that Elaine, like Florence, had nursed a wounded warrior, then fallen ill herself, made elaborate arrangements for her funeral, and written a letter to be read after her death. Arthurian legend thus gave him an opportunity to celebrate a heroic woman of his day, as he had celebrated male heroism in 'The Charge of the Light Brigade'.

Malory (XVIII, xv) had passed lightly over Elaine's nursing of Lancelot, making clear that she did it from purely amorous motives; but Tennyson makes her do it on principle:

> 'The gentler-born the maiden, the more bound,
> My father, to be sweet and serviceable
> To noble knights in sickness, as ye know,
> When these have worn their tokens. . . . '   (761-4)

Even more suggestive of Florence's triumph over the opposition of the doctors at Scutari is the passage where the medically expert hermit actually admits that Elaine's 'fine care' has 'saved' Lancelot's 'life' (856-8).

'Elaine' was published in June 1859. If it was intended as a delicate tribute to Florence Nightingale, it rather misfired. In January 1860 she published her *Notes on Nursing*, and Emily Tennyson immediately got a copy of it. There she found what must have read like a satire on her husband's poem:

> It seems a commonly received idea among men . . . that
> it requires nothing but a disappointment in love . . . to
> turn a woman into a good nurse . . . popular novelists of recent days
> have invented ladies disappointed in love . . . turning into the
> war-hospitals to find their wounded lovers, and when found,
> forthwith abandoning their sick-ward for their lover, as might be
> expected. Yet in the estimation of the authors, these ladies were
> none the worse for that, but on the contrary were heroines of
> nursing.

As if to prove that she was no Elaine, Florence remained alive for another fifty years.

III

'On Malory,' wrote Hallam Tennyson, 'on Layamon's *Brut*, on Lady Charlotte Guest's translation of the *Mabinogion*, on the old chronicles, on old French Romance, on Celtic folklore, and largely on his own imagination, my father founded his epic.' After extensive research, he strictly subordinated his narrative sources to his own purposes, taking what suited him, ignoring what did not, and creatively adapting any detail for which he could find a use.

The *Brut*, a Middle English verse history of England, which he read in Madden's edition, with a literal prose translation (1847), apparently suggested a parallel between the nativities of Arthur and Christ. Arthur is born at 'the time that was chosen', in fulfilment of a prophecy by Merlin, and is miraculously endowed by 'elves' with special virtues. His conception is also miraculous: Ygerne, his mother, lets Uther, his father, sleep with her, as he has been transformed by Merlin's magic into the image of her husband, Gorloïs. Zeus, the real father of Heracles, plays the same trick in the Amphitryon myth; and Tennyson's idea of making Arthur a partial analogue of Christ may have been encouraged by Layamon's nativity of Merlin (born to a nun impregnated by an incubus), by the Middle English spelling ('Nou was Arthur god king'), and by Madden's quotation from Giraldus Cambrensis: 'the Britons expect that Arthur will still come, just as the Jews expect their Messiah.' The chief function of the implied analogy is that in 'The Coming of Arthur' the doubts and disputes about Arthur's legitimacy come to symbolize the Victorian controversy about the truth of Christianity.

The *Mabinogion* served mainly to supply, in 'Geraint the Son of Erbin', the basis of 'The Marriage of Geraint' and 'Geraint and Enid'. Tennyson followed Lady Charlotte's version (1849 edition) quite closely, but improved the narrative technique, clarified the morality, and adapted the tale to fit into the total scheme of the *Idylls*. The literary changes include the substitution of the flash-back technique commended in Homer by Horace for the chronological order of the original, which starts *ab ovo* with an account of Arthur's court, listing the names of his eight porters, and then tells the story of Geraint's marriage to Enid, their estrangement, and their reconciliation. Tennyson begins with the events leading up to their estrangement, and then returns, via Geraint's harsh command to Enid to put on her 'worst and meanest dress', to his earlier, loving request that she should continue until their marriage to wear her 'faded silk' (130f, 760–2). The sadness of their estrangement is thus intensified by juxtaposition with the happiness of their first love.

The morality is clarified by making Enid's father the innocent victim of the wicked Edyrn, whereas in the original he was the first transgressor, by trying to cheat his nephew out of his property. The tale is fitted into the *Idylls* by attributing Geraint's suspicion of his wife to rumours of Guinevere's adultery ('The Marriage of Geraint', 24–32); by inserting Arthur's speech about the genuineness of Edyrn's repentance ('Geraint and Enid', 887–918), which shows the trustfulness of Arthur's character, while suggesting that his trust in Lancelot and Guinevere may be misplaced; and by the imaginative use of a seemingly pointless episode which concludes the story in the *Mabinogion*. There Geraint has to find his way through a hedge of mist, and after fighting with a mysterious knight, to blow a horn, whereupon 'the mist vanished . . . and all became reconciled to one another'. The hedge of mist is transformed (with the help of Lucretius and St Paul) into an image for Geraint's earlier state of delusion, and for one of the whole poem's central themes, the confusion of truth with falsehood:

> O purblind race of miserable men,
> How many among us at this very hour
> Do forge a life-long trouble for ourselves,
> By taking true for false, or false for true;
> Here, through the feeble twilight of this world
> Groping . . . .   ('Geraint and Enid', 1-6)

The oldest of the 'old chronicles', Nennius' *Historia Britonum* (early ninth century), provided the details of Arthur's 'glorious wars' ('Lancelot and Elaine', 284–309); but the gloss that appears in some thirteenth-century manuscripts of it, stating that Arthur was 'cruel from his boyhood', was naturally ignored. Geoffrey of Monmouth's *Historia Regum Britanniae* (twelfth century), which began the process of romanticizing the historical Arthur, seems to have had little effect on the story of the *Idylls*, apart from giving 'historical' authority for suppressing Malory's statement that Modred was Arthur's son by his own sister. Another of Geoffrey's works, however, recording 'the prophecies of Merlin', was owned by Tennyson, and contributed interestingly to his poem. The prophecy that under the heathen Saxons the British 'mountains' shall 'be levelled as the valleys' (translation of 1842) is given a new meaning when Merlin is muttering under his breath about Vivien's habit of projecting her own weaknesses on others:

157

And they, sweet soul, that most impute a crime
Are pronest to it, and impute themselves,
Wanting the mental range; or low desire
Not to feel lowest makes them level all:
Yea, they would pare the mountain to the plain,
And leave an equal baseness.   ('Merlin and Vivien', 823-8)

Similarly the prophecy that Arthur's 'death will be doubtful' develops deeper significance when dying Arthur says: 'all my mind is clouded with a doubt' ('The Passing of Arthur', 426). In some notes for the *Idylls* (Cambridge University Library) Tennyson copied out not only this prophecy, but also a story from another twelfth-century chronicler, Giraldus Cambrensis, who claimed to have witnessed the discovery of the bones of Arthur and Guinevere at Glastonbury, which he identified with the 'insula Avallonia' ('the island-valley of Avilion'). Among the female bones was found, intact, a tress of golden hair; but 'when a monk laid greedy hands on it, and picked it up, it all immediately fell into dust'. The story merged in Tennyson's mind with a rather similar story told in 1840 about the opening of an Etruscan tomb, to produce the passage in 'The Holy Grail' (379-439) where Percivale, before he becomes a monk, sees a series of objects, including a woman who opens her arms to meet him, 'fall into dust'.

In 'old French Romance' (which he probably met first in the extracts quoted by Southey in his edition of Malory) Tennyson found, besides the story of the two Guineveres, further encouragement to make Arthur typify Christ, in the statement that Ygerne was 'la plus belle Crestienne qui jamais fut cree apres la Vierge Marie', and support for the truth-falsehood theme in the interpretation of 'Excalibur' as 'il vrai'; but the chief thing he took from this source was the picture of Vivien as a thoroughly evil character. In Malory (IV, i) Nimuë imprisons Merlin under 'a great stone' partly in self-defence, because he always 'lay about the lady for to have her maidenhead', and partly in fear of him 'because he was a devil's son'. In the *Merlin* Romance, however, she is treacherous and vindictive: Southey quotes her as justifying her action on the grounds that Merlin's gossip has made Morgain call her 'harlot', the word which in 'Merlin and Vivien' (829-43) makes her stand 'Stiff as a viper frozen'. The snake imagery attached to her by Tennyson comes from her boast, in one of Southey's extracts, that she is 'the white serpent' of which Merlin had prophesied; and her extraordinary writhings round Merlin (236-40) have been traced to their source in the illustration heading the relevant chapter in Southey's Malory, which shows a man trying to extricate himself from the coils of a huge snake with a scarf round its neck, and a tongue darting towards his face. This doubtless contributed to Tennyson's characterization of her as the incarnation of slander: the image of a sharp sword for a slanderous tongue is used by Lancelot to Pelleas ('Pelleas and Ettarre', 564–5). According to Hallam Tennyson, the Romance supplied the name 'Vivien', instead of 'Nimuë', which the poet first used; though Matthew Arnold had already called her 'Vivian' in 'Tristram and Iseult' (1852), which Tennyson possessed.

Tennyson's research into 'Celtic folklore' was far from superficial. He read about Welsh history and literature in such works as the *Myvyrian Archaiology of Wales* (1801) and E. Davies's *The Mythology and Rites of the British Druids* (1809); he made a tour of Wales in 1856, seeking out the local antiquarian wherever he went, and systematically picking his brains; and he learned enough Welsh to decipher such texts as Thomas Price's history of Wales, the *Hanes Cymru* (1842), the *Mabinogion*, and Llywarch Hen's elegy on the death of Geraint. In the *Myvyrian Archaiology* he was introduced to the *Triads,* one of which included Afallach (Avilion) among 'the three perpetual harmonies' of Britain, and possibly suggested the important music imagery of the *Idylls.* Davies's account of the 'Helio-Arkite' religion probably explains why Vivien is a sun-worshipper ('Balin and Balan', 433–53); and his quotations from Taliesin's poetry about Dylan (Son of the Sea) or Ail Ton (Son of the Wave), followed by mention of 'the Druidical opinion,that *fire* and *water* would, at some period, prevail over the world', may have resulted in the story of Arthur's appearance, as a naked baby, on a fiery wave ('The Coming of Arthur', 376–84). The wave was 'a ninth one' because 'Every ninth wave is supposed by the Welsh bards to be larger than those that go before' (*Eversley*), an idea corresponding to the Greek belief about the third wave (*trikumia*), used by Julius Hare in the passage already quoted from *Guesses at Truth*, along with the Roman *fluctus decumanus* (tenth wave), as an image for the 'epoch-making master-mind' which periodically appears to further human progress.

'Geraint and Enid' concludes with Geraint crowning 'A happy life with a fair death', as in some lines of Llywarch Hen which Tennyson translated in his preliminary notes for the *Idylls* (Cambridge University Library): 'in Longporth was slain Gerynt a man beloved . . . in Longporth where he was slain for Arthur, a man beloved . . . .' The last

159

phrase acquires special significance when read as a coda to a poem about a man who, because he distrusted his wife's love, made himself so un-lovable.

Arthur's birth and death are both marked by the gnomic statement, which was once intended to be used a third time, as the last line of the *Idylls* ('The Coming of Arthur', 410; 'The Passing of Arthur', 445; *Poems*, p. 1754): 'From the great deep to the great deep he goes'. Here Tennyson epitomizes a 'Bardic system' explained in the notes to Southey's *Madoc*, in which all 'Animated Beings' progress from 'the Circle of Inchoation' 'in the Great Deep', through the Circle of 'Liberty in the State of Humanity', to 'the Circle of Happiness' in Heaven.

From Malory's *Le Morte d'Arthur* (which he probably read first in Wilks's bowdlerized text of 1816, and later studied in Walker's unex-purgated edition of the same year, a present from Leigh Hunt in 1835) Tennyson took the main outline of his narrative, and a few of his finest verbal effects, e.g. Gareth's controlled response to Lynette's sneers: 'I shall assay' ('Gareth and Lynette', 763), the eerie description of the castle of Carbonek ('The Holy Grail', 810-15), and the poignant bre-vity of the statement that the dead Elaine 'lay as though she smiled' ('Lancelot and Elaine', 1154). He rejected Malory's blow-by-blow accounts of tournaments and single combats, and all meaningless ele-ments of magic or the supernatural. Thus Balin's fratricide is related to a defect in his personality, not to his keeping a sword that is fated to kill the man he loves most in the world (II, ii); and his 'dolorous stroke', which in Malory (II, xv-vi) is inflicted on King Pellam, demolishing a castle and destroying three counties in the process, becomes, in Tenny-son's prose sketch for 'Balin and Balan' (*Memoir*, vol. 2, pp. 134-41), the stroke with which Balin kills his brother, 'which first shook to its base the stately order of the Table Round'.

Malory is full of humour, often fairly crude, as when Lancelot, during a siesta designed to build up his strength before an important tournament, is accidentally shot in the buttock by an incompetent huntress, so that he cannot sit in a saddle; or when he innocently goes to sleep in what turns out to be a young lady's bed, and awakes to feel her lover's 'rough beard kissing him'. This type of humour is allowed into the *Idylls* when Sir Sagramore, like Pickwick, goes to bed in the wrong room by mistake, and sleeps all night 'A stainless man beside a stainless maid' ('Merlin and Vivien', 718-43); but the joke is functional in a condemnation of Vivien's habit of always thinking the worst of other people.

Since Tennyson had 'always pictured Arthur as the ideal man' (*Memoir*, vol. 2, p. 128) he overlooked much of his behaviour in Malory: his slaughter of 45,000 men in a single day; his responsibility for a massacre of innocents closely resembling Herod's; his failure on three separate occasions to intervene when Guinevere is going to be burnt alive; his encouragement of Tristram and Isoud's adultery; his fathering of an illegitimate son on 'Lionors, a passing fair damosel'; and his fathering of Modred by intercourse with another 'passing fair lady' which he takes to be merely adulterous, but finds to be also incestuous (I, xix–xx). The expurgation of this incident, which in Malory is the crime that causes his downfall, was condemned by Swinburne (1872) as removing 'the keystone of the whole building' and destroying 'the Hellenic dignity and significance' of the legend, by eliminating a tragic *hamartia* comparable to Oedipus' incest, or Agamemnon's sacrifice of Iphigenia.

Merlin's character is similarly improved: he is relieved of responsibility for the virtual rape of Ygerne, and converted from a would-be seducer of Vivien into a tired old man who, in a moment of weakness caused by deep depression, yields to her, not merely because he is physically excited by 'her touch', but because he is 'overtalked and over-worn' ('Merlin and Vivien', 938–64). Gareth, in Malory, marries Lynette's sister, having tried 'to abate' his 'hot lusts' with her before the wedding. Lynette disapproves of such conduct and keeps interrupting them, for which Tennyson rewards her by making Gareth marry her instead. Malory's Elaine asks Lancelot to be her 'paramour' if he will not be her husba d: Tennyson's is content merely to 'follow' him 'through the world' ('Lancelot and Elaine', 932–4). Lancelot objects that this would only lead to scandal.

Two of Malory's characters are systematically devalued. Gawain, though explicitly contrasted by Malory with the honest Gareth, as being 'vengeable, and where he hated he would be avenged with murder' (VII, xxxiv), is turned against Lancelot by genuine grief for the death of his brother (XX, x), and before he dies, he writes Lancelot a magnanimous letter of apology (XXI, ii). Tennyson's Gawain has no redeeming qualities: he is nothing but a 'light-of-love', 'Light . . . in life, and light in death' ('Pelleas and Ettarre', 353; 'The Passing of Arthur', 56). Malory's Tristram is a brave, courteous, generous and scrupulously chivalrous character, whose life-long love of Isoud is caused by a potion that he drinks with her before she marries his uncle, Mark; whose own marriage to Isoud of Brittany is never consummated, because on the wedding-night he remembers his first love, and is suddenly 'all dismayed' (VIII, xxxvi); and who, when murdered by 'that traitor king', Mark, is lamented by 'every knight that ever were in Arthur's days' (XIX, xi). Tennyson suppresses the story of the potion, and makes Tristram a heartless cynic and philanderer, who threatens, if only in jest, to strangle Isolt if she acts on his own ethic ('Free love - free field - we love but while we may'), and regards 'the vows', which are the basis of Arthur's attempt to improve human nature, as 'the wholesome madness of an hour' ('The Last Tournament', 712; 275; 649-94). He represents, in the *Idylls,* the greatest threat to Arthur's aspirations, and the forces in Victorian society and thought which Tennyson thought most inimical to spiritual progress.

Other features of Malory that he adapted less radically, but most effectively, to his own purposes include two passages (XIX, i; XX, i) linking human affairs with seasonal change, which are developed into the symbolic time-scheme of the *Idylls*, starting at 'the New Year' and ending 'at midnight in mid-winter' (*Eversley*); the image of Fortune's Wheel (XX, xvii; XXI, iii), which is the subject of Enid's song ('The Marriage of Geraint', 345-58) and underlies the cyclic pattern of the whole poem; and the story of the Red Knight (VII, xiii-xvii), who explains his bad behaviour as caused by love of 'a fair damosel'. Tennyson attributes his own Red Knight's savagery to bitter disillusionment about love, and about the ideals of the Round Table, caused by Pelleas's experience with Ettarre and Gawain, a quite different story in Malory (IV, xxi-iii). There Pelleas is consoled by 'the damosel of the lake', and lives happily with her ever after. Tennyson's method of ending the story, with Pelleas 'reeling back into the beast' and becoming the Red Knight, seems rather more plausible.

In spite of its title, the climax of *Le Morte d'Arthur* is the ascent of the sinful Lancelot into heaven, first announced by the Bishop's 'great laughter' in his sleep. Then follows a glowing obituary from Sir Ector, and Lancelot's funeral (rather as the *Iliad* ends with the funeral of Hector). In writing a poem that really centred on Arthur, Tennyson was handicapped by the need to substitute for the moving last farewell of the guilty lovers (XXI, ix-x) a farewell scene between an injured husband and a penitent wife; and to end with the picture, not of a warm, human character, but of 'ideal man'. He brilliantly overcame the latter handicap, and humanized his superhuman hero at his death, if not always in his life, by making him, like Socrates (and Oscar Wilde's Ernest), know that he knows nothing:

'But now farewell. I am going a long way
With these thou seëst – if indeed I go
(For all my mind is clouded with a doubt) – '
                              ('The Passing of Arthur', 424–6)

IV

Virgil and Milton wrote first pastoral, and then epic. Tennyson, wish-ing to follow their example, was probably encouraged by the upsurge of interest in Homer which began in the 1840s, became conspicuous by 1857, when a reviewer in *Blackwood's* wrote that Homer was 'in danger of becoming the fashion', and culminated in Matthew Arnold's *On Translating Homer* (1861), the immediate cause of Tennyson's 'Speci-men of a Translation of the Iliad in Blank Verse' (1863). The fashion originated in the controversy provoked by Wolf's suggestion (1795) that Homer was not a single poet, but merely the name for a compila-tion of numerous short poems, preserved by oral recitation, and rather inadequately unified by later editors: a view developed by Lachmann, and attacked by Gladstone in the *Quarterly Review* (1847). The Homer boom resulted in unprecedented numbers of articles on Homer and Homeric translation, and of English versions in a variety of styles and metres. Other products were Clough's mock-Homeric *The Bothie of Tober-na-Fousich* (1848), and Matthew Arnold's 'Sohrab and Rustum' (1853), subtitled 'An Episode', Aristotle's term for self-contained sections of Homeric epic. Bulwer Lytton's *King Arthur: An Epic Poem* (1848–9) tried to cash in on the vogue, but was really mock-Arthurian and quite un-Homeric, being written in the metre of *Venus and Adonis*, and in a flippant style sometimes resembling that of Byron's *Don Juan*, as when Gawaine, about to be roasted and eaten by the goddess Freya, appeals to the Utilitarian criterion: 'THE GREATEST PLEASURE OF THE GREATEST NUMBER.'

Tennyson, of course, wished to write a classical, not a Lyttonian epic. The *Idylls* were to resemble the *Iliad* in relating the fall of a great city and civilization, the *Aeneid* in presenting a hero with a divine, historic mission threatened by the woman that he loves (Dido, Guinevere), and *Paradise Lost* in explaining the loss of ideal happiness through sin and disobedience.

'Homeric echoes' came first. Wolf's theory suggested that an epic could be gradually assembled from a number of short, self-contained poems (Lachmann's *kleinlieder*), a process begun with 'Morte d'Arthur'; and a notebook apparently dating from the 1830s (Harvard) shows Tennyson trying on, as it were, the singing-robes of the Homeric bard. It contains six lines of Homeric Greek hexameters, and an uncompleted seventh crossed out, as if in the process of composition. The subject is the spell-binding effect on his audience of the bard Demodokos, who is asked to sing what he has 'heard of the deeds and sufferings of Odysseus on the wide sea'. Demodokos, most of the phraseology, and two complete lines come from the *Odyssey*; but the passage itself appears nowhere in Homer. It was not until this century that the function of Homeric 'formulas' (prefabricated chunks of metrical language which could be used for a number of different contexts) began to be understood by scholars, as an aid to oral improvisation. Tennyson, however, seems already to have grasped the principle, and to have cast himself in the role of an oral poet, holding a live audience enthralled by his extempore story-telling, as he had done in his youth at Somersby, and again at Cambridge. The conception appears in the *Idylls* in such phrases as 'he that tells the tale' ('Geraint and Enid', 161), and in the recurrent use of quasi-Homeric repeated lines and phrases.

Perhaps the most striking of the many Homeric echoes in the *Idylls* is the final battle in the mist, in which 'friend slew friend not knowing whom he slew' and the fallen 'Looked up for heaven, and only saw the mist' ('The Passing of Arthur', 95–117). Though it recalls, like Arnold's 'Dover Beach' and Clough's *The Bothie* (ix, 51–4), the night-battle in Thucydides vii, the fighting in a mist, the looking up to heaven, and the 'cryings for the light' are primarily modelled on a passage in the *Iliad* (xvii, 645–7) which Longinus quoted as an instance of the sublime. There Ajax prays to Zeus to disperse the mist, and 'kill us in the light'. His prayer, unlike those of Arthur's knights, is answered.

Virgil and Milton also contributed numerous details; but the most important influence on the final literary form of the *Idylls*, as implied by their title, was Theocritus.

His contemporary, Callimachus, thought it anachronistic, in the urban, cosmopolitan, and literary society of Alexandria, to imitate the long Homeric epic, and declared 'a great book is a great evil'. Here he disagreed with another contemporary, Apollonius Rhodius, who wrote a four-volume epic, the *Argonautica*. Theocritus, however, took the same line as Callimachus, and preferred to write only short poems, with a strong descriptive and pictorial element, and a highly wrought style. Of his four works in this mini-epic genre (*Idylls* xiii, xxii, xxiv,

xxv) three relate to Heracles, and as Andrew Lang observed (1880), 'it
is not impossible that Theocritus wrote, or contemplated writing, a
Heraclean epic, in a series of idyls'. This was Tennyson's final model.
Rejecting as cacophonous Edmund Lushington's title, 'Epylls of the
King' (*Memoir*, vol. 2, p. 130), he adopted the name of Theocritus's
poems, retaining the Greek double l, to distinguish it from his own, and
Theocritus' pastorals, and pronouncing the *i* as in *idle*, according to the
current pronunciation of the initial *ei* in the Greek *eidullion*, doubtless to
stress the word's meaning (a little picture), and its reference to Theocritus. He rephrased Callimachus' epigram ('I thought that a small
vessel, built on fine lines, is likely to float further down the stream of
Time than a big raft'; *Eversley*), and composed a modern equivalent of
Theocritus' *Heracleid*. In his edition of Malory, Southey had twice
pointed out the similarity between the myths of Heracles and of Arthur,
both of whom were born as a result of supernaturally disguised adultery, were successful in twelve great ordeals, and died in consequence of
their wives' sexual attractions. Theocritan influence on the text itself is
most clearly visible in the image used to describe Geraint's muscles
('The Marriage of Geraint', 76-8), which comes from *Idyll* xxii, 48-50,
and in the curious picture of Balin and Balan sitting beside a fountain
('Balin and Balan', 21-9), which is modelled, like several features in the
following passage, on lines 34-106 of the same *Idyll*.

The influence of classical epic combined with that of mediaeval
Welsh poetry. In his book on the Druids, Davies had written:

> Amongst the most curious remains of the old Bards, we may class
> those metrical sentences, called *tribanau*, or *triplets*. . . . The most
> singular feature of these versicles is, that the sense of the first two
> verses has no *obvious* connection with that of the last. The first line
> contains some trivial remark, suggested by the state of the air . . . or
> the like. To this is frequently subjoined, something that savours
> more of reflection; then the third line comes home to the heart,
> with a weighty moral precept, or a pertinent remark upon men and
> manners (p. 77).

One such *triplet* was translated as follows: 'It rains without, and here is a
shelter – What! the yellow furze, or the rotten hedge! Creating God!
why hast thou formed the slothful!' (p. 76). Merlin's 'riddling' rhymes
in 'The Coming of Arthur' (402-10) are an accurate imitation of this
ancient form:

> 'Rain, rain, and sun! a rainbow on the lea!
> And truth is this to me, and that to thee;
> And truth or clothed or naked let it be.

The content of the second line was apparently suggested by a poem of Taliesin, on which Davies commented: 'He seems to say – Though one may be right, it does not follow that the person who thinks differently must be wrong' (p.525); and Davies's remark that *'three* was a sacred and mystical number amongst the Druids' (p.79) probably explains the use of a three-line stanza for the songs included in seven of the *Idylls*.

V

'Poets are wrong', said Aristotle, 'who write *Heracleids, Theseids* and so on, under the impression that because Heracles was one man, their plot will be automatically unified' (*Poetics*, viii). He had just explained that a poetic action must have 'a beginning, a middle, and an end', and went on to suggest the desirability, in epic as well as tragedy, of a plot containing *peripeteia* (reversal) and *anagnorisis* (recognition). Dr Tennyson's library included a copy of the *Poetics*, and the poet followed Aristotle's prescription in the *Idylls*. Between his 'beginning' ('The Coming of Arthur') and his 'end' ('The Passing of Arthur') he placed ten *Idylls* under the general title of 'THE ROUND TABLE'. By presenting his 'middle' as a circle, he almost invited the reader to see these *Idylls* as a revolving Wheel of Fortune, on which Arthur is first raised, and then, as in his fearful dream in Malory (XXI, iii), flung down into 'an hideous deep black water', full of 'serpents, and worms, and wild beasts, foul and horrible'. Thus the whole central action is a large-scale *peripeteia* (literally a 'falling round'), and Guinevere, at the end, has her own personal *peripeteia* combined with an *anagnorisis*, when, having rejected Arthur as insufficiently human, she recognizes too late that he, not Lancelot, is the man she loves, because he is 'the highest and most human too' ('Guinevere', 644). 'Tragedy tries to keep within a single revolution of the sun' (*Poetics*, v). Tennyson applies the idea imaginatvely to the patterning of his epic. In 'Gareth and Lynette' human life is pictured in terms of a single day, both in the names of the knights to be overcome, 'Morning-Star', 'Noon-Sun', 'Evening Star', and 'Night' or 'Death' (619–23), and in the rock-engravings: 'Phosphorus', 'Meridies', 'Hesperus', 'Nox', 'Mors' (1174–5); and the same symbolism is implied in the structure of the whole poem. In 'The Coming of Arthur' (99) he can see 'even in high-day the morning star'; twilight is falling when the last battle ends, and he dies at midnight. Parallel to the diurnal time-scheme is the annual one already mentioned, beginning on New Year's Day and ending in mid-winter.

Within these unifying patterns of narrative are many unifying patterns of theme and image. The man-beast theme outlined earlier appears first ('The Coming of Arthur', 10-25) in conjunction with a garden-wilderness image: Arthur's cultural experiment is a garden created in a vast expanse of wild country, and always liable to be invaded or overgrown by nature in the raw. The image, which may perhaps be traced to Tennyson's gardening activities at Farringford, and to Horace's gardening metaphor 'you may expel nature with a fork, but it will keep on coming back', anticipates Thomas Huxley's use of it in *Evolution and Ethics* (1894) to express the eternal opposition between the 'cosmic' and the 'ethical process'.

Equally pervasive is the truth-falsehood theme, which includes the sense of fidelity versus treachery. In the first sense it is initially concerned with the problem of discovering the truth about Arthur's origin: is he legitimate or illegitimate, a true king or a false one? In the second, it appears from the outset in the contrast between Arthur's trust in Lancelot ('The Coming of Arthur', 129-33) and Lancelot's disloyalty. In 'The Passing of Arthur' the king, dying because of Modred's treachery, calls even Bedivere 'untrue', while Bedivere sees that 'the true old times are dead'; and death comes without bringing either of them any certainty of the truth. Between the first *Idyll* and the last, the theme may be traced through a highly inventive series of variations.

The epistemological aspect of the truth-falsehood theme is frequently expressed by the image of mist. Doubts about Arthur's authenticity are seen in Leodogran's dream ('The Coming of Arthur', 424-45) as a 'haze' that partially conceals 'a phantom king'; and Camelot is first glimpsed only fleetingly 'through the mist' ('Gareth and Lynette', 184-93). Guinevere's last sight of Arthur is again of a 'phantom' king disappearing into the mist ('Guinevere', 596-601); the final battle is fought in 'a deathwhite mist', and Arthur dies with his whole mind 'clouded with a doubt' ('The Passing of Arthur', 95, 426).

The whiteness of the mist associated with Arthur and his whole enterprise connects with a pattern of colour imagery, in which white represents the eternal. Plato (*Phaedrus*, 247) had called the eternal reality 'colourless', and Shelley had developed the idea (*Adonais*): 'Life, like a dome of many-coloured glass, Stains the white radiance of Eternity', and Browning, in 'Numpholeptos' (1876), made elaborate symbolic use of the prism. Similarly, in the *Idylls* the Lady of the Lake, who, as Tennyson observed (*Eversley*) 'in the old legends is the Church', and is associated with Christ ('The Coming of Arthur', 290-3), wears 'white samite, mystic, wonderful', and the female spectators of the Tournament of the Dead Innocence are 'white-robed'; but their haste to revert to multi-coloured clothes immediately afterwards ('The Last Tournament', 147, 216-39) symbolizes the general reversion to purely earthly values which, in connection with Tristram and the Red Knight, culminates in a horrible cataclysm of redness ('The Last Tournament', 406-87). The pattern concludes with Guinevere's realization that, although she had turned from Arthur to Lancelot in search of 'warmth and colour', saying 'The low sun makes the colour', the 'highest' could also be 'most human' ('Lancelot and Elaine', 120-34, 'Guinevere', 633-56).

The most important unifying image, however, is that of music. It evidently arose from thoughts of the Homeric poet-harper Demodocus, the myth of Orpheus, and musical delights which, in the Charlemagne romances, make Avalon like a paradise for Ogier and for Arthur. In notebooks of Tennyson's Cambridge period, now at Harvard, he copied extracts relating to all these topics, including eighteen lines from the Middle English romance *Sir Orfeo*, and also attempted to draw a flute, a harp, and a violin. Though 'not thought to have an ear for music', he loved Mozart, and at Cambridge 'played himself a little on the flute' (*Memoir*, vol. 1, p.77). Thus at an early stage the idea of music was associated for him with Arthur, especially as the constellation Lyra was also called 'Arthur's harp' ('Gareth and Lynette', 1281).

To summarize briefly the ubiquitous music symbolism of the *Idylls*: Arthur's attempt to 'manufacture Cosmos out of Chaos' (to adapt Carlyle's metaphor for Tennyson's own poetic attempts in 1844) is seen as the creation of music out of discord, an insubstantial and precarious balance of conflicting forces, which has to be constantly recreated. Thus Camelot (as in the Amphion myth) is 'built To music, therefore never built at all, And therefore built for ever' ('Gareth and Lynette', 371-4). 'Arthur's music' is gradually silenced by such disruptive elements as Vivien, herself the 'little rift within the lute' of her own song ('Merlin and Vivien', 387-90), and Tristram, the 'false harper', who substitutes an ugly music of his own, itself 'broken' when Mark murders him ('The Last Tournament', 260-84, 724-48). In each of the first eleven *Idylls* except 'Geraint and Enid' (which was originally only half of 'Enid', separated from the other half in 1873) there is a song: in 'The Passing of Arthur' the music has ceased, but for the wailing from his barge, as it floats away, 'like some full-breasted swan . . . fluting a wild carol ere her death' (433–40).

VI

Written over half a lifetime, *Idylls of the King* has the massive grandeur of a Gothic cathedral (as his architect friend Knowles suggested) along with its inequalities. It contains much of his finest verse; intellectually, it is a brilliant synthesis of classical epic, mediaeval legend, and personal reactions to the life and thought of his age; and it is only because of the modern reluctance to read any long poem as a whole, and to take any ethic seriously which cannot readily be squared with the doctrines of Freudian, Jungian or Behavioural psychology, that the impressiveness of Tennyson's achievement is not yet widely recognized. As a powerful image to remind us what very thin ice all civilization rests on, the poem has a permanent value; and while we may not share its attitude to sex, we can hardly pretend that its warning against the social dangers of hypocrisy, so necessary in his period, is wholly irrelevant in ours.

10

Later Works

Arguing that Homer composed the *Iliad* before the *Odyssey*, Longinus called the former mainly dramatic, the latter mainly narrative, 'which is typical of old age'. Dobell described Tennyson as a man who looked as if he might quite well have written the *Iliad*, but his later career hardly corresponded with that of Longinus' Homer. The work produced during the last thirty-five years of his life certainly included, besides the *Idylls of the King*, many purely narrative poems; but it also included, in addition to some brilliant metrical experiments and a few of his finest lyrics, seven stage plays, and numerous dramatic monologues.

II

Encouraged, no doubt, by the example of Clough, who had spent a great deal of time devising English equivalents for Horace's lyric metres and for Homer's hexameters, and provoked by Arnold's lumbering hexameter translations from the *Iliad* (1861), Tennyson published (1863) 'Attempts at Classic Metres in Quantity'. The best was 'Hendecasyllables', which, while displaying his mastery of Catullus' 'dainty metre' (14), subtly suggested that his exasperation with those 'ninnies of critics', as he called them (Lewis Carroll, *Diaries,* ed. R. L. Green, 1953, p. 126), was quite violent enough to justify an attack as obscenely abusive as Catullus xvi, an outburst of rage against his critics Aurelius and Furius. Equally suggestive was the imitation of the metre of Catullus lxiii in 'Boädicea' (1864). Catullus' poem describes how a young man turns himself, by castration, into 'a bastard woman': Tennyson's barbarous heroine has been turned by anger into a virago, who denounces the 'tender effeminacy' (62) of the Roman males, and wants

170

the Roman females made to look as unfeminine as herself: 'Chop the breasts from off the mother ...' (68). Though 'Boadicea was always a heroine of his' (*Materials*, vol. 2, p. 303), the poem, contemporaneous with several on the theme of forgiveness, seems designed to convey the ugliness of revenge.

Catullus' farewell to his dead brother (ci) and his delighted greeting ('Hail, beautiful Sirmio') to the small peninsula on which he had a villa (xxxi) combined with a visit to Sirmione (1880) to suggest a form of lament for Tennyson's brother Charles, 'Frater Ave atque Vale' (1883); and the tribute to the poet's first great literary model, 'Milton', was appropriately written in Alcaics, a metre in which Milton had composed a Latin ode at the age of sixteen. Another great model, Virgil, was celebrated (1882) in a metre clearly intended to recall that of Horace's *Ode* (I, iii) wishing Virgil a prosperous voyage to Greece.

Two other lyrics show the same fusion of the literary and the personal. 'Merlin and the Gleam' (1889), a cross between an *Odyssey* and a *Pilgrim's Progress*, incorporating Arthurian material, and in some respects resembling Arnold's *The Strayed Reveller* (1849), ambiguously allegorizes a retrospect of Tennyson's poetic career; and 'Crossing the Bar' (1889) perfectly epitomizes his final attitude to death, a mixture of fatalism, stoicism and doubtful optimism, through the image of starting a voyage into the unknown at evening. The poem is thus a natural sequel to 'Ulysses', written half a century before.

III

Tennyson's plays are a human, rather than a literary, triumph. One cannot help admiring the courage, energy, adaptability, and sheer intellectual power of a man who, starting virtually at sixty-five (since the early *The Devil and the Lady* was clearly not intended for the commercial stage), could acquire so much competence in an unfamiliar and technically difficult genre; but admiration for the playwright is not quite enough to make the plays really enjoyable. However, his three stage-successes deserve investigation.

The Falcon (produced 1879) was based, like 'The Lover's Tale' (published, after several piracies, the same year), on the *Decameron* (Day Five, Novella Nine). There a young nobleman, Federigo, having impoverished himself by extravagant efforts to win the love of Giovanna, is finally visited by her with a request for his one remaining treasure, his falcon, to satisfy a whim of her desperately ill son. Federigo has to tell her that she has already eaten the bird for lunch, as he had no other food to offer her. Coventry Patmore had versified the story in 'Sir Hubert' (1844), and Tennyson followed Patmore in romanticizing the whole sequence of events. Boccaccio's hero falls in love with a married woman, and tries to seduce her. She, being 'as chaste as she is beautiful', resists him, and finally marries him, when her husband and son are dead, not because she wants to, but because her brothers pester her to marry someone, and she recognizes Federigo's 'worth'. Patmore's never reveals his love until both husband and son are dead, and Mabel (Giovanna) practically proposes to him. Tennyson's falls in love with Giovanna when she is fifteen, but does not tell her so, or even start sending her anonymous presents, until she is already a widow. She returns his love, but dare not marry him, because of a 'feud between our houses' (*Oxford*, p. 716), as in *Romeo and Juliet*, and a brother, as in Keats's 'Isabella' (also from Boccaccio), who will not let her marry a poor man. Finally, however, her love overcomes her fear of her brother, and the one-scene play ends happily, with a prospect of recovery even for her sick son.

The Cup (1881) dramatizes a story in Plutarch's *The Virtues of Women* (xx) about a Galatian priestess of Artemis called Camma, who punishes her husband's murderer and her own would-be seducer, Sinorix, by pretending to accept his proposal of marriage, and then, as part of the wedding-ceremony, making him drink with her a cup of poison. Tennyson makes his villain a Galatian collaborating with the Roman occupying forces, an Epicurean, contemptuous of religion, and, by implication, a Victorian scientific materialist, when he speaks of a human embryo as 'a thread within the house of birth', and a Pateresque aesthetic philosopher, when he defines the function of 'the passions' as 'To warm the cold bounds of our dying life' (*Oxford*, p. 711; 707), or, as Pater put it (1879) to 'burn always with' a 'hard, gemlike flame' in 'this short day of frost and sun'.

The theatrical dénouement in the temple is prepared for by some effective touches of dramatic irony, as when Camma tells Synorix: 'I will be faithful to thee till thou die' (p. 711); and the two-act quasi-operatic melodrama concludes with the dying Camma employing the image of 'Crossing the Bar': 'I will go . . . On my last voyage . . .' (p. 713).

The historical basis of *Becket* (published 1884) seems to have come chiefly from conversations with J. R. Green, and from the first volume of his *History of the English People* (book 2, chapter 3), which Green gave Tennyson, presumably on publication (1877). This was the source of such details as Henry's restlessness: 'If I sit, I grow fat' (*Oxford*, p. 650), and Becket's reference to his own secular costume: 'Why – look – is this a sleeve For an archbishop?' (p. 649). The idea of interweaving Becket's historical career with the legend of Henry's mistress, Rosamond Clifford, had probably been suggested long before by George Darley's verse-play, *Thomas a Becket: A Dramatic Chronicle* (1840). According to Hallam Tennyson, the 'germ' of *Becket* was the lyrical monologue, 'Rosamund's Bower' (*Poems*, p. 735) 'written before 1842'. In his Preface Darley had pointed out the *'stage-effectiveness'* of Becket's character and fate, the dramatic possibilities of his having 'so precise a counterpoise' in the character of Henry II, and the advantage of acquiring, even by a slight anachronism, 'the interest of a gracious female character' (Rosamund). The play ends with the ghost of Rosamund appearing at the head of Becket's bier, and reproaching Queen Eleanor for having murdered her. *Becket*, while sharing with Darley's largely ridiculous melodrama several characters, features, and phrases, generally avoids its absurdities, but retains some traces of its 'stage-effects'. It ends, for instance, with 'flashes of lightning' (apparently historical) which show Rosamund 'kneeling by the body of Becket'.

Sir Richard Jebb, the editor of Sophocles, thought *Becket* 'a drama of great power, finely conceived and finely executed'. Judged by the non-realistic standards of Greek tragedy, the treatment of Becket's conflict with Henry justifies this verdict, and may be compared, in its basic conception, with Sophocles' *Antigone*, where a clash between religious and political convictions, both sincerely held and arguably right, causes the martyrdom of the protagonist. It may also be compared with T. S. Eliot's treatment of the same theme, *Murder in the Cathedral*, which probably owes its Four Tempters to the fourfold temptation scene in *Becket* (I, iii, *Oxford*, pp. 658-9).

Better than the plays are the dramatic poems. The argument between hope and despair in 'The Two Voices' is taken up again in 'The Ancient Sage' and 'Vastness' (1885). The former, somewhat similar in structure to Act II of Arnold's *Empedocles on Etna* (1852), is a dialogue between a cheerful old philosopher and a gloomy young sceptic recalling James Thomson's *The City of Dreadful Night* (1880), and, in his view of old age, Juvenal's *Satire* x. The old man's faith rests partly on such subjective experiences as Tennyson's 'Passion of the Past', and his mystical trances (212-39). 'Vastness' is a one-sided dialogue in which faith speaks only two lines, but has the last word. The pattern resembles Herbert's religious poem 'The Collar'.

The most interesting dramatic poems are the monologues. These include seven in Lincolnshire dialect, beginning with 'Northern Farmer, Old Style' (1864) and ending with 'The Church-Warden and the Curate' (1892). Founded on first-hand knowledge gained in Tennyson's youth at Somersby, with only minimal help from literature (he owned a copy of William Barnes's *Poems of Rural Life in the Dorset Dialect* (1847) which contained a lyrical monologue by a farmer, 'I got two viel's', and a dialogue about a 'sly wold feller, Farmer Tup'), these highly original poems show a capacity for humorous, subtle, realistic, and utterly unsentimental characterization. Perhaps the best is 'Owd Roä', in which a father tells his son how a dog rescued him as a baby from a burning house. In his enthusiastic tribute to the dog, the speaker unconsciously reveals himself as an affectionate father but completely callous husband, who let his wife catch ' 'er death o' cowd', while he was busy resuscitating the animal (113–14). The difficulty of mastering the dialect words and the phonetic spelling of these poems can be easily overcome in a very few minutes; the reward is a great deal of pleasure, and the discovery of a quite unexpected aspect of Tennyson's personality and talent.

The dialect poems often touch on tragedy obliquely, through humour; but in two other monologues the approach is grimly direct. 'Rizpah' (1880) is spoken by a dying working-class woman to a well-meaning but narrowly religious lady visitor, whom she receives with a convincing mixture of suspicion, fear, contempt, and imaginative sympathy. In a brief remission of delirium she recalls how her son was hanged for stealing 'one purse', and how she collected his bones one by one, as they fell from the gallows, and buried them 'by the churchyard wall'. The poem was a powerful protest against the social system, and also against the type of religion that emphasized sin and punishment, rather than 'compassion, mercy and long-suffering' (60–76). 'Despair' (1881), based, like 'Rizpah', on a real incident, is spoken by a man who has tried, with his wife, to commit suicide. She has been drowned, but he has been rescued 'by a minister of the sect he had abandoned', to whom the monologue is addressed. The man bitterly resents his rescue, and promises to 'escape' the minister 'at last', and kill himself properly. The poem, which vividly conveys the horror of the moment when husband and wife walk hand in hand into the sea, expresses Tennyson's dismay at the prevalence of two attitudes to religion which seemed equally productive of despair: agnosticism, and the type of Calvinism which pictured 'a God of eternal rage' (21–40).

IV

Longinus was right, however, to this extent: the most notable productions of Tennyson's later years were in narrative form. One group of
poems related, with great energy and an infectious sense of excitement,
historical feats of heroism ('The Revenge', 1878; 'The Defence of
Lucknow', 1879; 'The Charge of the Heavy Brigade at Balaclava',
1882). Another injected new meanings into classical myth. 'The Death
of Oenone' (1892), based on the sequel to Homer's epics written by
Quintus Smyrnaeus, probably in the fourth century AD, centres on
Oenone's remorse at having refused to forgive Paris immediately before
his death. Tennyson died with the works of Shakespeare in his hands,
and although he could no longer read, it was not accidental that the
book was open at *Cymbeline,* of which the final message is: 'Pardon's the
word to all'. 'Demeter and Persephone' (1889), based on the Homeric
Hymn to Demeter, makes Aeschylus' idea in *Prometheus Vinctus,* and
Keats's in 'Hyperion', that primitive gods are superseded by more
enlightened ones, carry the modern thought expressed in *Essays and
Reviews* (1860) that religions, like all living creatures, go through a
process of evolution (126–36).

'Lucretius' (1868), the most interesting poem in this group, has
several different levels of meaning. On the surface it is a tribute to one of
Tennyson's favourite poets, paid in the form of a brilliant pastiche of
Lucretius' style and content, authenticated by constant near-quotations
from the *De Rerum Natura.* At a deeper level, it is an oblique protest
against changing contemporary attitudes to sex: Lucretius' disgust at
the overpowering sexual urges which have been aroused in him by his
wife's 'philtre' is partly expressive of Tennyson's own distrust of sex (as
in 'The Vision of Sin', 1842), and of his sense that the human beings of
his period were 'reeling back into the beast': an image used by Lucretius
when he feels that 'some unseen monster lays His vast and filthy hands
upon my will, Wrenching it backward into his . . .' (219–21). This
protest is simultaneously concerned with questions of literary decorum.
Since his theme requires him to approach the pornographic in order to
make the reader feel Lucretius' sexual excitement, Tennyson does
approach it, but no more closely than this poetic purpose justifies. Here
he was probably reacting against what he thought the inartistic crude-
ness of Swinburne's handling of sex. According to Oscar Browning
(*Memories of Sixty Years,* London, 1910, p. 117) Tennyson once remarked, after reading the passage about the naked Oread (188–206):

'What a mess little Swinburne would have made of this!'

The poem also makes a political comment. Lucretius lived at a time when constitutional government by aristocrats or *optimates* (both words derive from words meaning 'the best') was being superseded by arbitrary dictatorships based on the power of the mob. This transfer of political authority from the best to the many was being repeated in Tennyson's own age, and he adapted the legend of Lucretius' suicide to symbolize the sinister aspect of democracy. Jerome's version of Eusebius' *Chronica* (fourth century AD) said merely that Lucretius had been sent mad by a love-potion, without mentioning how he came to drink it: Tennyson makes the poet's wife responsible. Mistakenly imagining that her 'master' has ceased to love her, she, 'wrathful, petulant', 'destroyed him' with a drug (1-23). It is the case of a stupid inferior frustrating the high purposes of a superior; and the analogy with the democratic process is deliberately emphasized by a simile (adapted from one in Keats's 'Hyperion', i, 227-58), comparing the baser thoughts intruding on Lucretius' mind because of his wife's action to 'crowds that in an hour Of civic tumult . . . throng, their rags and they The basest, far into that council-hall Where sit the best and stateliest of the land' (164-72). Thus 'Lucretius' implies what Arnold made explicit in *Culture and Anarchy* the following year: that we should be ruled by a government representing, not the 'ordinary self' of the 'Populace', but 'our best self '.

Finally there is a religious meaning. Tennyson ingeniously converts Lucretius from a denouncer of religion into an indirect defender of it, by making him realize that his view of the gods is inconsistent (113-16), and that his whole poem (which Jerome said was written 'in the intervals between fits of insanity') is, in its statements on religion at least, merely a product of mental confusion. He meant, he says, to prove 'That Gods there are, and deathless. Meant? I meant? I have forgotten what I meant: my mind Stumbles, and all my faculties are lamed' (116-23). There is also the implication (with reference to Lucretius' third book) that if there is no life after death, suicide is the only answer. As he told Knowles, without a belief in personal immortality he saw no point in living: 'I'd sink my head tonight in a chloroformed handkerchief and have done with it all')*Reminiscence*, p. 169).

In a class of its own is the semi-allegorical 'The Voyage of Maeldune' (1880). 'Founded on an Irish legend. A.D. 700', with touches derived from the *Odyssey* and from Lucian's *True History,* and a general pattern of frustration recalling the Prologue to William Morris's *The Earthly Paradise* (1868), it describes a fantastic voyage, undertaken to avenge a murder, and ending with the murderer left unpunished: 'I saw him and let him be' (128).

The theme of forgiveness is central in the first of three 'Idylls of the Hearth', 'Sea Dreams: An Idyll' (1860). The spelling of 'Idyll' in the subtitle evidently refers to the chief literary source, Theocritus *Idyll* xxi, about two poor fishermen sleeping in a hut by the sea. One dreams that he catches a golden fish, and decides in his dream to retire from fishing on the strength of it; but when he wakes up and tells his friend about it, he is given the sound advice: 'Keep on looking for fish of flesh, or you'll die of hunger, in spite of your golden dreams.' Tennyson translates this gold-flesh antithesis into something like 'don't think about money; think about people'.

The other literary source is Juvenal *Satire* xiii, an attempt to console a man for the loss of a large sum of money through the dishonesty of a trusted friend. The satirist argues, first, that the thief will be condemned and punished by his own conscience, and secondly that only a petty mind cares for revenge. The first argument is paraphrased in the poem (168-73); the second, in the form of a Christian plea for forgiveness, is the poem's chief moral.

The literary sources are cleverly combined with Tennyson's own experience of having been cheated out of £3,000 by Dr Allen. The poor fishermen become a poor city clerk, holidaying at the seaside with his wife and baby. The golden fish becomes a Peruvian gold-mine in which the clerk has been persuaded to invest his savings by an unkind carica-ture of Dr Allen. The dreams of husband and wife refer not only to the illusory gold, but also to the decline of Christianity in the period, imaged by the erosion of cathedral-like cliffs by the waves, and to the replacement of true Christianity (as in 'Rizpah' and 'Despair') by creeds that pictured God as a vindictive torturer (Tennyson's friend, F. D. Maurice, had been deprived of his Chair at King's College, London, in 1853 because he denied the doctrine of Eternal Punishment).

'Sea Dreams' is usually dismissed as sentimental, because of the 'baby song' with which it ends ('What does little birdie say?'); but this is entirely functional in the complex pattern of a poem which constructs, out of the most diverse materials, a parable of the Christian ethic, and appropriately ends with a reflected image of the *Sacra Famiglia*.

The two other 'Idylls of the Hearth', 'Aylmer's Field' and 'Enoch Arden' (1864), were based on stories written out for Tennyson by Thomas Woolner, 'The Sermon' and 'The Fisherman's Story', included in Amy Woolner's *Thomas Woolner* (1917, pp. 219-25, 208-12). The

177

East Anglian setting of both tales probably suggested Crabbe, whose 'hard pathos' Tennyson greatly admired (*Memoir,* vol. l, p. 210) as a literary model.

The first story is named from the funeral sermon 'preached at the burial of the only child of a wealthy Suffolk baronet', denouncing the 'pride and avarice' of her parents, which has caused her death and her lover's, in 'such a storm of passion' that the mother has a fit and dies a few days later, and the father becomes 'almost an imbecile' till his death. The Rector is thought of as the avenging angel to wreak judgment upon those hardhearted ones who caused all the desolation; but Tennyson rejects this idea. His Rector calls for pity, rather than vengeance, and makes the political point (the poem is subtitled '1793') that, considering the atrocities committed in the French Revolution, it is no time to excite popular anger against aristocratic oppression (751-83).

The influence of Crabbe shows itself in the moralizing introduction (as in 'Procrastination'), in the sharply ironical tone (especially in comments on the parents), in a verbal echo from 'Delay has danger' ('sickly sun', 30), and in the use of Biblical allusion. Just as Crabbe points the final moral of 'Procrastination' by incorporating a phrase from the parable of the Good Samaritan, Tennyson stresses the Christian moral of his poem by incorporating in the sermon the equivalent of the words on the Cross, 'forgive them, for they know not what they do' (782), and some words referring to Judas in the *Acts* (i, 18-20), which imply that Aylmer's Field is 'the field of blood', bought for 'thirty pieces of silver' (786, 846-53).

Another literary influence was Juvenal's *Satire* viii, an attack on pride of ancestry which is generally paraphrased by Leolin (381-86), and probably suggested (viii, 76-8) the image used to describe the mother's sudden collapse when her stronger husband shows signs of breaking down (806-11). Woolner's account of the young hero's hard work at studying law (which doubtless recalled Arthur Hallam's studies at Lincoln's Inn) seems also to have attracted certain features of Samuel Smiles's account in *Self-Help* (1859) of Lord Eldon's early life, which may also have suggested the reference to a 'blacksmith-border-marriage' (263).

Although the parents first appear as caricatures reminiscent of Sir Leicester Dedlock in Dickens's *Bleak House* (1852-3) and Lady Bertram in Jane Austen's *Mansfield Park* (1814), their reactions to the sermon are described most movingly, and so are the lovers' parting and period of separation. In spite of some laboured rhetoric, and some excessive efforts to make the prosaic poetical, 'Aylmer's Field' remains a most impressive performance, which successfully conveys Tennyson's passionate indignation at the thought of young love being thwarted by parental 'pride and avarice'.

'The Fisherman's Story' gave Tennyson much more scope, since its parallels with the *Odyssey* allowed him to give it the character of a mini-epic. If Odysseus had come home after twenty years to find Penelope married, he would probably have killed the adulterous pair with the same sense of conscious virtue as that with which he killed the suitors; but perhaps a modern 'strong heroic soul' ('Enoch Arden', 909) would feel morally compelled to do otherwise?

Tennyson deliberately increased his 'Fisherman's' resemblance to Odysseus, by supplying equivalents of several features in the Homeric narrative. Odysseus is brought home to the harbour from which he sailed, with a number of presents from his recent host: Enoch is given money by the officers and men of the ship that lands him there. Odysseus is then surrounded by a mist (*Odyssey*, xiii, 189): so is Enoch with a 'sea-haze' (666-77). As Penelope at last embraces Odysseus, her joy is compared to that of shipwrecked men, swimming for their lives, at the first sight and touch of land (xxiii, 233-40): Enoch, instead of embracing his Annie, welcomes death as gladly as a 'stranded wreck' welcomes the sight of a life-boat (824-8). Odysseus is told by Teiresias (xi, 134-6) that death will come to him 'from the sea', when he is surrounded by prosperous people: Enoch dies in poverty, though his wife is well-off, after hearing a loud 'calling of the sea' (904). Enoch's association with Odysseus is further stressed when he tells Miriam Lane: 'let me hold my purpose till I die' (871), recalling the words of 'Ulysses' (59-61): 'my purpose holds To sail beyond the sunset. . . until I die'.

Since Enoch is a hero of a Christian, not a pagan, stage of human history, his name connects him with Shakespeare and the Bible. In *Genesis*, 'Enoch walked with God: and he was not; for God took him' (v, 24). The 'translation' of this God-fearing patriarch evidently suggested the idea of Annie's Bible-inspired dream, which she interprets as meaning that he is sitting happily in Heaven, though it really means that he is stuck on a South Sea island. This ironical use of extra-sensory perception, in which Tennyson believed, and which also figured in 'Aylmer's Field' (578-98), replaces Woolner's statement: 'no news whatever came of her husband, beyond the fact that the ship in which he was returning from China was wrecked in the Southern Seas, and all hands lost.'

A more significant association of Enoch Arden with the Bible is an implied resemblance to Christ. The vision of Annie with her new family through the window causes Enoch an 'agony in the garden' (754–87); his words to Miriam Lane, 'I am the man' (848), remind us of Pilate's words before the Crucifixion, 'Behold the man' (*John*, xix, 5); and Enoch's dying words and posture are clearly an allusion to Christ's (*Matthew*, xxvii, 50).

The theme of unintentional bigamy, with the awkward moral questions it raised, was popular in the 1850s and 1860s; but Tennyson probably began to think of it in connection with Crabbe's 'The Parting Hour' (1812), which seems to have contributed to *In Memoriam* (xli, 5–8). In this *Tale*, suggested by the adventures of Crabbe's brother William, the hero sets off for 'a Western Isle' in the hope of making enough money to marry his childhood sweetheart, having urged her not to be seduced by 'that fawning Philip' (the name of Annie Arden's second husband). She waits for ten years, then, being assured of her lover's death, marries someone else. When he finally returns, after forty years, having also married someone else in his travels, he finds his first love a widow, and they live together in a sad, but faithful, Platonic 'friendship'.

Crabbe's poem raises the moral, though not the legal, problems of the innocent bigamous marriage, and these are the problems handled in 'Enoch Arden'. Some reviewers were shocked by Tennyson's apparent willingness to condone bigamy, while modern readers tend to question whether Enoch's altruism was necessarily the right answer, or alternatively, whether it would not have been kinder to leave Annie believing that he had died long before her second marriage. The variety of possible reactions to the poem's moral line indicates Tennyson's success in presenting a type of problem which is true to life in the sense that it is impossible to solve satisfactorily.

Two features of the poem's admirable construction deserve notice, the use of dramatic irony, and the use of symbolic landscape. The three children, Enoch, Annie and Philip, play at first in a state of innocence, which foreshadows the complexities of their adult life, as when they play at 'keeping house': Enoch and Philip quarrel about whose 'wife' Annie shall be, and she promises to be a 'wife to both' (23–36). The three children playing house in a primal paradise, which already has its causes of discontent, point forward to the three shipwrecked men, Enoch and his two companions, keeping house in earnest, in another seaside cave, and living, 'ill-content', in an 'Eden of all plenteousness' on a lonely island 'in a lonely sea' (546–58). More subtly the 'yellow sands' on which the children play (2) recall Ariel's song of carefree enjoyment in *The Tempest* ('Come unto these yellow sands, And then take hands: Curtsied when you have, and kiss'd...'), with its funereal sequel ('Full fathom five thy father lies...Sea-nymphs hourly toll his knell'), suggesting what Annie will one day tell her children, and Enoch's 'costly funeral' (911).

This much ridiculed conclusion is, like that of 'Sea Dreams', entirely right in its context, rounding off the poem's epic character by echoing the last line of the *Iliad*, and also pointing the final irony. As Tennyson explained (*Eversley*), 'The costly funeral is all that poor Annie could do for him after he was gone. This is entirely introduced for her sake....' The absurdity of such gestures, whose only function is to relieve the feelings of the living, was perfectly clear to the poet. When his mother was buried, the year after 'Enoch Arden' was published, with 'a plain cross' marking her grave, he wrote: 'All of us hate the pompous funeral we have to join in, black plumes, black coaches and nonsense. We should like all to go in white and gold rather, but convention is against us' (*Memoir*, vol. 2, pp. 18–19). Thus the last two lines, by stressing the hideous sense of impotent guilt that Enoch's kindly-intended 'heroism' must have inflicted upon his wife, forces the sensitive reader to recognize the extreme complexity of the moral questions raised by the poem.

The symbolic landscape is depicted in the opening lines (1–9):

Long lines of cliff breaking have left a chasm;
And in the chasm are foam and yellow sands;
Beyond, red roofs about a narrow wharf
In cluster; then a mouldered church; and higher
A long street climbs to one tall-towered mill;
And high in heaven behind it a gray down
With Danish barrows; and a hazelwood,
By autumn nutters haunted, flourishes
Green in a cuplike hollow of the down.

A chasm between 'cliffs' which have been 'rent asunder' is the image used in Coleridge's 'Christabel' to describe how two close 'friends in youth' 'parted – ne'er to meet again!' (90–5); here it seems to objectify the 'putting asunder', not by man, but apparently by God, of a married couple (*Matthew*, xix, 6). The 'yellow sands', as already indicated, suggest kissing followed by death. Philip's mill is higher than 'the

181

mouldered church', because his marriage, which the outdated ecclesiastical ethic would condemn, is somehow sanctioned by a higher authority. The 'gray down' with its 'Danish barrows' hints at the miseries of human life and death as seen in perspective by a superhuman eye. The down becomes 'the waste' at the moment of his agonized renunciation of reunion with his wife and family (733); but this moment, for all its desolation, marks the highest point of his spiritual development.

The 'hazelwood' 'haunted by nutters' reminds us of Wordsworth's 'Nutting', which describes the poet's 'sense of pain' at having desecrated a hazelwood in his boyish egotism:

> Then up I rose,
> And dragged to earth both branch and bough, with crash
> And merciless ravage: and the shady nook
> Of hazels, and the green and mossy bower,
> Deformed and sullied, patiently gave up
> Their quiet being . . . .   (43–8)

It is when 'the younger people' are nutting that Philip sees Enoch and Annie 'sitting hand-in-hand', and, though heart-broken, 'Had his dark hour unseen', and made no attempt to desecrate the 'sacred fire' of their love (61–79). It is again when 'the younger ones' 'bent or broke The lithe reluctant boughs to tear away Their tawny clusters' that Philip makes his first proposal to Annie (374–418); but he still reverences the 'sacred fire' of her first love, and is careful not to 'break or bend' her 'reluctance'. At the climax of the poem it is Enoch's turn to refrain from 'merciless ravage'. He has his own 'dark hour unseen', and is equally careful not to 'shatter all the happiness of the hearth'. He holds a green 'branch', not of a hazel, but of a yew; not to drag it down, but to support himself through his ordeal of non-desecration (753–66).

While the hazelwood seems to represent the idea of self-denial and reverence for the divine element in human love, the 'cuplike hollow' in which it rests evidently serves to emphasize the parallel between Enoch's prayer after his agony in the garden ('Too hard to bear! . . . '), and the prayer in Gethsemane, 'let this cup pass from me' (774–82, *Matthew*, xxvi, 39).

'Enoch Arden' is frequently dismissed as a sentimental product of Tennyson's decline, too well adapted to the tastes of a lower-class reading public. It is really one of his great artistic achievements.

11

Reputation

'Modern fame is nothing . . . ,' said Tennyson in 1865. 'I shall go down, down! I am up now' (*Memoir*, vol. l, p. 513). Attached, like King Arthur in Malory, to a revolving Wheel of Fortune, he began at the very bottom (as far as the critics and general public were concerned), being regarded, poetically speaking, as a bastard. By 1843 he had swung up far enough for Nathaniel Hawthorne to use the word 'Tennysonian' as a term of praise. By 1865 he was indeed 'up', the acknowledged king of English poetry; but the downward swing described in Arthur's nightmare was just about to start, with Alfred Austin playing the part of Modred (1869). It was in the 1920s, after the publication of T. S. Eliot's *The Waste Land* (1922), that the wheel turned completely 'up so down', precipitating Tennyson into the 'hideous deep black water' of fashionable contempt, with every critic 'taking him by a limb'.

Having passed his nadir, he began to be carried very slowly upwards; and Harold Nicolson tried (1923) to accelerate this movement by jettisoning, as useless lumber, practically all of Tennyson's works except the short lyrics. The expedient worked so well that in 1946 W. H. Auden thought it prudent to throw out Tennyson's intellect too: 'He had the finest ear, perhaps, of any English poet; he was also undoubtedly the stupidest; there was little about melancholia that he didn't know; there was little else that he did.'

By then such desperate action was quite unnecessary. Common sense was already reasserting itself, with timely support from American scholars like W. D. Paden (1942), and later from Edgar Shannon and E. D. H. Johnson (1952).

In recent years, the two publications which have done most, by making the facts about Tennyson's life and poetry widely known, to raise his reputation, are the immensely informative and delightfully written biography by his grandson, Sir Charles Tennyson (1949), and the splendid annotated edition of the poems by Christopher Ricks (1969).

It is now no longer regarded as a sure sign of discriminating intelligence to sneer at Tennyson. He is being taken very seriously, like other Victorian writers, by academic critics, and 'the common reader' is once more at liberty to enjoy him without serious risk of being thought eccentric or hopelessly old-fashioned; but two factors still prevent him from standing quite as high in public estimation as he deserves. The first is the curious, but persistent, notion that we are a superior species to the Victorians (a notion often revealed in television interviews by the constant use of 'Victorian' as a general-purpose term of abuse). The second is inadequate understanding of the literary and historical context in which his poems were written. Great as he is, and much as he has to offer the modern reader, he is not a twentieth-century poet, either in his poetic method or in his manner of thought, and some recent critical attempts to turn him into one are merely misleading. By explaining in some detail how his poetry relates to previous literature, especially classical, to his own experience, and to the ideas and events of his period, I have tried to arm the reader against this misconception, so that the wheel may carry Tennyson at least a fraction of a degree higher. 'Man is so small!' he told Allingham (*Diary*, p. 89), 'but a fly on the wheel'; and any attempt by an individual to affect the machinery driven by the 'Great Wheels' would have seemed to him highly ridiculous. But I would rather he thought me a fly with delusions of grandeur, than what he thought a contemporary source-hunting critic, Churton Collins: 'a louse upon the locks of literature!'

Chief Publications of Tennyson's Poetry

Poems by Two Brothers, Louth, 1827.

Poems, Chiefly Lyrical, London, 1830.

Poems, London, 1833 (date on title-page: actually published December 1832).

Poems, 2 vols, London, 1842.

The Princess; A Medley, London, 1847

In Memoriam A. H. H., London, 1850

Ode on the Death of the Duke of Wellington, London, 1852.

*Maud, and Other Poems,*London, 1855.

Idylls of the King ('Enid', 'Vivien', 'Elaine', 'Guinevere'), London, 1859.

Enoch Arden etc., London, 1864.

The Holy Grail and Other Poems (adding 'The Coming of Arthur', 'The Holy Grail', 'Pelleas and Ettarre', 'The Passing of Arthur' to *Idylls of the King),* London, 1870 (date on title-page: actually published December 1869).

Gareth and Lynette etc. (adding 'Gareth and Lynette' and 'The Last Tournament' to *Idylls of the King),* London, 1872.

Queen Mary, London, 1875.

Harold, London, 1877 (date on title-page: actually published December 1876).

The Lover's Tale (completed), London, 1879.

Ballads and other Poems, London, 1880.

The Cup and The Falcon, London, 1884.

Becket, London, 1884.

Tiresias and Other Poems (completing *Idylls of the King* with 'Balin and Balan'), London, 1885.

Locksley Hall Sixty Years After etc. (including *The Promise of May),* London, 1886.

Demeter and Other Poems, London, 1889.

The Foresters, London, 1892

The Death of Oenone, Akbar's Dream, and Other Poems (posthumous), London, 1892.

The Works of Alfred Lord Tennyson Poet Laureate, London and New York, 1894.

The Works of Tennyson, annotated by the poet, ed. Hallam, Lord Tennyson (The Eversley Edition), 9 vols, London, 1907–8; 6 vols, New York, 1908.

Poems and Plays (Oxford Standard Authors), London, New York and Toronto, 1965.

The Poems of Tennyson, ed. Christopher Ricks, London, 1969.

A Variorum Edition of Tennyson's 'Idylls of the King', ed. John Pfordresher, New York and London, 1973.

Bibliographical Notes

This study is based chiefly on the primary sources mentioned in the list of abbreviations on page xiii; but I am deeply indebted throughout to Sir Charles Tennyson's *Alfred Tennyson* (1968), and to Christopher Ricks's annotated edition of the Poems (1969). Other books and articles which have supplied information, or suggested lines of research, and which the reader may also find helpful, are as follows.

Chapter 1   The Age

Ideas and Beliefs of the Victorians (B.B.C. Talks), 1949; J. H. Buckley's *The Victorian Temper*, 1951; Walter E. Houghton's *The Victorian Frame of Mind*, 1957; Sir Llewellyn Woodward's *The Age of Reform 1815-1870* (Oxford History of England), 2nd edn, 1962; G. Kitson Clark's *The Making of Victorian England*, 1962; J. F. C. Harrison's *The Early Victorians 1832-51*, 1971; Geoffrey Best's *Mid-Victorian Britain 1851-75*, 1971.

Chapter 2   The Poet

Joanna Richardson's *The Pre-eminent Victorian: A Study of Tennyson*, 1962; George O. Marshall Jr's *A Tennyson Handbook*, 1963; Christopher Ricks's *Tennyson*, 1972.

Chapter 3   Early Poems

W. D. Paden's *Tennyson in Egypt: A Study of the Imagery in his Earlier Work*, Lawrence, Kan., 1942; F. E. L. Priestley's *Language and Structure in Tennyson's Poetry*, 1973.

Bibliographical Notes

Chapter 4   *Poems* 1833

Lionel Stevenson's 'The "High-born maiden" symbol in Tennyson' (1948), and G. Robert Stange's 'Tennyson's Garden of Art: A Study of "The Hesperides"' (1952), both reprinted in *Critical Essays on the Poetry of Tennyson*, ed. John Killham, 1960.

Chapter 5   *Poems* 1842

Robert Langbaum's *The Poetry of Experience: The Dramatic Monologue in Modern Literary Tradition*, 1957; William E. Fredeman's 'St Simeon Stylites', *University of Toronto Quarterly*, vol. 38 (1968).

Chapter 6   *The Princess; A Medley*

John Killham's *Tennyson and 'The Princess': Reflections of an Age*, 1958.

Chapter 7   *In Memoriam A. H. H.*

E. B. Mattes's *'In Memoriam': The Way of a Soul. A Study of Some Influences that Shaped Tennyson's Poem*, 1951; John Dixon Hunt's *Tennyson: 'In Memoriam': A Casebook*, 1970; Alan Sinfield's *The Language of Tennyson's 'In Memoriam'*, 1971; Ward Hellstrom's *On the Poems of Tennyson*, 1972.

Chapter 8   *Maud*

R. C. Schweik's 'The "Peace or War" Passages in Tennyson's "Maud"', *Notes and Queries*, vol. 205 (1960); R. W. Rader's *Tennyson's 'Maud': The Biographical Genesis*, 1963; Philip Drew's 'Tennyson and the Dramatic Monologue: A Study of *Maud*', in *Tennyson*, ed. D. J. Palmer, 1973.

Chapter 9   *Idylls of the King*

F. E. L. Priestley's 'Tennyson's *Idylls*' (1949), reprinted in *Critical Essays on the Poetry of Tennyson*, ed. John Killham, 1960; Kathleen Tillotson's 'Tennyson's Serial Poem', *Mid-Victorian Studies*, (1965); John D. Rosenberg's *The Fall of Camelot: A Study of Tennyson's 'Idylls of the King'*, 1973.

Chapter 10   Later Works

Peter Thomson's 'Tennyson's Plays and their Production', in *Tennyson*, ed. D. J. Palmer, 1973; P. G. Scott's *Tennyson's 'Enoch Arden': A Victorian Best-Seller*, Tennyson Society Monographs, 1970.

Chapter 11   Reputation

J. D. Jump's *Tennyson: The Critical Heritage*, 1967; E. D. H. Johnson's descriptive bibliography of Tennyson in *The Victorian Poets: A Guide to Research*, ed. F. E. Faverty, 2nd edn, 1968. Isobel Armstrong's *Victorian Scrutinies: Reviews of Poetry 1830-1870*, 1972.

The fullest up-to-date bibliography is John Dixon Hunt's in *English Poetry: Select Bibliographical Guides*, 1971. B. C. Southam's *Tennyson* (Writers and their Work, 1971) gives a brief critical account of Tennyson's poetry, and a useful select bibliography.

Index

Index

Hone, William, 85
Horace, 18, 19, 50, 72, 77, 84, 89,
  116-18, 126, 138, 144, 148, 156, 167,
  170-1
Hughes, Thomas, 11, 13
Hunt, Leigh, 91, 160
Hunt, William Holman, 9
Huxley, Thomas, 12, 13, 152, 167, 174

Indian Mutiny, 11, 13
Ireland, 1, 8, 17
Irving, Henry, 15, 16, 32

Jebb, Sir Richard, 173
Jerome, St., 176
Johnson, E. D. H., 183
Jones, Sir William, 90
Jowett, Benjamin, 12, 29, 33, 120
Jung, Carl Gustave, 169
Juvenal, 31, 90, 99, 101-2, 142, 173,
  177-8

Keats, John, 4, 21-2, 49, 50, 51, 70,
  94-5, 121, 130, 172, 175-6
Kemble, John, 55
Kingsley, Charles, 140, 142, 154
Knowles, James, 31, 77, 89, 127, 169, 176

Lachmann, Karl, 163
Laing, A. G., 41
Lamarck, Jean Baptiste, 109, 124
The Lancet, 134
Landor, Walter Savage, 24
Lang, Andrew, 164
Laplace, Marquis de, 108, 129
Layamon, 156
Layard, Sir Austin Henry, 145-6
Lear, Edward, 29, 31
Lecky, William Edward Hartpole, 85
Lincolnshire, 1, 34, 38, 46, 60, 174
The Literary Gazette, 97
Llywarch Hen, 159
London Review, 23
Longinus, 164, 170, 175
Lucian, 38, 60, 176
Lucretius, 36, 40, 45, 57, 64, 67-8, 73-4,
  79, 90, 93, 121, 157, 175

Lushington, Edmund, 26, 93, 103-4,
  126, 165
Lushington, Franklin, 139, 141-2
Lushington, Henry, 29, 103, 141-2
Lyell, Charles, 9, 108, 123-5, 134, 149
Lytton, Edward George Bulwer, 26,
  163

Mabinogion, 156-7, 159
Macready, William Charles, 24
Madden, Sir F., 156
Maidstone, 3, 102, 104
Malory, Sir Thomas, 78-9, 149-50,
  155-62, 165-6, 183
Malthus, Thomas Robert, 7, 95
Manchester, 142
Marston, John, 90
Marx, Karl, 8, 9, 13
Maurice, Frederick Denison, 9, 11, 20,
  62, 101-2, 107, 177
Mechanics' Institutes, 3, 104
Merlin (prose romance), 150, 158
Metaphysical Society, 12
Michelangelo, 114
Mill, James, 3
Mill, John Stuart, 3, 4, 9, 14, 23, 74, 152
Millais, John Everett, 9, 29
Milnes, Richard Monckton (first
  Baron Houghton), 21, 24, 70, 121
Milton, John, 19, 37, 39, 51, 66,
  117-19, 149, 163-4
Mitford, Mary, 81
Moore, Thomas, 40
More, Sir Thomas (St), 75
Morning Post, 134
Morris, William, 16, 176
Moschus, 64, 119
Moxon, Edward, 22, 26-7, 29, 56
Mozart, Wolfgang Amadeus, 168
Murray, Hugh, 41
Myvyrian Archaiology of Wales, 159

Napoleon III, 11
Nennius, 157
Newman, John Henry, 153-4
Nicolson, Sir Harold, 183
Nightingale, Florence, 10, 21, 59, 154-5

193

Index

196